HAS
CHRISTIANITY
FAILED
YOU?

Books by Ravi Zacharias

HAS CHRISTIANITY FAILED YOU?

RAVI ZACHARIAS

ZONDERVAN®

ZONDERVAN.com/
AUTHORTRACKER
follow your favorite authors

ZONDERVAN

Has Christianity Failed You?
Copyright © 2010 by Ravi Zacharias

This title is also available as a Zondervan ebook. Visit www.zondervan.com/ebooks.

This title is also available in a Zondervan audio edition. Visit www.zondervan.fm.

Requests for information should be addressed to:
Zondervan, *Grand Rapids, Michigan 49530*

Library of Congress Cataloging-in-Publication Data

Zacharias, Ravi K.
    Has Christianity failed you? / Ravi K. Zacharias.
       p. cm.
    Includes bibliographical references.
    ISBN 978-0-310-26955-7 (hardcover, jacketed)
    1. Apologetics. I. Title.
BT1103.Z345   2010
239'.7 — dc22
                                       2009051033

Published in association with the literary agency of Wolgemuth & Associates, Inc.

Cover design: Scott Lee Designs
Cover photography: Shutterstock
Interior design: Beth Shagene

Printed in the United States of America

10 11 12 13 14 15 /DCI/ 23 22 21 20 19 18 17 16 15 14 13 12 11 10 9 8 7 6 5 4 3 2 1

To my dear friend, Mark Pu,
whose candor and concern for an authentic Christianity
have made a profound impact on my life.

Thank you, friend.

CONTENTS

ACKNOWLEDGMENTS

It is a privilege for me to team up with Zondervan again. I am always impressed by how earnestly the team at Zondervan works to craft every book with the reader in mind. The effort required makes me a more disciplined writer by the time each manuscript is complete. My thanks to them for all their help, in particular to John Sloan and Dirk Buursma. I am again thankful to Wolgemuth and Associates, especially to Andrew, as he has been a great guide at every stage. As always, my research assistant Danielle DuRant did all the digging for source notes and references and provided valuable interaction as the book progressed. Any reader of my books knows there is the ever present and labor-intensive effort of my wife, Margie. She is the final editor. Her best writing hours are late at night; my best hours are early in the morning. Now with a completed manuscript we can breathe a sigh of relief and synchronize our lives again. That I warmly welcome with gratitude!

There are a few more whom I shall leave unnamed but for whom I am immensely grateful. They are the ones who candidly and courteously shared with me why they had struggled with their faith and why, for some of them, the belief had failed them. I earnestly pray that as they read this, God will rekindle that flickering light and bring new life where there seems none. My hope is that I will see them all in the presence of the Lord, when he shall wipe away every tear, answer every question, and fill every void. The God I believe in is more than able to do this. This book is a feeble step to point to a solid Rock. That Rock is Jesus. My total gratitude goes to him for enabling me to write.

HAS CHRISTIANITY FAILED YOU?

Some time ago, our ministry held an open forum at the beautiful Fox Theater in Atlanta, Georgia. Some of my younger colleagues asked me to consider addressing the topic "Has Christianity Failed You?" My first reaction was surprise that they thought such a topic would be of interest to a diverse audience. They were even more surprised by my surprise. The disappointment in Christianity they had heard expressed by so many of their friends was supported by the questions raised in scores of letters received at our ministry. (It is said that for every person that writes a letter, there are probably a thousand who feel the same way.) Many of their contemporaries, having found new hope and meaning in Christ, had begun to experience tension between what they believed and what they were seeing around them or experiencing themselves. Uncertainties about their faith had grown and weariness had begun to creep in. What had been a vibrant and dynamic faith had become defined by nothing more than a circle of friends and range of activities. They concluded that, especially for the younger generation, this was not a topic we should keep from addressing.

So I agreed, even though I was still not sure to what degree people would be drawn out into the open. During the weeks before the forum, our videographer took his camera to record the responses of several people who had renounced the Christian faith they had once held. One was a man who had been rejected by Christians because of his gay lifestyle. Another had fallen into adultery, and though she had repented, she had never felt accepted by Christians at church again. Some said they had been disappointed in Christianity because they found it intellectually untenable in an age of reason.

To my total surprise, on the day of the event we had a capacity crowd of four thousand people — with more people lined up outside, willing to pay a higher price for a ticket to get in. I had seen "scalpers" at ball games but never at a Christian "talking head" event. Some of those who had been interviewed made a point of attending the event so they could see if there was an acceptable answer to their disappointment. If this crowd was any indication, the sense that Christianity has failed is real and troubling and pervasive.

Why are so many today not only living with silent doubt but actually leaving the "evangelical fold" for something else? Is there something wrong with the message, with the communicator, with the hearer — or with all three? Is it time to ask ourselves some hard questions about what it means to be a follower of Jesus Christ? Why does it seem that God has made it so hard to continue believing, regardless of one's education, personal experience, or standing in society? Such skepticism is not representative of just those who are hostile to the faith; it also represents many who are honestly asking questions. This book is an attempt to respond to both of these groups, within and outside the Christian faith. More to the point, I believe, is whether it is actually possible to still make sense out of life once one has denied one's faith in Christ or has shunted him aside.

In the end, the answers that are given and received must be both felt and real, with the added impetus that God is nearer than one might think. He desires that we sense him very near to us and not distant from us. But the assurance of his nearness comes at a cost, just as is true for any relationship of love and commitment. Of the thirty-seven years that my wife and I have been married, the three most difficult years in our marriage were those during which I set aside my calling as an itinerant evangelist and, at the request of my denominational leadership, took up a seminary professorship as my principal contribution to the work of the church. Going against my inner calling was difficult, and in the end I realized that when one is outside the will of God, one's other commitments can also be put at risk and one's most important relationships can become dry and lifeless. To be in the place where God wants you is indispensable to enjoying the blessings God offers.

The question raised in this book — *Has Christianity failed you?* — is an even deeper challenge than it may appear. It is not merely that Christianity may not be what some thought it would be (that sounds more like a question of felt need); the real question is one of intellectual coherence, and that is much deeper. Former evangelical Robert M. Price takes to task Rick Warren's bestselling book, *The Purpose Driven Life*®, and responds with one of his own, *The Reason-Driven Life*. Price puts the sword to evangelical faith and twists it with delight. In powerful words and with boastful scholarship, he declares that evangelicals have been intellectually hoodwinked or are existentially hypocritical. Every chapter is laced with mockery of what he claims to have once believed as an evangelical and reveals his anger for having been "taken in." I would venture to suggest that large numbers of people would concur with him as many of our young people in particular are finding themselves trying to survive the terrifying high seas of their faith journey without chart or compass.

When Noah was building his ark, God gave him detailed instructions for everything: how high, no higher; how long, no longer; what species to include and in what numbers — details ad nauseum. But when all had been done according to God's instructions and the door was finally shut, it must have been a terrifying experience to realize there was no sail or rudder on this ark. Who was in control?

Is Christianity a mindless game in which we are hurled into the storms of life with false assurances, or are the instructions we have been given so detailed that we can anticipate what the storms of belief will be like, know who is in control, and what to do when we reach solid ground? In the end, rather than it being Christianity that has failed, could it be that we will be startled to find out it is the church that has failed, not Christ?

This book is for Christians and skeptics alike. I pray it will make a difference in how each person who reads it sees Jesus, how they see themselves, and how they see the way life is to be lived and thought through.

God does not disappoint us. We often disappoint him and ourselves. There is a road to recovery; there is direction to the center of his place for us. I hope the following pages will point to the rudder and the sail we have been given and, most important, to the Captain of this ship called Life.

1

WHO IS JESUS?

Three little boys were arguing about whose father got home faster from work each day. The first boy boasted that his father was a former Olympian middle distance runner and ran in record times. He left work at 4:00 p.m. every afternoon, and although his home was three miles away, he would grab his briefcase and run all the way, reaching home by 4:15. The second boy was not to be outdone. His father, he said, had competed in professional auto racing, and once he put his foot to the pedal, nothing could get in his way. He also worked three miles away and also left work at 4:00 but reached home by 4:05. The third one was just chuckling at all these boastful claims. He knew he had them both beaten. His father, he said, actually worked five miles away from home. He left work at 4:00 every afternoon and got home half an hour before he left work, at 3:30. He worked for the government.

With my apologies to all those in civil service, the point I want to make is that it is human nature to lay claim to something that is exceptional or superior to everyone else, whether it is one's culture, a great landmark building, or a skilled leader. Our skyscrapers are higher than your skyscrapers; my culture is better than your culture; my culture is *older* than your culture; my dad is stronger or smarter or faster than your dad — so goes the game of one-upmanship.

To those who feel that Christianity has failed them, I ask, Have you sometimes wondered whether that's all there is to religion too — one culture claiming that its values are better than another's or that one's faith is superior to someone else's faith? Are all religions basically false? Are all religions basically true? Are all religions merely ethnocentric prejudices camouflaged by spiritual talk?

After years of belief as a Christian, I have to reluctantly and sadly admit that sometimes this does seem to be the case. Some religions do lay claim to a superior heritage by virtue of a superior birthright. Islam, for example, touts the language of the Qur'an as the supreme linguistic expression so that reading it in any language other than Arabic deprives the reader of experiencing the miracle. The prophet of Islam is specifically the prophet of Arabia, and yet he is supposed to be supreme over the world of revelation. If religion can be reduced to "bragging rights," it is a very deadly game, isn't it? People give their hard-earned money and their valuable time to pin all their hopes for the eternal — and, oh, so much more — on that belief. What one deems to be of ultimate value exacts a cost in proportion. Indeed, a close scrutiny of some religions will show that many religious claims are indeed all about the "son bragging about the father," resulting in questions about the father himself.

Something else about religion that is equally discomfiting to many is its claim to exclusivity. But this ought not to surprise us, because truth by definition must exclude that which contradicts it. When someone claims their religion is superior to other faiths but cannot support the claim, we should ask what this claim of supremacy looks like when it is applied to matters of life and destiny. And it is even more important to ask these questions before walking *away* from a belief once held as the dearest of commitments.

At a recent forum in India, I was asked why someone with an apparently passionate commitment to his or her belief in Jesus Christ would suddenly "come out of the closet," declaring this belief untenable. For some, it may very well be that the Christianity that has resulted in disappointment may have been nothing more than a boast that "my father is better than your father" rather than having been a true faith that has been lost after examining the claims of Christianity with an honest heart and mind and finding it wanting.

Before we can talk about some of the existential problems some people believe they have experienced with Christianity, we must begin this discussion by taking a close look at the claims of Jesus and their implications — who is Jesus and what does he teach (and Christianity by extension) — for this is the only way to determine that it is really Christianity that has failed and not something or someone else. Matthew tells us that Jesus placed a little child among the leaders he was developing, his disciples, and declared, "The kingdom of heaven belongs to such as these" (Matthew 19:14) — meaning, without the simple faith of a child we cannot see heaven. At the same time, he won the commitment of the scrutinizing mind of Saul of Tarsus, who knew and had done all that the law required for salvation. An honest examination of Jesus' pronouncements readily demonstrates that they uniquely transcend all cultural distinctives and can be powerfully confirmed by human need, longing, and observation, across cultures and language groups.

A great many books are being written about this Jesus today, even by those who disavow his historic assertions. After all, in the fallout of postmodernism one can make anyone say anything about anything, bereft of the text or the context. Physician and author Deepak Chopra has cleverly written two books on Jesus, one he admits is a complete work of fiction, though you can be sure he has a real motive in doing so, and the other in which he says that Jesus finally gained enlightenment in his pursuit of the ultimate. Though he claims to greatly admire Jesus, such twisted writing betrays the truth taught by Jesus and distorts history.

Once we understand Jesus in his *own* words and measure his claims and promises against our deepest needs, we will be surprised at just how personal and magnificent he really is — the way and the truth and the life (John 14:6) — rather than being merely the focus of deviously rendered fictitious story lines.

C. S. Lewis's conversion story, *Surprised by Joy*, describes this precisely. Lewis says that his greatest realization after he had finally recognized who Jesus is and what he offers to every human heart was that he had not come to a place or accepted a belief; he had come to a *person* — and that person is the very person of God.

The spiritual talk of today is all about ideas and feelings; Jesus' message, on the other hand, is about the person and presence of God. The spiritual talk of today minimizes fact and maximizes the mystical; Jesus always connected experience to fact. The spiritual talk of today engages in seductive double-speak; Jesus presented the truth as absolute, even when it was uncomfortable to hear — never making mysticism the ultimate goal but putting it in the context of what was real. The spiritual talk of today employs clichés that endanger the spirit by making truth secondary to what feels good; Jesus taught that feeling his presence is only possible because of the fact of his existence. The spiritual talk of today claims to be generously accepting of all faiths, while in reality — with a prejudice that disregards reason and misplaces faith — it undermines the only faith that truly teaches tolerance.

The message of Jesus goes beyond mere religion or belief and dramatically alters our way of thinking and being. He challenges all of humanity to taste and see that he is good and to take to heart the truth that his word abides forever.

Some time ago, I attended a football game in my home city of Atlanta. Through the courtesy of one of the players, we were seated close to the team's bench. Years before, I had watched a game from the nosebleed section, and I remember thinking how small the players looked and how vast the playing field appeared. This time, however, I was so close to the players that I could almost hear them breathing, and I was quite surprised by how big they were and by how small the field really was.

When we are close enough to the Jesus of history that we can look at history from his perspective, we actually see how mighty and strong he is and how navigable life is with him as the captain.

GIVING A "FACE" TO JESUS

Growing up in India, I heard his name many times. In the Hindi language, his name is *Isa Masih*, which is transliterated from "Jesus the Messiah." Christians are called *Isaiis* (pronounced *Is-**ah**-ees*), meaning "Jesus Ones" or "Jesus Followers." Christmas is *Bada Din* — the Big Day. Yes, I heard the name of Jesus. But apart from associating him with going to church and with the festivities of Easter and Christmas, his name meant nothing to me.

His picture hung in our home at eye level in my parents' bedroom, which was the larger of the two small bedrooms in our home in New Delhi, India. My earliest memory of that picture is that my mother never opened her eyes in the morning until she had first reached for her glasses and positioned them on her face. Only then would she turn toward the picture and open her eyes, so that the face of Jesus was the first thing she saw every morning. It was a ritual for her, and in a culture where superstition abounds, those fears and habits are subtly passed on from generation to generation. So when I was in a crisis, I would go into her room, lean on the little chest of drawers, look at the picture, and make my petition. If I were sure that nobody would see me, I would even kneel in front of it and mutter a quick plea for help, especially at examination time. I remember it well — a faded, green-hued version of the most famous of all paintings, Warner Sallman's *The Head of Christ*. Back then, however, it was just a picture to me, a talisman.

Artists have drawn pictures, painted canvasses, and sculpted images of Jesus as they see him. It's odd, isn't it, that the most revered personality in history, whose birth is the point of reference for our calendar and whose life is described as "the greatest story ever told," has left us no picture of himself? Just as the most defining moment of our lives, our own births, cannot be recalled, the most supreme name in all of history, honored by millions, is ultimately faceless to us.

I also recall, as a young teen, seeing an American movie magazine that ended up in our home through some American friends. I remember seeing a picture of an actor seated on a chair, his face in his hands, and the bold caption above the picture reading, "Dare I, a sinner, play Christ?" For years, no movie production ever showed Jesus' face, just his back or his body from his shoulders down. Modern authorities in the field of communication would consider this a huge lapse; after all, isn't a picture worth a thousand words? God indicated that the contrary is true. It is not *seeing* that is all important; it is the act of *recognizing* that brings together much more than mere sight.

One of the fascinating stories in the book of Exodus pictures Moses on the verge of leading the people of Israel from bondage in Egypt into the Promised Land (Exodus 33:12 – 23). It has been a long and arduous journey; the Israelites have lost many lives and faced severe deprivations. Moses goes off alone to pray and pleads with God, "Show me your glory."

What an amazing request, considering that Moses has already experienced the series of miracles that had brought them from slavery to that point! No one could have doubted that a supernatural hand had guided them. From escaping the Egyptians at the Red Sea to the revelation of the Ten Commandments to the provision of their food and clothing along the journey, this horde of humanity would never have made it without divine intervention. Yet Moses still asked to see God's face, even being so bold before God as to insist that he would not cross over the Jordan River without being assured of God's presence.

God gave an even more amazing response to Moses' request: "You cannot see my face, for no one may see me and live." And so he told Moses, "There is a place near me where you may stand on a rock. When my glory passes by, I will put you in a cleft in the rock and cover you with my hand until I have passed by" (Exodus 33:20 – 22). Thus, Moses would see the "back" of God but not his face. It might have been like walking into a room and knowing someone is there, perhaps smelling their cologne or perfume or hearing them breathing, even hearing a voice, but not being able to see the person — maybe something like Dorothy's first meeting with the Wizard of Oz.

Perhaps if we are able to understand why God has kept his face from us, we will have a clue to why we must learn to recognize him and sense his presence through his words and deeds rather than through his physical features. I venture two bold reasons. First, if we could see God's face, his defining physical features would necessarily be very different, depending on what part of the world we are in. In the East, it would become all about the image itself rather than the person, and the image would become the focus of adulation. The clothes he wore, his hairstyle, anything even remotely connected to his facial appearance would become a fetish and the object of worship to which the superstitious or spiritually minded would cling. The idolatry of the means as an end would be inescapable.

During a visit to India's southern state of Kerala, I was driven to a city with the tongue-twisting name Kodungallur. Kodungallur is famous for one thing: It was here, according to tradition and even some historical references, that the apostle Thomas is said to have arrived in India in AD 53. Famed writers of early Christian history such as the Venerable Bede and Gregory of Nazianzus, among others, have made reference to Thomas's trip to India. The oldest denominational Christian church in India bears the name of Thomas — the Mar Thoma Church. I walked around the site of Thomas's disembarkation and let my imagination wander until a caretaker offered to show me one of the relics of the apostle that was near the altar, encased in a glass vault behind a heavily locked door. As she unlocked the door to the vault and I moved toward the relic, the voluminous sound of a hymn broke out — a security measure that alerted the keepers of the shrine that somebody was close to the relic. The guide bowed her head for a moment and touched the glass with her hand; she then touched her heart and kissed her hand in reverence. Inside the vault, on the other side of a magnifying glass, was a small bone from the right arm of the apostle. (After his martyrdom in India, Thomas's body was sent to Rome, but in more recent times, the pope authorized a piece of bone from Thomas's remains to be sent to the historic shrine.) As I stared at that little piece of bone that was about two inches long, I couldn't help but wonder not only about its authenticity but about Thomas himself. Needless to say, stories of this bone's magical powers abound. The Eastern mind invents the fantastic and reveres fetishes and relics as the means to its belief. Over the years, millions have made their pilgrimage to that spot, touched the vault, and kissed the glass barrier that separates them from that small piece of bone.

In the West, a slightly different scenario might unfold if we knew exactly what Jesus looked like. Yes, there would be those who, like their counterparts in the East, would truly reverence the object rather than the

Savior, but I also believe that the financial rewards of its commercialization would be enormous. Can you imagine what would have happened if James, the half brother of Jesus, had opened up a memorabilia shop to sell pictures of Jesus? Rather than being reduced to his own image, in the West God would be reduced to our image. Expositions of his face would abound, each expert claiming different insight. There would be, in all probability, multiple attempts to isolate and replicate any DNA that might still cling to any artifact. Could you imagine a Jesus look-alike contest? One can only pity the winner at Christmas! Before long, lobbyists would demand a transgendered rendering of the Christ. Why was he male and not female — or neither? And God forbid if he were a white male.

Our demand for infinite knowledge is insatiable, and to think there is a Being who is beyond our capability of dissecting and studying scientifically is more than some of us can handle. Think about it. Is there any other language in the world like English in which so many versions of the Bible are available, each new translator claiming a unique perspective on the truth? Each one adds a little more information to the picture until what becomes important to us is how we view God rather than how he views us. Too many have so humanized God and deified man that we can scarcely tell the difference any more. Books of this nature become bestsellers because they assure us that God is just one of us. But the ramifications of this familiarity are dangerous and destructive. We have tried to reshape God to become relevant to us rather than finding out how we must become relevant to him. We in the West simply cannot live with the possibility that God has purposely left himself clothed in mystery until we are able to "recognize" who he truly is. We have tried to conform him to our image rather than the other way around, and objects of spiritual significance exact a disfigurement of stupendous proportions.

There may be a second reason that God has kept his face from us. Billy Graham, the noted evangelist, likes to tell of a time he was staying at a hotel in a Pennsylvania town. As the elevator door shut on him and a couple of his colleagues, another passenger in the elevator said, "I hear Billy Graham is staying in this hotel." One of Dr. Graham's colleagues pointed to

Dr. Graham and said, "That's him." There was a moment of uncomfortable silence while the man looked Dr. Graham up and down, and then he said, "What an anticlimax!"

Sometimes it is better to keep the mystery intact. Though knowing what Jesus looks like would fulfill a longing within us, I am convinced it is a longing that can only be met when our minds and hearts have been lifted to a far higher level in which we could contain that transcending, awe-inspiring reality. Instead, God has disclosed himself in descriptive terms that give us enough information to be able to know who he is, and he has hidden enough of himself for us to learn the balance between faith and reason. No earthly relationship with an infinite, transcendent God can exist without maintaining these two aspects.

In the Hindu faith, there is a defining story of a young man coming to a sage to inquire what life is all about. The sage asks the youth to go to a nearby tree and pick the fruit. When he has done so, the sage directs him to cut up the fruit. Then he instructs him to remove one of the seeds and break open the seed. Finally, the wise man asks, "What do you see inside the seed?" "Nothing," is the reply. "Well, young man," returns the sage, "just as that tree emerged from nothing, so from nothing is this thing we call life. The more you know about it, the more you will find that life and its source are reduced to nothing."

Now to be fair, the sage could have meant that nothing is not really "nothing" — that the source of all existence is an intangible reality, some life-giving force. But it is here that the Christian faith makes a serious departure from Hindu teaching. Far from teaching that all existence comes from nothing, the gospel of John begins this way:

> In the beginning was the Word, and the Word was with God, and the Word was God....
>
> The Word became flesh and made his dwelling among us. We have seen his glory, the glory of the One and Only, who came from the Father, full of grace and truth.
>
> JOHN 1:1, 14

This series of assertions in John 1:1 harks back to the beginning of the book of Genesis, where we read: "In the beginning God created the heavens and the earth." *Bereshith bara Elohim* — in the beginning God. On these three Hebrew words, all else hangs. The created order does not declare "nothing" as its ultimate cause, nor does it acknowledge merely a force behind the cause. There is a *person* behind the cause. A person is more than the physical; personhood involves essence of thought, will, and feeling — a thinking, willing, and feeling entity in relationship. God created a quantity we call the universe. He created an entity we call humanity. The quantity — or thing — he created did not have a mind. The entity he created did have a mind. That is the heart of the human story. It is the mind that holds together the confluence of values and teaches us to value both the quantity and the entity in proper relationship. It is the mind that frames questions of moral significance and purpose. It is the mind that sees not just the face of the person but the person behind the face. It is the mind that holds memories and processes texts within contexts, so much so that when the mind has become disconnected from those memories, we wonder who the person is anymore.

CONNECTING THE BODY
AND THE MIND

Which of us, given a chance, would not want to see this Jesus of history? The noted talk show host Larry King was once asked to identify the one person across all of history that he would have liked to interview. "Jesus," he answered. To see him, to touch him, to *recognize* him — that would be the pursuit, wouldn't it? The apostle Paul writes, "No eye has seen, no ear has heard, no mind has conceived what God has prepared for those who love him" (1 Corinthians 2:9).

And one day we shall know God as we are known by him. What do we know about ourselves? We know what we feel, what we long for, whom we love, hate, judge. In short, everything we know about ourselves, we know through our senses. But still our knowledge of ourselves is partial. God is the only one who knows us comprehensively. By denying him and his existence, we reject the one person who knows us completely, with the result that we truly become strangers to ourselves and to others. C. S. Lewis rightly said, "I believe in Christianity as I believe that the sun has risen, not only because I see by it, but because by it I see everything else."[1]

If we have become strangers to ourselves and to others — and, in effect, cannot recognize the truth about ourselves — why do our questions assume that we are able to reason comprehensively enough to be able to recognize and understand God? The implication in our disenchantment with Christianity is that God is not who we thought he was or who we thought he ought to be. He doesn't do things the way we think he should or thought he would. *He has not lived up to our expectations.*

Our minds seek answers that will satisfy us and make us comfortable. Why, asks the one with the gay lifestyle, is my lifestyle not accepted as normal? Why, asks the one who has committed adultery, is the way back so fraught with moral condemnation? Why, when I have been wronged, do I expect everyone to accept my side of the issue? In short, we establish an "ought" from what "is" and consider those who do not agree with us to be wrong. Are we not supposing that it would be a better world if we were treated according to the terms *we* feel or think we merit?

THE HUMAN DILEMMA

I believe two propositions summarize the basic struggle we have over our expectations of God and demonstrate at the same time that Jesus is the answer to that dilemma. The first is that the world is made for the body; the body is made for the soul; the soul is made for God. The second proposition comes from Thomas Merton: "We cannot be at peace with others because we are not at peace with ourselves, and we cannot be at peace with ourselves because we are not at peace with God."[2]

The first statement — that the world is made for the body, the body for the soul, and the soul for God — is drawn from three realities: the world, the body, and the soul. Merton's proposition draws from three different realities — our fellow humans, ourselves, and God. Both of these propositions describe a "transactional relationship": how an individual relates to the physical world and to others who comprise one's personal world. Isolation from these is not a possibility. Even if a man were to live alone on an island, he would talk to himself and relate to the physical world around him, as was beautifully portrayed by Tom Hanks in *Castaway*. Man is not a completely self-contained, unidirectional being. The questions that haunt us always come from two directions: (1) How do we make sense of this physical world we find ourselves part of? and (2) How do we make sense of the spiritual yearnings we have and the earthly relationships that make up our lives?

Even as I write this, I realize there is no place to set my feet and feel completely secure in this world. The world seems to be in turmoil. I was scheduled to write in a secluded setting in Thailand. But just two days before I left the United States, the airports in Bangkok were shut down. Thousands stormed the new multibillion-dollar airport in protest against their political leadership, and all international travel was shut down for days. Thailand is a Buddhist country, and Buddhism is supposed to reflect the heart of peace. Not at that moment. So I was diverted to New Delhi. But India was reeling from the violent terrorist acts of Muslim radicals, who took over two of the most beautiful hotels in Mumbai and slaughtered two hundred innocent people in the process. They were followers of Allah "the compassionate." As my two experiences demonstrate, is it any wonder that the world looks at both politics and religion and mocks them for being bereft of answers? Both seem to use people as a means to accomplish their own ends. Or the reverse happens: people use both politics and religion only to accomplish their own ends.

For years, a common phrase heard in the West has been "Jesus is the answer." Tired of that glib statement, cynics respond with their own question: "But what is the question?" Asserting that we Westerners have come of age and no longer need religion, we are passionate in our declarations that all religions are equally false and therefore should all be consigned to the dustbins of history. But while we proclaim that all religions are equally false, it is interesting that Christianity is perceived by many today to be more false than the others and more deserving of rejection. The feather in the cap of this condemning judgment against Christianity is that many in the fold of skepticism claim to have once been believers in Jesus but have come "out of the closet," confessing that they simply no longer have any belief. God is but the vestige of an idea they once enjoyed but have now cast aside with certainty. Jesus is nothing more than an ideal that inspired music, art, and architecture. As a person he really does not matter. His historical existence is, at best, moot. Like a snake shedding its skin and leaving it behind to mingle with the dust of the earth, God is no longer of any consequence. In fact, since God is actually a product of our own primitive or immature imagination, we have discovered that, in reality, it is he who needs us in order to exist; we don't need him.

This skepticism about God arises from what we perceive as unanswered questions about life. But in spite of our skepticism, our hearts still beat with those persistent, unanswered longings, and in desperation or cynicism our minds continue to ponder the deep issues of our existence.

THE QUESTION
OF ALL QUESTIONS

I do not believe that we will ever be able to understand the depth of our own questions until we first understand ourselves, the questioners. We are like the young man in a Q&A session who, after some discussion, finally said, "What, then, am I asking?" Further, I do not believe that we will ever understand who we are until we understand who Jesus is, for our encounter with him, this "faceless" figure, defines what it means to be human. So before we can even discuss Christianity and whether it has failed us, let us first consider who Jesus is.

The twentieth-century Scottish preacher James Stewart makes a powerful statement when he talks of the mystery of Jesus' personality as the "startling coalescence of contrarieties":

He was the meekest and lowliest of all the sons of men, yet he spoke of coming on the clouds of heaven with the glory of God. He was so austere that evil spirits and demons cried out in terror at his coming, yet he was so genial and winsome and approachable that the children loved to play with him, and the little ones nestled in his arms. His presence at the innocent gaiety of a village wedding was like the presence of sunshine.

No one was half so compassionate to sinners, yet no one ever spoke such red-hot, scorching words about sin. A bruised reed he would not break. His whole life was love, yet on one occasion he demanded of the Pharisees how they ever expected to escape the damnation of hell. He was a dreamer of dreams and a seer of visions, yet for sheer stark realism he has all of our self-styled realists soundly beaten. He was a servant of all, washing the disciples' feet, yet masterfully he strode into the temple, and the hucksters and moneychangers fell over one another from the mad rush and the fire they saw blazing in his eyes.

He saved others, yet at the last, himself he did not save. There is nothing in history like the union of contrasts that confronts us in the gospels. The mystery of Jesus is the mystery of divine personality.[3]

A *contradiction*, according to the Random House Webster's College Dictionary, is "a statement or proposition that denies another statement or itself and is logically incongruous"; a *contrariety*, however, holds two aspects of an issue in balance and in tension without violating the logical congruency of either. In the contrarieties within Jesus, we see how he represents the answer for all the tensions we feel within ourselves. For example, the gospel of John refers to Jesus as being "in the beginning," and also as being "with" his Father (John 1:1 – 2). How could he have always been and yet come to be? This contrariety of Jesus' eternal existence and historical existence has made it at once both difficult and most relevant.

The prophet Isaiah tells us, "To us a child is born, to us a Son is given" (Isaiah 9:6). Please note that the Son was not born; the *child* was born. The Son was not born because the Son always existed. The incarnation of the Son as the child lying in a manger is the embodiment of the Eternal One who came to reveal and connect this mind/body struggle of ours, this struggle to connect who we are as material beings with who we are as spiritual beings.

JESUS THE SON

Jesus' "sonship" is qualified in four ways. When we come to terms with these qualifications, we are better able to understand why we think, and why we struggle, the way we do. Those four qualifications give us the relational terms that ought to engage our attention and enable us to recognize him as the sole answer to all of our questions about meaning, purpose, pain, and destiny.

Son of David

The first description of Jesus as a man is clearly his ethnic lineage. In the tenth chapter of Mark's gospel, we find the story of a blind man named Bartimaeus. Look at his name carefully: Bar-Timaeus. Ironically, we really do not have a name for him. He is simply "son of Timaeus," which is what his name means. His only identity in the story is through his father. In that time and culture, it was not uncommon for a son to be named in relation to the father, as in Simon Bar-Jonah. This method established "bragging rights" within a culture. In the present-day Middle East, after the birth of a son, a parent is often known as "mother of . . ." So here we are introduced to the blind son of Timaeus, and Bartimaeus cries out, "Jesus, Son of David, have mercy on me!" (Mark 10:47). Notice he not only addresses Jesus by his name but also recognizes his lineage — his Jewish ancestry and descent from King David, the greatest of Israel's kings.

No monarch in Israel is more revered than David. If one were to go back in time to the great prophets — Isaiah, Jeremiah, Zechariah, Ezekiel, Amos, and Hosea — they all predicted that the Messiah would be a *Son of David*: "Of the increase of his government and peace there will be no end. He will reign on David's throne and over his kingdom, establishing and upholding it with justice and righteousness from that time on and forever," wrote the prophet Isaiah (9:7). There could have been no political vision higher than to restore the throne of the beloved and revered King David, who triumphed over the challenges and threats of his day with courage and humility. Because of David, his people were respected in their time.

There is something unique in this acclamation. Jesus was from the line of Jewish kings, but he did not come as the King of the Jews. When Pilate sentenced him to crucifixion, he ordered a sign to be nailed to the cross over Jesus' head that read, "JESUS OF NAZARETH, THE KING OF THE JEWS", even though the priests protested the designation Pilate had given Jesus and demanded to have it removed (John 19:19 – 22).

There is irony here. Pilate saw Jesus as a would-be Jewish king, sentenced to death under Roman law for treason. It's interesting that this Roman saw Jesus in a greater light than did the Jews themselves. That Pilate recognized Jesus as a king was a slap in the face to the Jewish authorities because *they* did not recognize him as a king. When Jesus rode into Jerusalem on a donkey on Palm Sunday, the crowd did want to crown him as their king, but he roundly rejected their designs for him because he had not come to earth to lead one nation in its political pursuits. He was absolutely clear when he said to Pilate, "My kingdom is not of this world" (John 18:36).

Yet Bartimaeus cried out to Jesus by his name and title, implicitly recognizing him as the heir to the throne of David. Jesus' designation as "Son of David" suggests both his ethnicity and the political hopes of his people. Bartimaeus recognized who Jesus was. The Jews of Jesus' day, suffocating under the scourge of Roman rule, longed for ethnic supremacy and a political identity. But Jesus rejected these aspirations with the not-so-subtle reminder that they were secondary to the nation's spiritual malady. He reminded his listeners, as he would later tell Pilate, that his call was not to one particular nation, nor was his kingship one of political power. Rather, it was to rule in the hearts of men and women who understood his higher call for us to be citizens of heaven and sons and daughters of God.

This was hard for some Jews in that day to accept, and it is hard for those of us today who desperately wish for political solutions to our national problems. But here again there is a balance. It is not that political solutions are not important; rather, it is that when it comes to moral issues, political solutions are, at best, superficial. In time, they will be whittled down, fade, and be replaced. Slavery can be made illegal, but racial prejudice may still remain. The caste system may be outlawed in India, but intercaste marriage is still deemed to be a step down. Human beings will always find ways to divide and create hierarchies. Such is the plight of the human heart.

Go back for a moment. The blind son of Timaeus called out to Jesus, the Son of David, to heal him. Jesus looked at him and asked a rather obvious question: "What do you want me to do for you?" (Mark 10:51). "Rabbi, I want to see," he responded. With that one simple declaration he revealed every yearning of his heart, for Jesus says, "Your faith has healed you" (verse 52). The affirmation given to this blind man was the first acknowledgment of his own identity. It was *his* faith rather than someone else's faith, and it was his *faith* in Jesus that was responsible for his healing.

This is the first clue to transcending ethnicity. One may call to Jesus out of his ethnic and cultural distinctive, but one's ultimate transformation comes in that personal dimension of trust apart from any cultural elitism. "Teacher, I want to see." No matter what one's race or station in life, we come to him to see beyond the immediate and to be freed from the tyranny of the moment.

A Contrast of Visions

A few years ago, I visited Jerusalem while researching a book on Islam. I asked for and was granted a personal appointment with the Grand Mufti of Jerusalem. (In terms of political appointments within Islam, this position is considered the third highest: the first is the Grand Mufti of Mecca, and the second is the Grand Mufti of Medina.) Unfortunately, my visit with the Grand Mufti was painful at best. To every question I asked, his answer was one of two: "Jesus came to the Jews," or, "If it's in the Qur'an, it's true." But the core of his belief was that only those who spoke Arabic could really understand the Qur'an and that only a Muslim had the right to quote it. It is utterly amazing to me that Muslims believe that access to the Qur'an is restricted by both language and affirmation, and yet, Islam is a religion for the world. All of his answers were ultimately swallowed up in the world of political theory and ethnic superiority.

Those realities are inescapable to the Muslim today. To believe in the superiority of the culture within which "the last and the greatest prophet" revealed "the perfect book" in a "distinctive language" is built into the fabric of the worldview of any Muslim. This is the world of pride and prejudice. This is what happens when we think we are "the favored sons and daughters of a prejudicial God." So many world conflicts abound today over matters of race and ethnicity, each considering itself superior to the other. One can argue from the beginning to the end of each day about what it means to be a Christian, or what it means to be a Muslim or a follower of any other religion, including atheism. The bottom line will always haunt: *What is the political and cultural vision of this religion?*

Thomas Sowell, senior research fellow at the Hoover Institute of Stanford University, has written a book called *A Conflict of Visions*. In his introduction, he writes, "Visions may be moral, political, economic, religious, or social. Where visions conflict irreconcilably, whole societies may be torn apart. Conflicts of interests dominate the short run, but conflicts of visions dominate history."[4]

An Invitation to Freedom and Trust

As the Son of David, Jesus never envisioned a political structure for his people with him as the leader. The politics of Jesus were spiritually foundational, not morally dictatorial. He desired to rule in the hearts of men and women with the imperative of love and truth, not with the sword and the imperatives of fear and legalism. The world of Islam or any other worldview or religion that enjoins a political theory rules with a rod of fear and threats. The call of Jesus is an invitation to freedom and trust. I am free only inasmuch as I can trust my fellow human being. If I cannot trust those around me, I am not free. We must know the one to whom we belong and who calls us all to the same purpose. Only when I am at peace with the Son of David can I be at peace with myself, and only then will I be at peace with my fellow humans and truly free.

Let me illustrate. Our family has always had a dog. I am the kind of person who enjoys having a dog, provided the distance is always maintained between man and animal. All furniture and food prepared for the consumption of humans are off-limits for the dog, as far as I'm concerned (but with kids who treat dogs as immediate family, it's hard to win out). For many years we had a beautiful Border collie that we brought home from England. We named him G. K. in honor of one of my favorite authors, G. K. Chesterton (much to the dismay of the British Kennel Society, which did not think G. K. was a suitable name for a member of such a distinguished canine species). So they settled for Chester in their records. But we ignored that stricture — he was G. K. We were privileged to have him for twelve great years. He was obedient to the core, loyal to the end, and disciplined to the point of making humans look bad.

In the last year of his life he was diagnosed with cancer. One afternoon, I saw him lying in the entryway to our bedroom, barely breathing and unable to respond when I spoke to him. I phoned my wife, Margie, and told her G. K. seemed to be in his last hours, if not minutes. She rushed home from our daughter's house, for G. K. was really Margie's dog. When he heard her car pulling into the driveway, he strained to turn his head. His neck craned toward the garage, and as the door opened, he realized it was her. I saw an amazing expression in his eyes of loyalty and love. He struggled to get up on all fours and somehow hobbled over to her and collapsed at her feet. Anyone who had seen the kind of love and devotion he displayed would have had to wipe away the tears.

The Bible makes a remarkable comment about the allegiance of an animal: "The ox knows his master, the donkey his owner's manger, but Israel does not know, my people do not understand" (Isaiah 1:3). What does it mean to be a person? Surely it must at least mean that if even an animal can recognize its master, we must also see ourselves in a relationship to the author of our lives, who gives us the distinctive of personhood that transcends all race and ethnic barriers. We relate, we love, we care, we belong. The rule of affection, trust, and love is something intuitively woven into our beings. That is why it is reprehensible for a parent to betray a child and why cruelty to the animal world is seen as inhuman, because as humans, we are supposed to value the created order, and the weakest among us who cannot speak for themselves must be spoken for.

The plea "Jesus, Son of David, have mercy on me!" elicited the ultimate compliment when Jesus asked Bartimaeus what he wanted from him. "To see," came the answer. In echoing this response, we break free from our ethnicity and our assumed privilege of race. The gospel writer in Matthew 26, reminds the reader that David himself in Psalm 110:1 referred to Jesus as his Lord when he said, "The LORD says to my Lord: 'Sit at my right hand until I make your enemies a footstool for your feet.'" Here comes the contrariety: The Messiah is called the Son of David when, in effect, David's greatness lay in the fact that he recognized the lordship of the Messiah. It was not that Jesus was the Son of David but that David, by faith, was Jesus' son. The vision of God for humanity is that we might see his claim on us as an invitation to live and love, transcending all ethnic and cultural boundaries, not because Jesus is David's son, but because he is the instrument of power over all other power, of essential worth over political ideology, of human need over ethnic arrogance. He has eradicated every barrier of race and culture and position in life. David was a king, but in the eyes of God he was a child of God.

Son of Man

We go beyond political and ethnic claims to Jesus' claim to full humanity. Of all the titles that Jesus could have selected, the one he used most of himself was "the Son of Man" (eighty-two times in the New Testament). All of the occurrences (with one exception) are in the gospels, and all but two are from the lips of Jesus himself. The one exception is when Stephen used it, moments before his martyrdom: "I see heaven open and the Son of Man standing at the right hand of God" (Acts 7:56). The other exception to Jesus' usage of the term is when the crowd reacted to Jesus' prediction of his crucifixion by saying, "We have heard from the Law that the Christ will remain forever, so how can you say, 'The Son of Man must be lifted up'? Who is this 'Son of Man'?" (John 12:34).

Clearly this was a title Jesus considered to be very significant. Understanding this term, then, ought to be taken seriously and distinctively from the definition given by secular humanism of what it means to be human. In the previous section, we saw the person of Jesus (the Son of David) transcending cultures and ethnic barriers to underscore our existence as children of God. In the title "Son of Man," we see both the glory and the shame of the universe and all the transcending uniqueness that underscores the essence of every human being, cutting across gender. Conceived by the Holy Spirit and born of a woman, Jesus actually has no male ancestry, yet he is called "the Son of Man." In Psalm 8:4, David asks, "What is man that you are mindful of him, the son of man that you care for him?" In Jesus' mission as the Son of Man, we also see the ultimate horror of who we can become when we throw away the mirror for our souls.

I do not intend a theological study of this title here, so I shall resist digressing, as tempting as it might be.[5] Suffice it to say, there are many implications of its usage. Let me mention just three here.

First, by the title "Son of Man," we are reminded of the significance of humanness. By identifying himself with humanity, what dignity and nobility Jesus has given us!

Second, Jesus identified himself with this term in the third person; rather than saying "I" he referred to himself as "the Son of Man." He is clearly making a distinctive identification here. The writers of the Bible often use a prophetic passage to give the background or context of a statement before applying it in the present or to the future. Peter did this on the day of Pentecost, as recorded in the book of Acts:

> Amazed and perplexed [by what they saw taking place], they asked one another. "What does this mean?" ...
>
> Then Peter stood up with the Eleven, raised his voice and addressed the crowd: ... "No, this is what was spoken by the prophet Joel: ..."
>
> ACTS 2:12, 14, 16

Another example is Jesus' address at the synagogue in Nazareth. He did the expected when he accepted the scroll of the prophet Isaiah that was handed to him. Unrolling it, Luke says he "found the place where it is written: 'The Spirit of the Lord is on me, because he has anointed me to preach good news to the poor ...' " (Luke 4:18, quoting Isaiah 61:1). But then he did the unexpected; he rolled up the scroll, gave it back to the attendant, sat down, and said, "Today this scripture is fulfilled in your hearing" (Luke 4:21). He took what they knew and were expecting, calling to their memories the context, and announced its fulfillment in the present — in himself. Imagine the scene! This is once again a typically Eastern way of speaking of one's self — in the third person. He identified himself as the fulfillment of the prophecy while retaining the distinction of the eternal Son, now in incarnate and temporal form, by using the third person.

Third, the term "Son of Man" in Ezekiel and Daniel was used in a particular sense. The following reference in Daniel is instructive:

> In my vision at night I looked, and there before me was one like a son of man, coming with the clouds of heaven. He approached the Ancient of Days and was led into his presence. He was given authority, glory and sovereign power; all peoples, nations and men of every language worshiped him. His dominion is an everlasting dominion that will not pass away, and his kingdom is one that will never be destroyed.
>
> DANIEL 7:13 – 14

This is a key passage for understanding the expectations people had for the Son of Man, which are clearly messianic. But note something remarkable. In the period of history between the Testaments, writings about the Son of Man became politicized and power driven. Instead of a focus on worship, it turned to judgment, domination, glory, ownership, control — everything we consider to be the trappings of absolute power.

Some years ago, I was privileged to address the heads of state in a particular continent at their first annual Prayer Breakfast. I arrived, but unfortunately my suitcases didn't. After checking into the hotel and making contacts to try to get my luggage to this remote city before the breakfast the next morning, my bags finally arrived in my hotel room around 3:00 a.m. I was able to arrive at the venue a few hours later suitably dressed, although not very calm in my spirit. Each president made his appearance amid great pomp and circumstance; a convoy of high-priced automobiles, black-suited security men wearing dark glasses, and ladies bedecked in great finery befitting the power of their station formed the entourage of each leader. As the breakfast began and one speaker after another welcomed the guests and spoke to their common issues, it became obvious that the continent was in serious trouble, rife with life-threatening disease and, in most countries, poverty beyond description. I sat at the head table through all this, my head swirling with fatigue, emotion, and questions. Were we real or fake? Did we really care, or was this politics as usual? After my talk, one president said to me, "Our cumulative wisdom is unable to meet the daunting challenges of our time." No more sobering assessment could have been made.

That night, my son, a colleague, and I went out for dinner and were served by a pleasant young waiter named Ernest. He was very cordial, and we had a good conversation with him. As we were about to leave, he said, "Sirs, if you ever come back to my country, would you please bring me a pair of shoes?" He lifted his foot to show us that the soles of his shoes were worn through. He said he had to walk for over an hour to work each day, and his shoes were constantly wearing out because they were of such poor quality. I asked him what his size was and suggested I could mail him a pair, but he quickly pointed out that they would never make it past the post office. So all we could do was take his contact information and promise to bring him some shoes if we were ever to come back.

It was dark by now, and as we walked back to the hotel my son, Nathan, said, "Dad, Ernest's shoe size is the same as mine. I have a brand-new pair of Doc Martens in my room." He had just bought them in England a few weeks previous. I said, "What do you want to do?" He said, "I think I'll take them back to the restaurant." So we wrapped them up and walked back the way we had come. When we entered the restaurant, we asked for Ernest and handed him the package. Curious, he opened it and looked inside as the other waiters crowded around to see what he had. With great excitement he pulled out the shoes and tried them on. They were a perfect fit. Our eyes filled with tears as the other waiters high-fived him. Our only regret is that we didn't have a pair to give each of them.

The contrast between our experience of the morning and this experience at night was literally night and day. In the bright setting of power we had sensed darkness, and in this dark setting of simplicity we had been touched by the light.

Now this story has everything to do with the Son of Man. We are told that "the Son of Man came to seek and to save what was lost" (Luke 19:10). Who is Jesus? He has identified himself with every human being regardless of culture, color, or belief. He is in the face of every human being. Jacob betrayed his brother Esau and stole his blessing from their blind father, Isaac (Genesis 27). When the moment of reckoning came more than twenty years later and Jacob came face-to-face with his brother, he begged for Esau's favor and said, "To see your face is like seeing the face of God" (Genesis 33:10). The Son of Man crosses barriers and cultures because we are all made in God's image.

But the Son of Man came to suffer and to be crucified. Mark and Luke both quote Jesus as saying that it was for this reason that he came to earth as a man (Mark 8:31; Luke 9:22). Not only did he love every human being, especially the downtrodden; the core of his message is that he came to embody the rejection and suffering of every person who has ever lived. Most of the times that Jesus used this title were in the context of his suffering and crucifixion. When Jesus told Peter that he would have to suffer and die, Peter thundered back that it could not possibly be so (Matthew 16:23). Peter could not imagine such a scenario taking place because his expectations were only that the Son of Man would come as a conqueror, a ruler, the personification of unrelenting power. Now he was being asked to accept the Son of Man as a suffering servant and a crucified Messiah? That the Messiah would suffer at the hands of his own creation and be mocked for his "powerlessness" was unthinkable!

Our experience of power is that it is used to subdue its opponents with greater strength and authority than they have. But Jesus demonstrated that true power means restraint and mercy. He redefined power, and suffering became something that was not only the lot of the weak but the personal choice of the Almighty. It is this picture of Jesus that the world can never seem to grasp. We think that the rhetoric of politicians will solve all of our problems. A new face, a new voice, a new eloquence — "change" becomes the mantra. The entourage follows the voice, and hopes become rife once again.

How wrong and simplistic we have become! True leadership only comes with an understanding of the Son of Man and his mission and vision because in our quest to understand him, he reveals to us the inner workings of our own hearts. He endured suffering himself to underscore our inner tragedy. We need not just political change; we need a change of our hearts — and only the Son of Man, who identified himself with us and personified both our glory and our shame, can accomplish that.

Son of God

No title is more recognized as properly belonging to Jesus than "the Son of God." Although it is mystifying, it also reveals the very being of God; for God, who is one in essence, reveals himself by this title as a being in relationship — a Trinity. This revelation of God as a being in relationship has led to a misunderstanding of God and to great misrepresentation. Any fisherman knows that one and three are not the same. Any thinking person knows that to talk of three persons in one essence defies any analogy except to a psychologically deranged person.

It is here that I think the Christian message has the only answer to the greatest question in philosophy, a question that has been asked since the time of the early Greeks: How does one find unity in diversity? Academics and cultures have both pursued an answer. But with the concept of three in one within the very person of God, we find that three individual wills aligned in one essence is precisely how God has disclosed himself — unity in diversity. And as we have been created in God's image, it is precisely this relationship within the Godhead that provides the possibility of relationship among us.

No illustration will ever fully capture this; many have been tried and have fallen short. But let me make one more attempt. The Bible describes marriage as the sacred coming together of a man and a woman in a consummate and exclusive relationship: "and they will become one flesh" (Genesis 2:24). When the consummate sexual act is completed and the woman is impregnated, at that moment of conception (whether she realizes it or not) there are actually three persons within one being — the woman, the seed of her husband, and, between them, the third person, the child. The woman is no longer responsible only for herself, for she is carrying her husband's distinctive DNA that, joined with her DNA, will engender the distinctive third person with his or her own DNA. In a strange and mystical but factual way, there are three in one. We claim to understand this process of conception, but all we do is create constructs of self-referencing meaning and think we have solved the puzzle. We may as well describe why a plane flies while ignoring the aircraft's designer and how he met the terms of the laws of aerodynamics. I ask a very simple question: If in our finitude, we can understand this concept of three-in-one in procreation, is it really impossible for the Creator, who is infinite, to be three in one sense and one in another sense?

Every hunger of the human heart — whether for love, for an explanation to human suffering, or for a way to understand death — has at its root the assumption that people and their relationships have intrinsic value. By calling himself "the Son of God," Jesus demonstrates that God is a relational being whose plan is to conform us as individuals to the image of his Son (Romans 8:29), and as a fellowship of believers to the relationship between the Son and the Father — "that they may be one as we are one" (John 17:11; Jesus' prayer to the Father before his arrest and crucifixion).

Savior

Among the numerous other titles Jesus carries is "Savior" — "the one who saves." Once again, every expectation within the historical context of Jesus' coming was for one who would save his people as a nation, a cultural community, and a favored people and deliver them from the oppression of Rome. Rome was the enemy. Rome had plundered them. Rome needed to be subdued. Isn't that the way it always is? It is always someone else's fault.

It is always someone else who is the problem. In his existentialist play *No Exit*, Jean-Paul Sartre described hell as "other people" — I'm all right; *you* are the problem.

Do you know the story of the man who was stranded on an island for a long time? When he was finally rescued, he was asked to explain the three structures on the island with him. "One is my home," he said, "and one is my church, and the other one is the church I used to go to."

Jesus says that the problem is *not* everyone else; the problem is within each of us. Attempting to satisfy the passions that rage inside us and the longings that motivate us, we invent spirituality, lean on political solutions, create new villains, turn our backs on Jesus, and blame a thousand tyrannies — but we never come to terms with the source of the problem deep within the heart and inclination of every human being. No matter our accomplishments or successes, our failures or shortcomings, the greatest struggle we face is within ourselves.

Some years ago, Canadian author Douglas Coupland wrote a book titled *Life after God* in which he reflects on the experiences of his own generation, a generation in which the majority have given up on God and pursued life according to their own goals and values apart from God, with varying degrees of success. But when he ends the book, he catches his readers completely off guard:

> Now — here is my secret:
>
> I tell it to you with an openness of heart that I doubt I shall ever achieve again, so I pray that you are in a quiet room as you hear these words. My secret is that I need God — that I am sick and can no longer make it alone. I need God to help me give, because I no longer seem capable of giving; to help me be kind, as I no longer seem capable of kindness; to help me love, as I seem beyond being able to love.[6]

"I am sick." That is the malady. And Jesus came as the answer to the problem. He is the physician of the soul.

In a recent tragedy of enormous proportions, India's fifth largest high-tech company was dealt a blow of foundation-shaking news. The CEO and founder disclosed that the company books had been doctored for years to misrepresent the true picture. The billions the company claimed in profit were simply not there. The founder had engaged in a monumental game of deceit, and in his letter of confession and resignation he wrote, "I felt like I was riding a tiger, not knowing how to get off without being eaten."[7] His company is called Satyam, which, ironically, means "Truth."

On November 26, 2008, a gang of Islamic terrorists stormed the historic Taj Mahal Palace Hotel in Mumbai. After the carnage that took over two hundred innocent lives ended, one of the guests who had been at the hotel for dinner that night was interviewed by the media. An Indian-born English actor, he described how he and his friends were eating dinner when they heard gunshots. Someone grabbed him and pulled him under the table. The assassins came striding through the restaurant, shooting at will, until everyone (so they thought) had been killed. This man, however, found himself miraculously alive. When the interviewer asked him how it was that everyone at his table and in the room was dead and yet he was alive, his answer was sobering: "I suppose it's because I was covered in someone else's blood, and they took me for dead."

This is a perfect metaphor of God's gift through Jesus to each one of us. Because he paid the penalty for our sin — because we are covered in the blood of his sacrifice — we may have eternal life. The Jesus of history is the Jesus who meets all of humanity in the innermost regions of our hearts' hungers and in our minds' needs. He is the one who transcends cultures, boundaries, and circumstances. He is the one who by his identification with us has given us intrinsic value. He is the physician of our souls. He is the one who gives us eternal life through his own death and resurrection. He transcends all that divides us from ourselves, from each other, and from God — both the significant things and the insignificant things — and gives us the life for which he created us.

To recognize God's presence, his power, and his design in our lives is to understand that Jesus is who he says he is, to believe that true life can only be found in him. Jesus said to Thomas, "Because you have seen me, you have believed; blessed are those who have not seen and yet have believed"

(John 20:29). John writes, "These are written that you may believe that Jesus is the Christ, the Son of God, and that by believing you may have life in his name" (verse 31).

Who is Jesus? He is the Son of David, the Son of Man, the Son of God, and the Savior — not to defeat Rome, not to take care of "the other guy," not to abolish the other political party — he is the Savior, the only one who can deliver us from the tigers within our own deceitful hearts. This is Jesus. Knowing who he is makes the journey to a strong faith rational, even though the way is punctuated with times of struggle. In our ethnic, human, and relational conflicts, we can see what happens when we displace the one who transcends all these issues, and in breaking our relationship with him, we break it with each other and ultimately with ourselves. This rupture of serious ramifications often leaves us saying that our faith has failed us. Rather than pausing to see what we have done to the content and object of our faith, we lay blame at the doorstep of God.

2

WHAT DOES IT MEAN
TO BE A CHRISTIAN?

Now that we have laid the foundation for a discussion on whether or how
Christianity has failed us by first recognizing who Jesus is and why he
came, let us go on to answer the question of what it means to be a Christian
— a person who believes what Christianity teaches. If we do not know the
answer to this question, again we cannot answer whether or not Christianity has failed us. So, what does it mean to be a Christian? What are the
logical implications for our lives that follow from what Jesus taught by his
example and his teachings?

I want to explore the hidden realities of the story that follows and use
it to illustrate and point out how the Christian life works and why it works
the way it does. In this pluralistic society and new age of science, it is even
more important to know what it means to be a Christian. We often hear the
statement that all religions are fundamentally the same and superficially
different. But this is not true. All religions are fundamentally different
and only superficially the same at best. Neither are the sciences fundamentally the same and only superficially different, for we talk of exact sciences, behavioral sciences, phenomenology, ontology, analytic statements,
and synthetic statements. Indeed, there is a legitimate range within which
truth can be pursued and within which the verification processes of truth
claims can be justified. To reduce all religions to the superficial similarities among them and make those similarities definitive of the religions
themselves does injustice to both the belief systems and the believers who

subscribe to them and puts at risk nothing less than individual identity — and spiritual life or death.

It has been said that the language of lust and the language of love are much the same. Both say "I love you," but one says it for a night and the other for life.

Words and emotions repeatedly fall victim to the moment and must be tested. Listening carefully and understanding what someone says they believe requires the ultimate test, not just of knowledge, but of wisdom as well. Knowledge and wisdom are two different things, and we must come to understand the difference between believing something and knowing why it is believed.

Many will remember the tragedy that took place among the college community of Taylor University in Upland, Indiana on April 26, 2006. Returning to the campus late at night, several students and staff in a school van were crushed by a truck whose driver had fallen asleep at the wheel. Four students and one staff member were killed. In the ensuing confusion of pulling the bodies out of the twisted metal and identifying them, a most unexpected twist unfolded.

For five weeks after the accident the Van Ryn family sat at the bedside of the broken body of their daughter Laura, the lone student survivor. But as the days went by, they experienced a growing and troubling consternation. Laura was not answering their questions or relating to them in a manner that was consistent with who she was. Attributing it to the trauma and head injuries she had experienced, they kept hoping that her mind would clear and that their daughter as they knew her would return to them. But with each passing day, their uneasiness increased, until they finally realized that this girl they had nursed was not Laura; she was actually Whitney Cerak, one of the other students in the van. Laura Van Ryn had not survived the accident and was in fact buried under a marker that read "Whitney Cerak."

This incredible case of mistaken identity had happened because of the extreme disfigurement caused by the accident and by the fact that the girls actually resembled each other. The trauma for the two families is unfathomable. We have all heard of newborn babies who have been switched at birth, but who can calculate the psychological ramifications of the honest mistaken identity in a multiple tragedy such as this one? Whatever judgment may be made on how such a mix-up could have occurred, no one denies that it was an honest, unintentional mistake, made in the chaos and confusion of devastating emotional trauma.

The decisions we make during the throes of wrenching emotion sometimes have great ramifications. Thus, skeptics often cavalierly charge that those who believe in God only do so out of psychological need or emotional fear. How easy it is for them to choose to ignore the fact that many skeptics are skeptical about God for the equally distorting psychological reasons of hurt, pride, or just plain self-aggrandizement.

Truth, however, is no respecter of mistaken judgments. That is the strange symmetry, the painful and redeeming reality of the nature of truth. How often has each of us made a false decision or judgment based largely on emotion and realized too late what has happened? People have been incarcerated for a good part of their lives because of wrong judgments. Similarly, one's whole view of life can develop from erroneous thinking, sometimes resulting from great trauma. Thus, many have turned their backs on God because of a traumatic experience that may have colored their thinking or their ability to reason logically.

In Isaiah 1:18 the Bible records God's words: "Come now, let us reason together." So let us begin to reason together about what Christianity teaches about life and the world we live in with our minds and hearts open to the truths that will be discussed so that we can honestly answer whether Christianity has failed us.

THE CONFLICT OF THE MORAL AND THE SPIRITUAL

When philosophers present arguments for God's existence, they resort to the laws of logic and the rational inferences one may draw from them. Over the centuries, the most existentially powerful argument that continues to haunt the discussion on God's existence is the moral argument, which goes something like this:

> Objective moral values exist only if God exists.
> Objective moral values do exist.
> Therefore God exists.

This simple syllogism is then broken down, and each statement is examined against reality and against its relationship to the two other statements in the syllogism. The argument stands or falls based on how it holds up against reality. Some who challenge God's existence will often assert that even if this argument does sustain the existence of some transcending power, it still doesn't tell us who this God is or, more particularly, why this God is the God of the Judeo-Christian faith and not any other god. In effect, they are arguing, "Yes, I will accept the fact that objective truth exists. But why should it be the truth as you see it rather than as I see it? Why can't I reject your version of truth and replace it with my version of truth?"

If there is no reality against which to measure truth, these people are correct. But I would ask them: Is it legitimate for me to argue that whether the theory of gravity articulated by Newton applies to a person depends entirely on how that person has been raised to think? Why must I accept the theory of gravity that Newton stated and that science has accepted? Why can't I come up with my own theory of gravity? The answer, the scientist would say, is that Newton's theory best reflects reality. And I would say that the existence of God best reflects the reality of the world we see and live in.

Now if we grant that objective moral values do exist, why does that necessarily point to a personal God as Jesus taught? Consider the following: Every time a question with moral implications is raised, it is raised *by* a person or *about* a person, or both. Animals and plants do not raise questions about morality. This must at least mean that personhood is indispensable to moral reasoning. But if the notion itself of personhood is essentially worthless — which is the position to which naturalism is ultimately and undeniably driven — is there really any point in any discussion about morality? Such a discussion just for the sake of discussion is circular at best, and no conclusion can be sustained apart from an acknowledgment of an ultimate spiritual reality.

Skeptics who mock anyone who questions the validity of certain scientific laws also mock anyone who believes in spiritual laws; they do so because they believe there is no empirical value in the spiritual; that is, they cannot test or evaluate spiritual truth using a scientific method. If physics is the only reliable means of knowing anything with certainty, what does that say of the laws of logic, which are not properly in the category of science? They have declared metaphysics unreliable and yet they have borrowed logic and reason from the world of metaphysics in order to prove their purely scientific explanation for the physical world! Induction and deduction are not only scientific tools; they are also used to determine the truth of ideas. Setting apart science as the only certain discipline is itself not a scientifically verifiable fact.

Moral categories must exist with certainty; otherwise the very critique of God as being "immoral" is a self-defeating argument because if there is no morality, God cannot be immoral — no matter what he does. What is more, having decided that there is no value in the spiritual anyway, they cleverly lump all religious truth claims indiscriminately into one bundle, which is then subjected to their empirically exact sciences. Failing the test, they are all tossed out of the arena of fact.

Certainly they must know that not everyone who believes in God subscribes to the same belief system. If all who believed in God believed in the same God, the term would need no explanation and multiple religious worldviews would not have developed. All belief in God is not the same, which is why we run into the clutter and complexity of competing worldviews, each arguing its own merit. If the problem of evil is the single greatest challenge in the debate around God's existence, the problem of which God to believe in is a close second.

There are many ways one can respond to this question, and I have done so in my writings elsewhere. Here I want to simply present what the Christian faith affirms that makes it unique and true with regard to the basic issues of human identity and human worth. I will try to avoid using theological terms, since they are often unfamiliar and can result in confusion and resistance. I will simply go to the big ideas that shape the worldview of the Christian.

THE "CAUSE" OF THE FIRST CAUSE

I am a Christian because I believe that Jesus is who he says he is, and I have accepted his sacrifice as payment for my sin. Beyond that, the first and foremost assertion of Christianity is implied by the question, *What is man?* The answer the psalmist gives to his own question demonstrates a starting point for Christianity that is different from any other belief system, secular or religious, except for Judaism:

> When I consider your heavens,
> the work of your fingers,
> the moon and the stars,
> which you have set in place,
> what is man that you are mindful of him,
> the son of man that you care for him?
> You made him a little lower than the heavenly beings
> and crowned him with glory and honor.
>
> PSALM 8:3 – 5

These magnificent words were penned nearly three thousand years ago by a man marveling at the beauty and diversity of what he saw around him in nature — and yet recognizing the distinctiveness of a human being in contrast to nature.

A story circulated some years ago about Sherlock Holmes and his loyal friend and student Watson, who were together on a camping trip. After a good meal, they lay down for the night and went to sleep. Some hours later, Holmes awoke and nudged his faithful friend awake.

"Watson," he said, "look up at the sky and tell me what you see."

"I see millions and millions of stars," Watson replied.

"What does that tell you?" Holmes questioned.

Watson pondered the question and then said, "Astronomically, it tells me that there are millions of galaxies and potentially billions of planets. Astrologically, I observe that Saturn is in Leo. Horologically, I deduce that the time is approximately a quarter past three. Theologically, I can see that God is all-powerful and that we are small and insignificant. Meteorologically, I suspect that we will have a beautiful day tomorrow. What does it tell you?"

Holmes was silent for a minute before speaking. "Watson, you idiot!" he said with a measure of restraint. "Someone has stolen our tent!"

As funny as this story is, if we apply it to our present discussion, we see that an enormous robbery has taken place in which someone has stolen from you that which provides shelter or the covering for your life. It is not accidental that those who stick to a scientific single vision of ultimate reality start by denying a Creator, and from there, all of the disciplines are herded together to create a mentality that asserts that any worldview seeking a transcendent explanation for our universe is unwelcome in intelligent discussion. When science categorically and unconditionally insists to all who hunger for religious truth that there is no such thing, it has ceased to be science and is only revealing its hostility.

This, I'm afraid, is what is revealed by the stridency and belligerence of the "new atheists." They are not open or willing to go where the evidence leads, unless that evidence sustains their own naturalistic assumptions. They have covertly reduced all philosophical thought and deduction to — ironically — *faith*. Perhaps inadvertently, in denying a Creator they also deny the essential worth of creation and of the act of creating, which means, then, that all great art, music, architecture, and writing must be consigned to the ash heap, because the inspiration behind these great expressions and reflections of the transcendent is denied as non-real or faith (it cannot be scientifically or empirically studied or observed). The same must apply to all the great themes of love, beauty, truth, morality, justice, and the like, as they too cannot be empirically or scientifically studied and observed.

The starting points, then, of Christianity and naturalistic science diverge, and unfortunately the resulting conflict often brings more heat than light. For when the starting point of one belief system is an intelligent mind with a purpose and that of the opposing belief system is matter and randomness, the ending points are determined right from the beginning.

On a side note, I would like to say that certain people who held these beliefs of naturalism could have saved me a lot of reading. In my days of graduate studies the noted philosopher Antony Flew was the atheist with whom we had to contend. I spent hours coming to terms with Flew's arguments and all that he demanded of theism in terms of logic and proof. Because he was the most noted atheist of that time, it was imperative that we understood and were able to respond to his challenges.

Now times have changed, and Antony Flew finds himself in the position of writing against the vociferous atheists of our day because he contends that atheism is no longer a logically tenable position for him. He is willing, he says, to go where the evidence leads. In his book *There Is a God*, Flew reflects on an argument regarding the probability of human origin that he had to deal with in his younger days. The argument runs like this: How long would it take for an infinite number of monkeys pounding on an infinite number of typewriters to compose a sonnet by Shakespeare? (Believe it or not, this argument was based on an experiment conducted by the British National Council of the Arts.) A computer was placed in a cage with six monkeys, and after one month of hammering away at the keys and using the computer as a bathroom, the monkeys produced fifty typed pages — but not one single word. This is amazing, considering that the shortest word in English could be a one-letter word such as the letter *a* or *I*. But a one-letter word is only a word if there is space on either side of it. Flew points out that if one considers that there are thirty keys on a keyboard, the possibility of getting a one-letter word is one in 30 x 30 x 30, which is one in 27,000. If these attempts could not even result in one one-letter word, what is the possibility of getting just the first line of one of Shakespeare's sonnets, let alone a whole sonnet? Flew quotes scientist and author Gerry Schroeder on the sheer improbability of the random existence of the universe:

If you took the entire universe and converted it to computer chips — forget the monkeys — each one weighing a millionth of a gram, and had each computer chip able to spin out 488 trials at, say, a million times a second; if you turn the entire universe into these microcomputer chips and these chips were spinning a million times a second [producing] random letters, the number of trials you would get since the beginning of time would be 10 to the 90th trials. It would be off again by a factor of 10 to the 600th. You will never get a sonnet by chance — let alone the complete works of Shakespeare. The Universe would have to be 10 to the 600th times larger. Yet the world just thinks the monkeys can do it every time.[1]

For Flew, the sheer improbability that such an intricate design as we have in this universe is the product of mindless evolution is insurmountable; the universe must have purpose and design behind it.

As powerful an argument as statistical improbability is, a simple point I want to make here is that although the specifics may be different, this is not a new argument for the improbability of chance. Antony Flew knows this to be so. But I must add that no dyed-in-the-wool naturalist is likely to suggest that our universe could not have beaten such odds. They will say that just because it is improbable, it doesn't mean that the universe didn't happen this way — a view that vehemently resists both human limitation and the humility required to follow reason where it leads. Instead, they will wax eloquent, like Watson, on endless categories of convoluted descriptions of what "might" or "could" have happened, all the while ignoring the most obvious deduction or conclusion before them as to the origin of the universe — that it was a deliberate act of creation by an intelligent being. Stubbornly and deliberately ignoring that "the tent has disappeared," there is no way for naturalists to account for human relational hungers, so they refuse to recognize that these hungers are validated by the real fact that people relate to other people through a relationship.

To even think we could get a Shakespearean sonnet by accident assumes, first, that we have other sonnets to which we can compare the "accidental" one in order to know that it is indeed a Shakespearean sonnet and, second, that whenever we see intelligibility we assume intelligence. Even if the monkeys could have produced a sonnet by accident, we would still wonder at the intelligence behind the technology of the keys and the development of the alphabet, the aesthetics of this sonnet in comparison with other sonnets, and, to boot, whether the monkeys knew what they were doing.

The numerical impossibility actually defies even the "chance" analogy. And in the origin of the universe, as naturalism tells the story, there are no monkeys to begin with. The monkeys evolved from chemistry and energy after the universe already existed. There are no alphabets to be explained. There is no idea of a sonnet except as nonexistent monkeys pounding on nonexistent keys. All these assumptions are circular.

Let me illustrate this point a little differently through the fascinating story of George Frideric Handel's composition of *Messiah*. His career as a composer was on the verge of collapse, and he was naturally discouraged, feeling that he was a failure. The words for *Messiah* were given to him as a possible oratorio, and he decided to try one last time to compose a great piece of music. When he reached the text for the "Hallelujah Chorus" and began to reflect on the words, he said later that he saw the heavens opened and the great God himself. And as the great chorus reached its climax at the first public presentation of *Messiah* before the king of England, the king rose to his feet in recognition of the awesome power of the words and music combining to give honor to the One to whom honor is due. The convergence of intelligence, aesthetics, and the inspirational power of a transcending reality in the person of God has the power to bring even kings either to their feet or to their knees.

All of this is dismissed as mere nonsense by the skeptic. Not only does he take that which appears statistically impossible and try to make it actual; he takes the emotion and spiritual expression that is common to the human experience, and is therefore actual, and tries to make it farcical. Is it really possible to deny such a reality as that described by Handel's experience in writing the music for *Messiah* without even a twinge of doubt that perhaps there is more to life than science alone?

Is that not what happened to the Van Ryn and Cerak families? It was not just DNA that told them they had the wrong daughter. There was something else — something beyond science and matter. It was the intuitive certainty that comes from the collection of data — memory, affections, attachments, and numerous other contingencies that produce the distinctiveness of what we call "personhood." What if the Van Ryns had insisted that this was their daughter, even as the Ceraks denied it, steadfastly believing it — even though the girl herself claimed she was not their daughter and all the DNA evidence pointed to her being someone else? What if they had stubbornly refused to accept the truth just because they had been told by the coroner that their daughter had survived the wreck?

In this same way, the naturalist is simply compelled to deny the evidence before him that each human life is of worth apart from anyone else, with unique needs and a unique capacity to relate to others. In fact, within the setting of this tragic event for the Van Ryns, the Ceraks and the Taylor community, science and the sacred were forced to converge. The DNA testing only confirmed that the person before them was who she was claiming to be and not who she was believed to be by the Van Ryns. This intertwining of the disciplines with relationship that is both "intrapersonal" and "interpersonal," within and without, reveals a distinctiveness that we must recognize as sacred and inviolable. But this is denied repeatedly in naturalism, which insists that we just happen to be here, that we're all just "dancing to our DNA," as Richard Dawkins puts it. For the Christian, the awesome nature of the world we are part of does not point to brute science in isolation but to the Creator, a personal God who can and does relate to human beings.

NOT ALL PURPOSES WITHSTAND SCRUTINY

The other day I passed a clever billboard while driving to the airport — it was an advertisement for Chic-fil-A in which one cow was standing on the back of another in order to reach a blackboard on which it wrote, "$E=MC^2=$

Eat More Chicken." To be sure, Einstein had anything but eating more chicken in mind when he came up with that formula. But from the breadth and depth of a scientific understanding of energy to the respite of clever humor, human beings are each distinct in intellect and mind.

Now as we think about created entities created by a personal Creator, the whole realm of purpose is brought into focus. Many facets of what it means to be a person are shared among us, but each person is still unique. All of humanity shares some core characteristics; for example, we know that none of us have caused our own existence and that from conception to death we cannot survive independently of each other. Our lives are interdependent, even as we build our individual values, hopes, and dreams. Every pursuit we follow is either conditioned or driven by personal choice to express that individuality.

Here we are brought up short in the search for our own distinctive identity and destiny. Are we content to just be here, putting in time, or are we going to pursue the significance we intuitively sense we have? Our laughter, our tears, our sense of humor, our fears all point to an innate ability to think as an individual in abstract, caricatured, and concrete terms.

Let me shift our focus from the intellect to the mind. Pastor and speaker Reid S. Monaghan, summarizing the argument of Kevin Favero (an electrical engineer by training), provides a syllogism that gives a remarkable clue to the difference between how the mind works and how mere intellect works:

> If matter/energy is all there is, then there is no free will.
> There is free will.
> Therefore matter/energy is not all there is.[2]

Monaghan is pointing to that which is definitive of all that is basic about moral reasoning. We know that as human beings, we have the capacity to feel with moral implications and to think in paradigms. We make judgments all the time according to the way each of us views or interprets the world around us. Even if we do not agree with each other on what ought to be, we recognize that there must be an "ought," such as, "We all ought to behave in certain ways or else we cannot get along," which is why we have laws. In short, we ascribe to ourselves freedom with boundaries and assume that truth is a valid goal. As a rule, we implicitly grant that two mutually exclusive statements cannot both be true without some qualification. Our shared humanity in the context of our distinctiveness and of our ability to reason in moral terms is precisely what the Bible asserts in God's infinite capacity to create individuals with a hunger for community and a hunger for truth — indeed, a hunger for individual acceptance.

These contrarieties of individuality and community become part of our search for meaning and for meaningfulness. In other words, I am not absolutely free to pursue individual meaning at the cost of denying someone else the same prerogative. Life comes as a package deal, and there is mutual responsibility if we are to keep from destroying each other. More to the point, we reap within ourselves the consequences of our choices because of the laws we must live by. If we don't, there is a law of diminishing returns when we pursue pleasure for pleasure's sake. Both pleasure and pain have therapeutic and debilitating sides to them, for, as C. S. Lewis wrote, "God whispers to us in our pleasures,... but shouts in our pains; it is his megaphone to rouse a deaf world."[3] This is vitally important to remember. Christianity gives an explanation for these realities of life on this earth; naturalism does not.

To illustrate, a prominent public figure recently contacted me by phone. Both of us were overseas when he called me. Perhaps being miles from home provided him some sense of protection and enabled him to say what he wanted to say. As I listened to him speak, nothing he told me was any different from what I have heard thousands of times before. Perhaps the specifics were different, but the story was the same. He had climbed the pinnacle of success. He had experienced human emotions of the deepest kind. Yet he was like a ship on the high seas without chart, compass, or destination. The essence of what he said was that he was lost. His impressive credentials and his level of despair were totally incongruent. He was living as an icon of success in a make-believe public persona. Privately, both he and his world were falling apart.

But he is no different from any of us, if we will but admit it, for we are all totally lost in spite of our accomplishments, both as individuals and as a community. Why do we see this so often and yet continue to deny its implications? It seems we have to learn the same lessons over and over. But there can be no reproach to pain unless we assume human dignity; there is no reason for restraints on pleasure unless we assume human worth; there is legitimacy to monotony unless we assume a greater purpose to life; there is no purpose to life unless we assume design; death has no significance unless we seek what is everlasting. This is true across the board in human experience — across cultures, languages, and backgrounds. This is what Christianity teaches.

This man had told our common friend, "Please pray for my children. I am not sure what will become of them." As I heard him speak of his situation and his fears, I couldn't but help think of the Broadway play *Phantom of the Opera*. The words of the song "Music of the Night" speak volumes of how the darkness of night intensifies temptation. Under the cover of darkness not only are nefarious schemes hatched and implemented, but strange justifications are invented. In the darkness, the song says, it is easy to pretend that the truth is what we think it ought to be.

When everything is done only for the sake of appearances, the human mind becomes a factory of manipulated reasons to justify the horrendous. We make our own truths in the dark, and when daylight comes, we wonder what possessed us to do what we did and to think what we thought. Half a century ago, Aldous Huxley said that he wanted the world not to have meaning because if there were no meaning to life he was freed to his own choices for sex and politics. Is it for the same reason today that we wish to deny the Creator any room in the public place?

False religions have at least one redeeming aspect — those who follow them do so because they understand they have not found the answer within themselves. They acknowledge that as humans we are quite limited and cannot make it on our own. Even when we exalt ourselves, it is because we need to justify our existence. Sheer naturalism lives the ultimate lie of giving itself value by self-reference, insisting that it needs no one and no thing in order to justify itself or its existence.

The Bible says we distort truth to suit ourselves. Christianity makes it clear that we are created to conform to the image of God's Son, Jesus (Romans 8:29; 2 Corinthians 3:18). He is the blueprint for life. Each of us must either recognize that we are who God says we are or deny him, leaving ourselves with no point of reference or value, except as our individual cultures assign to us.

NOT ALL FAITHS
ARE CREATED EQUAL

Christianity is unique in another way. Not only are we redeemed and given individual value by God and a place in community; we are shown the only reasonable vantage point from which to know these truths. Let me explain.

How do we know what we know? How do we know that what we know is true? Let's look at this set of statements Reid Monaghan put up on his website:

> A plurality of persons and ideas is good.
> A plurality of religions is a brute fact.
> A plurality of gods is an idolatrous fiction.
> A plurality of contradictory "truths" is an impossibility.[4]

A plurality of contradictory "truths" is an impossibility. This statement is the bottom line. Contrast everything you have just read that Christianity teaches about origin and purpose with the worldview of every other religion or belief, and you will see there is a difference between Christianity and other religious thought. In the pantheistic scheme, every birth is a rebirth; life moves in a cycle. Fatalism is the inevitable result of such a view: what has been, will be, and what will be, will return. Why worry about the children? They may not have been yours last time around and will not be yours next time around. Just fulfill your karmic debt so that you have a smaller debt to pay when you start over the next time. And perchance if you return with a greater debt, no one, as far as you know, will be able to identify the reason for it. This is the ultimate game of "Who's on First?" — never being able to pin down where anyone stands or who we truly are.

Instinctively we know that names and individuality mean something. Pantheism takes away individual essence and offers in return existence without reference. It is the coroner burying a body without ever knowing its true identity. As one former Hindu said to me, "If every birth is a payment for the previous birth, and I have had only a finite number of births, what was I paying for in my first birth? Even the bank tells me how much I owe them. My karma tells me nothing." Karma is a cruel, silent creditor. It leaves you hanging on a thread, filled with a fearsome uncertainty about whether it will support you or break you.

Islam *does* give primary place to the Creator. But from there, everything spirals down until you are reduced to the existence of an automaton. Everything is *Insha'Allah* — the will of God. Man is only a pawn in the hands of a God with whom no relationship is possible. From an Islamic perspective, Kevin Favero's syllogism (see above) would read:

> God is absolutely sovereign.
> There is no free will.
> Therefore man is absolutely determined.

Thus, the poetic cynicism of Omar Khayyam in his *Rubaiyat*:

> 'Tis all a chequer-board of nights and days
> Where destiny with men for pieces plays:
> Hither and thither moves, and mates, and slays,
> And one by one back in the closet lays.

Islamic apologists, trying to convince themselves of some freedom in their belief while also retaining their belief in the absolute sovereignty under which they live, would write a syllogism as follows:

> God is all sovereign.
> Just submit to Allah.

> You will be weighed in the balances.
> You will be held accountable
> *as if you are sovereign over yourself.*
> A sovereign God will judge you.

Christianity is definitively and drastically different from all other reli gions. God is sovereign, to be sure. But Christianity teaches that in his sovereignty God has given humanity freedoms within built-in boundaries that bring fulfillment. No amount of goodness can justify us before a sovereign God, but his grace makes up for what our wills cannot accomplish.

THREE POSTURES

Here I am going to significantly diverge into an aspect of the Christian faith that is utterly unique. I use the term on purpose as it defines both *Christian* and *faith*.

It stands to reason that there are three postures from which we can make judgments about our own human nature and the nature of ultimate reality.

Sheer Determinism

The first is *sheer determinism*, which means we have no choice in how we think or believe since it has all been determined for us, either genetically or through environment, and we are locked into the very data over which we stand as judge, creating a stranglehold within the naturalistic framework. Naturalists use this same determinism that they believe has sovereignty over them to throw mud at belief in God by attributing belief to genetic makeup or by declaring, as American molecular geneticist Dean Hamer does, that "a person's capacity to believe in God is linked to his brain chemicals." Interestingly, the same claim is made about homosexuality. In other words, everything is related to molecular genetics. In response to this conclusion, philosopher and writer David Berlinski states, "If he [Hamer] has refrained from arguing that a person's capacity to believe in molecular genetics is linked to a brain chemical, it is, no doubt, owing to a prudent sense that once *that* door is open, God knows how and when anyone will slam it shut again."[5]

Hamer is voicing the default position of bioethical evolution — molecular genetics. He has no other option but to take that view. But in a scathing look at evolutionary determinism Berlinski, a secular writer, declares the following:

> A successful evolutionary theory of the human mind would, after all, annihilate any claim we might make on behalf of human freedom. The physical sciences do not trifle with determinism: It is the heart and soul of their method....
>
> When [experimental psychologist and cognitive scientist] Steven Pinker writes that "nature does not dictate what we should accept or how we should live our lives," he is expressing a belief — one obviously true — entirely at odds with his professional commitments.
>
> If ordinary men and women are, like Pinker himself, perfectly free to tell their genes to "go jump in the lake," why pay the slightest attention to evolutionary psychology?
>
> Why pay the slightest attention to Pinker?
>
> Either the theory in which he has placed his confidence is wrong, or we are not free to tell our genes to do much of anything.
>
> If the theory is wrong, which theory is right?
>
> If no theory is right, how can "the idea that human minds are the product of evolution" be "unassailable fact"?
>
> If this idea is *not* unassailable fact, why must we put aside "the idea that man was created in the image of God"?
>
> These hypotheticals must now be allowed to discharge themselves in a number of categorical statements:
>
> There is *no* reason to pay attention to Steven Pinker.
>
> We do *not* have a serious scientific theory explaining the powers and the properties of the human mind.
>
> The claim that the human mind is the product of evolution is *not* an unassailable fact. It is barely coherent.[6]

62

This scintillating response by Berlinski to the yes/no dance that science engages in with determinism reveals precisely why science ends up being executed by its own artillery when the discussion turns to freedom of any kind. In short, a belief in determinism becomes self-defeating in the face of any departure from the status quo, whether it is an issue of morality or of invention.

Total Transcendence

The second position from which we can make judgments about our own nature and the nature of ultimate reality is to claim *total transcendence*. We are so able to jump out of the box that the box itself is defined by our absolute objectivity. But seriously, aside from being arrogant, is it really possible to rise above reality so as to view it with pure objectivity? Is such self-transcendence really possible? If in the particular judgments we make *within our lives* we fall so abysmally short, how can we make such sweeping judgments on life itself? Is this not the conundrum the philosopher Peter Kreeft had in mind when he wrote, "Falling in love is a mystery. Getting to Mars is a problem."[7] According to the philosopher Gabriel Marcel, a mystery is "a problem which encroaches upon its own data."[8] In other words, we borrow capital from a debt we owe.

If determinism hangs itself by its own rope because it doesn't have the freedom to choose its destiny, self-transcendence jumps into the abyss of a free fall with nowhere to land. There is no solid ground for takeoff or landing. In short, in both determinism and self-transcendence, there is no certain position from which to view the landscape.

Semitranscendence

The only option left from which to make judgments about our own nature and the nature of ultimate reality is that of *semitranscendence*. From this vantage point we are able to view and make judgments in the proper interplay between faith and reason. We can trust our findings with certainty, but we are not so "outside the box" that the box is nothing more than an object of study.

Let me illustrate. Some years ago, I had the privilege of speaking at a colloquium hosted by a fine group of faculty members at Johns Hopkins University. The theme of the conference was "What Does It Mean to Be Human?" There were representatives from a diversity of perspectives delivering papers. Mine was to be presented from the perspective of Christianity. I would cover four basic ideas:

1. *Creation*. Christianity teaches us that each one of us has been created by God for a specific purpose.
2. *Incarnation*. The incarnation of Jesus is the essential splendor to which we are to be conformed.
3. *Transformation*. Because of my propensity to distort and refashion my destiny, I, a human being, am in need of God's grace and the strength to change my propensities.
4. *Consummation*. The consummation of the Christian life is in the communion that one enjoys with God and the final purpose beyond the grave.

From this paradigm for life I argued that both the glory of humanity and its shame made sense.

One can imagine the distress of some listeners and the acerbic questions to which I was subjected when the opportunity was given. What is ironic is that in all of the questions, whether they challenged or supported what I had said, my points were in one way or the other sustained. One of the most antagonistic questioners vehemently objected to my assertion that at heart we as human beings were basically self-driven — hence our bent to evil. The louder she argued, the more she proved my point. I recall that Malcolm Muggeridge once said that human depravity is at once the most empirically verifiable fact yet most staunchly resisted datum by our intellectuals. Reinhold Niebuhr declared, "No cumulation of contradictory evidence seems to disturb modern man's good opinion of himself."[9]

Now here is the point. Minutes before I presented my talk, Francis Collins, the codirector of the Human Genome Project, made his presentation. In closing, he prepared to show us two pictures on the screen. As he uncovered the first one, he told us it was the rose window from York Minster Cathedral in York, England. The beautiful design in magnificent colors was like a great jigsaw puzzle, each piece perfectly in place. One could only imagine the skill of the craftsman or craftsmen who spent so many hours fashioning all the tiny pieces of glass and fitting them together.

Then Dr. Collins uncovered the second picture. There were the two pictures, side by side, the second design even more complex and beautiful than the first. As we awaited his explanation, there was pin-drop silence. After a moment, Dr. Collins explained that we were looking at a cross section of human DNA. There was an audible, awestruck response as the audience drew in their breath and gazed in wonder at the pattern made by the more than three billion bits of information in that one strand of DNA. Dr. Collins responded by saying that he knew of no other way to end his presentation than to sing a hymn. And with that he picked up his guitar and sang.

As I sat entranced by what I was seeing, the thought came to my mind that it was because of the DNA strand I was seeing that I could see what I was seeing. That which held me in awe was the reason for which I could be awestruck. In other words, mine was a meaningful response in recognition of meaning, enabled by that which made my meaning meaningful. Only a semitranscendent point of reference makes that possible. This is the bequest of my Christian faith because in Christianity the God who created us in his image and assigns value to each one of us is a transcendent, intelligent Being.

That is why the candor of David Berlinski is commendable, as he does not claim to be speaking from a Christian perspective. After his one-line zingers questioning the rationality of Steven Pinker's academic sleight of hand, he ended the section by saying, "The idea that man was created in the image of God *remains* what it has always been: And that is the instinctive default position of the human race."[10]

So the psalmist asks the question in Psalm 8:

> When I consider your heavens,
>   the work of your fingers,

the moon and the stars,
which you have set in place,
what is man that you are mindful of him ...?

He then answers himself:

You made him a little lower than the heavenly beings
and crowned him with glory and honor.
You made him ruler over the works of your hands;
you put everything under his feet....
O LORD, our Lord,
how majestic is your name in all the earth!

The glory of what it means to be human is that we can celebrate the glory of the universe in its immensity and intelligibility. The universe cannot return that compliment.

When the starting point is matter, the mind can be nothing more than matter. The psalmist's question, "What is man that you are mindful of him?" remains a haunting problem for humanism where humanity is but a by-product of the universe. And why would anyone care about the by-product when you still have the original? In naturalistic humanism, the universe is supreme, not humanity.

Readers of the Bible will remember the story of the group of religious leaders who came to Jesus and asked him if it was all right to pay taxes to Caesar (Luke 22:21 – 25). Jesus responded to them with a question of his own. He asked them for a coin, held it up, and asked, "Whose portrait and inscription are on it?"

"Caesar's," came the response.

"Then give to Caesar what is Caesar's, and to God what is God's," Jesus said.

The interesting thing is that the questioners did not come back with a follow-up question. They should have asked Jesus, "And what belongs to God?"

Undoubtedly Jesus would have answered with another question: "Whose image is on you?"

Let me take this a step further. The other motive behind this question was to pit Jesus against Caesar. The truth is that they didn't want to pay the taxes to Caesar, and they were hoping that Jesus would either anger the people or Caesar by whichever way he answered the question. But Jesus' answers always went to the root of the question and not the cultural trappings of the question.

This is also essential to understanding the uniqueness of Christianity. We are confronted every day with a host of problems. As we face a range of issues, we struggle to grind out solutions. Jesus faced the same issues in the questions that were put to him, and again and again his answers went to the root of people's questions. Again and again they tried to trip him up. When they could not trip him by pitting him against Caesar, they pitted him against the religious leaders, asking, "Which is the greatest commandment?" (Matthew 22:25 – 40). Moses had given over six hundred laws. Tradition added an unmanageable burden by multiplying the caveats and contingencies to those six hundred laws until they needed experts to decide what a particular law actually meant. So when Jesus was confronted with the question, one might have expected he would either dodge the question or pick out one law that could be the anchor of all the other laws.

His answer was profound. He did not give them one law; he gave them two: "'Love the Lord your God with all your heart and with all your soul and with all your mind.' This is the first and greatest commandment. And the second is like it: 'Love your neighbor as yourself,'" he said. Then he added a footnote. "All the Law and the Prophets hang on these two commandments."

The first law — to love the Lord your God with all your heart and soul and mind — makes the second — to love your neighbor as yourself — a *necessary* sequel, and the second is only possible because of the first. Any other rationality for loving your neighbor would die the death of a thousand qualifications in the cultural wars that we fight all the time. David Berlinski is right when he says that the idea that man was created in the image of God is the instinctive default position of the human race. We are not the by-product of an impersonal universe. God has poured into our hearts a hunger for him and the ability to reason to remind us that if we don't follow this imperative, we end up demeaning ourselves.

From the Christian perspective, the only roadblock to this celebration of God and to life as he has made it to be lived is that because we have turned our backs on God, we are spiritually bankrupt. The way back to God and to life is not by a set of laws or a set of strictures. The way back to God and to the life he desires for us is to humble ourselves before him and recognize that in giving his Son, God has provided redemption for each individual soul. And with that redemption comes a new life of serving God and our fellow human beings. God has presented us with not just an idea but with connected truths that give us a broader context by which we are able to interpret our particular experiences.

- We are made by a personal God.
- We are fashioned individually but with a hunger for community.
- We are unable in our own strength to attain what it takes to live peaceably with God and our fellow human beings.
- We have a blueprint in the person of Jesus that points us to our ultimate destiny.
- We are able to know the blessing of awe and humility, both of which are prerequisites for human dignity and for recognizing our limitations.
- We are made to live by reason and faith that are so intertwined that they are the only reasonable way we can transcend ourselves.

To say "I am disappointed in Christianity" is more than merely to say, "This isn't what I thought it was going to be." Much more than that is implied and is at stake if one is truly disappointed in Christianity. To be disappointed in Christianity, one really has to say, "I am totally transcendent over reality and cannot see any ultimate purpose whatsoever." The judgments that are then made in accordance with such an assumption can no longer be made in the context of a Christian way of viewing things — the Christian worldview. Doesn't it make more sense to say, "I am assuming some things about life and about myself that I dare not assume if there is an ultimate purpose and cause for my life — and what's more, there are some things I cannot fully understand"? The shift from seeking God's ultimate plan to pursuing my own immediate desire is a shift of text from a context that is indispensable.

To dismiss all of life as ultimately random is to also dismiss the mind with which I make such judgments. The only position from which I can make valid judgments is from a semitranscendent vantage point. But this vantage point is only given to me by a moral, personal First Cause — God. Our names, our identities, our relationships, our destinies all hinge on this starting point. This is Christianity. It values the individual as having transcendent worth, giving the individual a glimpse of that transcendence without changing the distinctiveness of a God/individual relationship. Isn't that the way we even relate as children to an earthly parent? How much more so in a relationship with God.

3

POINTS
OF TENSION

Many of us have heard the story of the father who placed his little boy on a table and then told him to jump into his arms. As soon as the boy jumped, the father stepped back and allowed his son to fall flat on his face. As the son screamed in pain and looked at his dad for an explanation, the father said, "That was to teach you that you cannot trust anyone in this world." Although this is an unpleasant story we must ask ourselves whether the father's conclusion is correct. Is it true that you cannot trust anyone?

I believe this is a dangerous half-truth. If the father was determined to teach this lesson, he could have pretended for a moment that he was going to drop the boy but then held him tightly while he explained the lesson he was trying to teach: It is always prudent to be cautious before trusting someone, because you don't always know whether they deserve your trust until it is too late. It is often not until the end of the journey that you learn the true character of your companion.

However, total skepticism makes life impossible. If you can trust nobody, you would never use any public transportation, never go to a doctor, never deposit money in a bank, never eat any food, never step foot outside your door — and on and on goes the list. In fact, you might become so paranoid that you're afraid to even trust yourself.

I have in my possession an authentic one hundred million dollar bill. When I hold it up before an audience, as I have often done, I always see the same expressions on the faces in front of me: "What's the catch?" I can almost hear them say. Why are they dubious? First, because they know that no one in his right mind would walk around with one hundred million dollars in his wallet, and second, if he *was* foolish enough to do so, he certainly wouldn't broadcast it in a public meeting. I take a moment or two to listen to their speculations, as I insist that the bill is authentic. And it *is* authentic — an authentic Zimbabwean one hundred million dollar bill. There's a nervous muffled laughter among the audience — there really is nothing funny about the pitiable plight of the economically plundered citizens of Zimbabwe. Zimbabwe's inflation rate is in the quintillions, and prices double there every thirty-two hours. But the catch with this bill, although it is authentic, is what is written just above the denomination: *Valid on or before December 31, 2008.* Zimbabwean currency is reprinted every ninety days.

There is an old adage that asks, "If a Cretan tells you that all Cretans are liars, can you believe him?" I put a similar question to a reporter when I was interviewed about the present economic crisis. Before he began the interview, I asked him if I could pose a question to him. He was somewhat taken aback and seemed a trifle irritated. I asked him why we are convicting top executives of financial institutions for their relativism in financial matters when we have taught our students for years in all our colleges, including Ivy League schools, that ultimately there are no absolutes. Why are we judging them according to absolutes when we have told them that everything is relative and there *are* no absolutes?

Isn't that a fair question? It is cool in our society to ridicule those who hold to absolutes, yet we quickly turn on those who live by the implications of the denial of these same absolutes. In the West, for years we have believed implicitly, if not explicitly, that moral boundaries matter, that life at its core is sacred, and that in matters of marriage and finance, a person's word should be trusted — until we lost ourselves in the swirling storms of the cultural challenges in the 1960s and everything went up for grabs as the status quo was challenged on all fronts. Those of us who were in college at that time were shaken by professors who encouraged students in no uncertain terms to challenge the establishment. Not only were buildings burned;

a whole structure of values that had governed a culture for centuries was called into question and tossed out.

During that time and in the decades since, voices from both inside and outside have sounded our demise. Aleksandr Solzhenitsyn warned that the West is on the verge of collapse. "Between good and evil there is an irreconcilable contradiction," he said, but he was dismissed as being an anticommunist ideological dinosaur.[1] Now Solzhenitsyn's warning has caught up with us, and we are wondering what has happened. We have awakened from our self-induced lethargy to find ourselves under the authority of those who answered the call to rebel against all that we as a nation have stood for and believed in. Now, our culture's foundations are crumbling and prophetic warnings are doubly impugned when they are first unheeded and then forgotten when proven to have been justified.

We need to understand that the tensions of life will always be there, regardless of the options we choose to live by. Systems of values will always be on a collision course with one another, and we will always have to defend what we believe from the assault of a conflicting belief system. If we have no firm commitments and haven't already determined which of our national convictions are nonnegotiable, our whole system will implode under the weight of momentary decisions. It is critical, therefore, to preserve those convictions or values that have already been tested and have proven to be a firm foundation. Only then can we test conflicting realities against what has shown itself to be reliable so that the foundation is left intact. This is as true for individuals as it is for nations.

The writers of the Bible were not ignorant of these tensions, nor is the Christian faith a stranger to this challenge. Jesus himself presented the conflict to us in stark terms in the account of his testing in the wilderness by the enemy of our souls (Matthew 4:1 – 11). In every instance, each temptation was a dangerous half-truth. "Change these stones into bread, and the masses will follow you," was the first challenge posed by the Tempter. It is interesting to note that the challenge was constructed to appeal either to his power or to his word. In fact, in his second temptation, Satan used the words "it is written" to challenge Jesus to demonstrate his autonomy from any transcendent limitations (verse 6). Though Satan used the line "Did God really say?" in the garden of Eden, he used the line "it is written" with Jesus in the wilderness. Satan knew that he couldn't challenge Jesus on whether God had indeed said something or not, so instead he tried to strip what God had said from its context. You see, for the follower of Jesus, the linear logic of belief goes something like this:

> The character of God, in whom there is no contradiction, is unchanging.
> He has demonstrated his character in his Word.
> He has revealed his character through his Son.
> He has established the church to live out those truths and values.

Satan was smart enough to appeal to Jesus within that hierarchy, using the written word to appeal to the character of God and "reasoning" that the result would enlarge or benefit the church. Think of the greater number of followers Jesus would have had for a time if his appeal to them had been that he would provide for their basic necessities. Satan's temptation was on the basis of that to which Jesus was already committed — the promises and the power of God. He weighted the challenge with the attraction of its pragmatic impact on the short term.

The seduction of the lie that God makes everything comfortable for us is precisely the reason many have been unable to face the tensions they experience in living the Christian life. Further, because the church has not always lived out the truths it claims to believe, doubt has been cast on the unchanging character of God. It is interesting that Jesus does not challenge the assumption of the appeal that many would have been drawn to him if he had promised to provide for their short-term needs. And it is important to note that he placed what was written (and that which Satan was trying to distort) in the larger context of the truth. In short, sound bites are not the story. If we do injustice to what is written, we end up making an unjust conclusion.

Satan began this temptation with the phrase "it is written," and Jesus responded with the words "it is also written" — not to engage Satan in an argument but to position the temptation of his own will against the standard of *God's* will and thus test all options against that reality. The definition of relativism is that the value of any moment or idea is based on the circumstances that surround it or on the standard that is set by the majority. By definition, then, relativism is a slave to the moment. However, absolutes, which are true regardless of circumstances or popularity, make it possible for precommitted certainties to be the basis on which to interpret a specific moment or issue, giving value to all moments without sacrificing any.

There is an important application to this challenge to faith. In intent, Satan's challenge to Jesus is little different from a question I have often been asked: "Since God is all-powerful and loving, why doesn't he perform an irrefutable miracle, like causing a shrunken arm to suddenly grow to full length or a limb to grow back? Why are all so-called miracles so subtle?" The implication is that if God would do spectacular things, people would believe in him.

This is a valid question, and I assure you it is not one we Christian apologists haven't thought of. I believe there is an answer, which I will touch on later. But first let me get to the root of this problem — our desire for God to prove himself to us or validate our belief in him by performing miracles — as we struggle with various points of tension we experience in trying to live as a Christian.

IT IS WRITTEN —
THE LARGER CONTEXT

A young student wanted to challenge the establishment in his institution, so as he was writing his doctoral dissertation, he would make a sweeping statement and footnote it by saying something like, "As told to me by the elevator operator in a restaurant." Then he would make another sweeping statement and say, "As narrated to me by a taxi driver who drove me to the airport."

When his supervising professor read the first draft, he challenged the student. "What sort of academic paper is this? You can't just make statements and footnote them with such second-rate sources as conversations in a taxi or in an elevator."

"Why not?" challenged the student. "Why is something more authoritative just because I found it in some article or in a book?"

The professor sat quietly for a while and finally said, "All right. We'll leave it as you've written it. Let's see what happens when you do your oral defense of this dissertation."

Sure enough, when he submitted the dissertation and defended it before the faculty committee, they approved it. He was called back to be informed that they had accepted his work. "There is only one small exception we would like to make," they said. "We are granting you your PhD but will not be giving it to you in writing. You'll just have to take our word for it."

He had made his point and lost. They made their point and won. Statements that are made may be either right or wrong, but if they are to be taken seriously so that they can be examined and evaluated, they must go beyond casual conversation. More often than not, that which people agree has ultimate value is put in written form and subjected to tests for veracity. So let us consider and evaluate this idea that an irrefutable miracle would better accomplish God's purpose for all time.

Suppose God restored the arms of an armless man, what do you think would happen? Of course, the person with new arms would run around showing off the miracle, and the miracle would become the point of conversation on every talk show. But what if he was so excited that he grew careless and stepped in front of a speeding car while he was trying to cross the road to show someone his new arms? What if he were crushed by an oncoming vehicle? Would he ask for another miracle, or would he be content to know that at least he had experienced a miracle once? And what about other armless people who hadn't been given new arms — wouldn't they begin to demand that if God is really who he says he is, he would do the same miracle for them out of fairness? Ah, so just one miracle wouldn't be enough. We would need multiple irrefutable miracles, and I also suggest that a few generations later, no one would believe the story, even if it were written down.

In fact, there is a similar incident recorded in the New Testament, and nearly two thousand years later many people do not believe it. After a man was given his eyesight by Jesus, numerous other interpretations of how and why his eyesight was restored were offered by those who heard the story.

The story Jesus told of Lazarus and the rich man is pertinent here. You may recall that the rich man died and was in eternal torment, separated from God, pleading with Abraham to send someone to moisten his tongue. But Abraham told him this was impossible because the separation after death is permanent, and no one can cross from one side to the other. So the man made another request — that someone warn his five brothers what was awaiting them if they did not make provision for their souls. Again his request was denied because, he was told, they already had Moses and the prophets who had testified to the options after death — and they could read what they had said. The rich man countered by suggesting that if someone were to rise from the dead and go back to earth to warn them, they would listen. But Abraham replied that if they did not pay heed to Moses and the prophets, they would not give any credence to one who had risen from the dead (Luke 16:19 – 31).

During the time of Moses, indisputable miracles abounded, even through the agency of Moses himself, yet when it was time to finally cross the Jordan River into the land promised by God, even Moses' faith faltered. He was not at all sure that God was with them in this journey.

Virtually every great leader in the Bible struggled during times of testing or tension over what they thought God should do or say, even though they had recognized God's divine intervention earlier. If we are honest, most of us are no different today. You see, at first blush, the miracle seems the only way to win a following. But the fickleness of the human mind, our insatiable desire to always want "just one more," the ever-present reality of need, our desire to play God and hence to control God, the apparent "hiddenness" of God when we need him most — all these reasons that become even more urgent in intense situations make the plea for the arm to be reattached "just this once" highly suspect.

On the other hand, what is left to believe if we dispense with God and the miracle of life itself? We argue for the existence of things and continue to believe they exist, even though they are mathematically impossible. We default to the belief that ultimate cause is something physical, even though no physical entity, however sectioned, explains its own existence. We hunger for love and meaning, even though we believe they are constructs of the mind and of culture or conditioning. We believe that only the empirical world is true, yet we posit this belief in metaphysical terms. We believe that matter has produced mind but that the mind transcends matter. We believe that everything that comes into being must have a cause, yet we believe the universe is causeless. We assume intelligence behind intelligibility — except for the universe. We believe in humanity's ability to totally transcend the mind but are forced to concede that we are subject to an unbreakable determinism. We deny the absoluteness of good and evil, yet we fill our prisons with relativists who have believed this — often highly educated and successful citizens.

I am compelled to ask you: Which position believes most in the "god of the gaps" and which position relies more on faith?

Jesus responds to Satan's challenges of what is written with the assumption behind what is written. Someone has said that a text without a context is nothing more than a pretext. The context of Jesus' revelation about what constitutes life — whether for the Christian or for the unbeliever — is unmistakable, and he has made it clear that if we do not understand the very context of why life *is* in the first place, we will never understand the text of how to live it out. I'll start with the basics.

WHAT IS WRITTEN RATHER THAN WHAT IS FELT

Some time ago, I was in the city of Tirana, the capital of Albania, which for decades has been considered the most atheistic country in the world. After a meeting where I addressed the members of parliament, I was invited by the curator of the national museum to visit the museum for "a surprise you do not want to miss." Having traveled for decades, I have learned to be skeptical of effusive invitations that promise a "once in a lifetime" opportunity. His persistence and genuine sincerity led me to accept his invitation.

I arrived with my colleagues at the appointed time, only to be greeted by a roomful of people who were employees of the museum. The curator ushered me to the front of the room and asked me to share with the employees what I had said earlier before the members of parliament. For a moment, I was a bit frustrated that a carrot had been held out to me and that I had been manipulated into another speaking engagement. But he continued to assure me that a surprise of immense proportion awaited me. By this point I had given up on his promise, and so I spoke to the group before me out of my heart, knowing I was addressing people who had suffered under a dictator for many years.

After I finished, the curator invited me to sit at a table. In walked two or three men in police uniforms, followed by armed associates, and in their extended arms, as if carrying a fragile treasure, they carried and placed right in front of me manuscripts that were clearly very old. When I looked to the curator for an explanation, he told me that these were copies of the gospels personally translated and transcribed by Saint John Chrysostom in the fifth century, in perfectly justified columns of gold ink.

For a moment I was too overwhelmed to speak. Then he told me these manuscripts had been discovered in the tenth century during excavations of the foundations of a church, and that they would have been destroyed by the previous regime had it not been for someone who had hidden them.

I began to read, and it happened that the text was the story of the woman who had poured out her "riches" on the head and feet of Jesus, anointing his head with perfume, washing his feet with her tears and drying them with her hair (Matthew 26:6 – 13). I have always found it interesting that Jesus said that wherever the gospel would be preached, the story of what she had done to him as an expression of her faith would also be told.

Here was a woman of ill repute who had heard of Jesus of Nazareth. Gathering her spoils, most probably gained from selling illicit pleasure, she risked being shunned by those in the room in order to be where he was, willing to put everything at his feet in order to gain his forgiveness and a new life.

This simple expression of repentance and love was made part of the gospel narrative to show both the shame of the human struggle and the glory of the mercy of God toward anyone who comes to him with a contrite heart. In her wildest imagination, this woman would never have thought that two millennia later, somewhere in a museum in an atheistic land, an Indian-born preacher would be reading her story copied by the hand of a translator who had lived four centuries after the event was recorded. In the mix of this story, all the tensions of the Christian faith come together — the power of the Word and its transmission of the story over time, forgiveness in the face of the blindness and pain of evil, the restoration of human dignity in the stranglehold of an undignified lifestyle, God's acceptance of worship from a sincere heart, the challenge to a culture that had marginalized womanhood at the hands of those who treated adultery as a one-person sin.

The skeptic responds with all the "contradictions" or shortcomings they see in the written narrative, the Bible. Indeed, the literature shelves are full of books written by those who claim to have been believers, now turned skeptics, who know enough of the Bible to attack it and hold it up for ridicule but never seem to have understood the revelation of God in its context. One must weigh their challenges seriously.

The term *inerrancy* is used by those committed to the Scriptures to mean that the Word as originally written was completely devoid of error because it was revealed by a holy and perfect God. Two arguments are generally raised against this claim. The first is that if the Scriptures were inerrant only in their original form, which we do not have, what does it really matter anyway? To this I say that if the original revelation was imperfect, it would pose an even bigger problem. How would we be able to distinguish between what is perfect and what is imperfect?

The second argument used against the inerrancy of the original Scriptures is that if God was able to give a perfect revelation, couldn't he have also preserved it perfectly? Yet, more than three thousand years since the initial revelation, the farther into history we go as we discover older and older manuscripts, the fewer variant readings there are, even of miniscule differences. The beauty of revelation through human instrumentation is precisely the dialectic of God's way of working. The farther back we go, the greater unity of instruction we find to capture the story with power and relevance.

Any desire of those determined to undermine the Scriptures or smother the text has failed, and the Bible remains virtually intact. With all the polemics about how untenable some of the ideas in the Scriptures are, the critic repeatedly misses the larger point: How do the writings of forty authors in sixty-six books, living across fifteen hundred years, converge in the single person of Jesus Christ? The number of prophecies both preceding and succeeding his birth, the nature of his teaching, the purity of his life, his incredible ability to connect all the dots in history, the physical nature of his resurrection, his persuasive teaching on the absoluteness of love based on God's eternal purposes, and many other specifics make the debunking of his person nothing more than a will to disbelieve. This is why Jesus constantly chided his questioners, saying such things as "Have you never read in the Scriptures?" and "Are you not in error because you do not know the Scriptures or the power of God?"

The written Word documented and certified exactly who this person would be, where he would be born, how he would be born, what kind of works he would do, what manner of death he would die, what manner of miracle his resurrection would demonstrate, and the signs of his return. The written Word was finally embodied in the person.

A BRUTE PHYSICALITY
WITH SUBLIME HUNGERS

We start with the written Word, and then we move to the immense struggle we *feel* over physical needs and emotional longings. We hurt, we hunger, we yearn, we cry, we laugh, we are disappointed. Even here, within the pressures of the tension between what we believe and what we feel, God meets us. We live in this tent of insufficiency. But what a tent it is! The Scriptures talk about us being "fearfully and wonderfully made" (Psalm 139:14). Sometimes it is more fearful than wonderful. Indeed, it is reminiscent of the "fearful symmetry" that poet William Blake wrote about.[2]

I think back to a simple operation I had a while ago — simple in the sense that, for the expert performing the procedure, it was a routine laminectomy on the disc between my vertebrae at L2 and L3. He assured me that it was routine and that he did not expect anything untoward. As it turned out, that which was supposed to take ninety minutes took twice as long. During the procedure, the fibrous membrane (the dura) covering and protecting the spinal chord ripped. That dural tear immediately put the surgical team in an emergency mode because the hazard of not repairing it properly and completely could have consigned me to a life of pain. When the doctor explained his challenge to me later, he said it was like "trying to sew wet toilet paper together." For three days I had to lie on my back to allow the dura to heal. For those three days medical team members visited me repeatedly to ask whether I had a headache and whether I could see. What a great day it was for me when they finally told me I could get up.

What a wonder is the fearful symmetry of the human body! It is intricately designed — fragile and resilient at the same time. The more intricate a system is, the more vulnerable it is to injury. Thus the nature of our struggle between what we believe and what we feel defies simplistic explanations. Our bodies and minds are easily destroyed. The memories carried within are often unrecognized until a point of collapse brings to the fore the memory of the tragedy that has already taken place.

The British newspapers some time ago carried a sad story of deep depression told by the wife of a husband who suffered a breakdown. This is Rebecca Mackenzie's story about her husband, Alasdair:

> Early morning in November 2006 and I was enjoying the first night of uninterrupted sleep since giving birth to my son Bruce two months earlier. Suddenly, the bed shook and I was woken by my husband sitting bolt upright in bed looking panic-stricken.

Instantly awake, I thought something terrible had happened to the baby, but as I checked the Moses basket at the foot of our bed, he was still sleeping contentedly.

I turned back to Alasdair and it was clear immediately that he was having some kind of crisis. He started crying and then, for two hours, my big, strong husband — a man with a black belt in karate — sat on the edge of the bed and rocked back and forth, sobbing like a baby.[3]

The rest of the story described the ordeals and trauma of this young family as the husband and father experienced a nervous breakdown. It was difficult to read without tearing up and at some level feeling the suffering of someone as she watched her loved one emotionally die before her eyes.

C. S. Lewis wrote the following:

Most of a man's psychological make-up is probably due to his body: when his body dies all that will fall off him, and the real central man, the thing that chose, that made the best or worst out of this material, will stand naked. All sorts of nice things which we thought our own, but which were really due to a good digestion, will fall off some of us; all sorts of nasty things which were due to complexes or bad health will fall off others. We shall then, for the first time, see every one as he really was. There will be surprises.[4]

We often ignore the physical element of our makeup. But we must accept what the human body is, as well as accepting our own limited abilities to correct a situation that has gone wrong in our bodies. And when our physical or mental frameworks are not functioning as they should, we usually feel it in our spiritual realm as well. I know many people for whom chronic depression has resulted from chronic pain. The body becomes the source of the spiritual struggle that ensues. There is no denying this.

Yet if we try to displace God from the process, we will be tempted to consider that which is aberrant, normal, and that which is normal, aberrant. Instead of recognizing that the imperfections we see in the makeup of the human condition are the result of aberrance, some argue that such imperfections could only have resulted from a random universe — and some conclude, then, that all of life is random. While physical illness may cause spiritual illness, the spiritual has a stand-alone capacity in and of itself. The default position of the heart and inclination of the will is against God.

Within this same imperfect physical frame are prompts that normally warn us that our natural desires for immediate gratification are really not for our ultimate good. How many times have we treaded into dangerous terrain, knowing deep inside that what we are doing is not right, yet rationalizing and arguing our way deeper and deeper along the path? How often does the appeal to the eye outweigh the caution of the soul? How repeatedly do we fall for an enticement we know is a lie, convincing ourselves that this time it will turn out to be true? How many disappointments and regrets must it take to prove that Scripture is right when it states there is a way that seems right to a person, yet its ends are the ways of death (Proverbs 14:12)?

Sometimes the temptations we battle are the result of inherited characteristics, as in the case of a child born as a drug addict or an alcoholic because its mother was addicted to drugs or alcohol. Carrying this thought a step further, we know that one's upbringing has a remarkable bearing on one's behavior. Being raised in a violent home increases the risk of becoming a violent adult. It amazes me that we readily accept as true the physical or emotional results of birth or environment and deny the possibility that our natural inclination toward what is spiritually wrong is by virtue of our human environment or culture. The very condition of humanity worldwide reveals a bent toward that which is destructive.

Instead of spending hours debating where Cain got his wife and what kind of fruit Adam and Eve ate, or whether the snake walked upright or crawled horizontally along the ground, can we not see the point of the narrative? The temptation in the beginning of creation was clear: By playing God, we redefine good and evil. In rejecting the voice of God and the boundaries he has set for us, we have made ourselves the master ethicists, and all categories become subject to our sovereign pronouncements. The point of the narrative is the propensity of humanity from the beginning to deny the warning and justify our own autonomy to become the ultimate judge of all reality. This choice to reject God's authority and replace it with our own is now an inherited characteristic with which we all must struggle.

I come from the East, and most Eastern teaching is done with stories. We learn to refrain from pushing the story to its limits but seek to get to the heart of what is being said. The parables of Jesus' day had this characteristic, as do proverbs. You cannot drive in India without seeing proverbs painted on rickshaws or buses, making some point of wisdom. We learn through proverbs, as we understand that narrative is different. Stories that tell the truth can be replete with detail in order to get to the greater truth, but they are not trapped by the detail. The Bible is a book written primarily in Eastern motifs, so in its own context let's see what the written Word says about the tension we face within these bodies that house us.

WHERE CHRISTIANITY "FAILS"

In the physical realm, we wrestle in three areas: the struggle for security, the struggle with pain and suffering and brokenness, and the struggle for sexual fulfillment. Let us take these one by one and see why we experience problems in living out the Christian faith. I will address the second struggle in greater detail in the next chapter.

Security

The first is the struggle for security, which goes beyond the fear of violence. It begins with the longing for human touch, and it is an inherent need. The desire of a child for the arms of its parents is not something that is imparted. The same is said about people in their old age, that they long for the touch of a caring hand.

I once had a conversation with a therapist in my home city who, along with others, offers time and service several times a year to the neediest in society. On one occasion they brought in a vanload of young women from the inner city to pamper them with facials and massage therapy, just to let them know they were cared for. As the therapist was using special oils to massage the deformed legs and feet of one of the young women, the young woman began weeping. Concerned that she had hurt her, the therapist asked if she was using too much pressure. "No," the woman said, "but this is the first time anyone has ever touched my feet." The therapist was moved to tears as well.

I recently read the story of a young man named Darren, who seemed to be incorrigible. He had been in many halfway houses that had given up on him and expelled him. In one place, the staff had gone on strike and refused to return to their posts until Darren was sent elsewhere. He was a master car thief and ran with a band of young teens that could break into any car and do with it whatever they wanted. They were brilliant in their ability to destroy. It was finally decided he would have to be sent to a juvenile facility because no one in any of the halfway houses had figured out a way to control him. Finally one experienced youth worker decided to take on the challenge of helping this young man change for the good.

The first week in his new home, Darren shattered all the windows after he somehow got his hands on a BB gun. After several weeks, the youth worker was on the verge of giving up. Darren was told they really wanted it to work so they were laying down ground rules. If he violated them, he would have to leave. Darren made a valiant effort, but a couple of incidents happened that nearly pushed everyone over the edge. One of these incidents was a fight with another resident in the early hours of the morning that ended with Darren cornering the other boy with a weed cutter from the garden. Car thievery continued to provide his biggest thrill. One day, the youth worker saw five cars Darren had stolen and left in the church parking lot.

Darren had never experienced a stable family life. Abandoned as a young child, he had never learned to trust anyone. As the weeks went by, the chains of rebellion seemed unbreakable, in spite of a few hopeful moments. And then, one Sunday afternoon, something changed in Darren. The youth worker had invited him to his house for dinner with his family. At the appointed time, the man arrived with his four-year-old son, Michael, to pick Darren up for the outing. As soon as the little boy saw Darren, he ran toward him, wrapped his pudgy little arms around his legs, and gave him a big hug. As he proceeded to examine the contents of Darren's pockets, he found a big bundle of car keys. During the lunch, Darren allowed Michael to play with the keys. When the time came for Darren to leave and return to the facility, he looked at little Michael and asked him if he would like to keep the keys, as Darren's gift to him. Michael was elated, completely oblivious to the fact that a life was being transformed right before his eyes. The inveterate car thief handed over the keys of his trade in an irresistible response to the embrace of unconditional love. That afternoon, instead of heading out with his buddies to break into more cars, he headed to church and turned his life over to Jesus Christ. A hug from an innocent child melted a hardened heart.

In a world looking for security, if the church is going to be the church of Jesus Christ, it must learn the power of love before it is too late. To the man longing for a new arm, the disarming of a crime-bound young man and the new heart and mind given to him by Jesus may not seem like a miracle. But to the heart that once did evil and the hands that now spread goodness, it is the greater miracle.

This longing to be touched is also the reason many Christians question God when they struggle to live life well and in a manner that brings glory to God, especially when they are going through a time of darkness or fear. We would love to feel God's arms around us. We would love to feel the embrace of the Almighty when we are feeling abandoned and alone. How many times have we wished we could just hear his voice? To the true seeker, sooner or later God comes through, even though his touch may not be recognized until much later. You see, instead of spectacular manifestations of power, the same God who used the human hand to write the Scriptures and preserve the written Word uses the human touch of his children to restore broken lives around them. This is the way Jesus conquers sin.

George MacDonald made the following observation:

> Instead of crushing the power of evil by divine force; instead of compelling justice and destroying the wicked; instead of making

peace on earth by the rule of a perfect prince; instead of gathering the children of Jerusalem under his wings whether they would or not, and saving them from the horrors that anguished his prophetic soul — [Jesus] let evil work its will while it lived; he contented himself with the slow, unencouraging ways of help essential; making men good; casting out, not merely controlling Satan....

To love righteousness is to make it grow, not to avenge it.... Throughout his life on earth, [Jesus] resisted every impulse to work more rapidly for a lower good — strong, perhaps, when he saw old age and innocence and righteousness trodden underfoot [italics added].[5]

Pain and Suffering and Brokenness

Consider God's intervention on three different occasions, as related in the New Testament. We read in the story of young Saul of Tarsus, a terrorist committed to destroying the infant church, that Jesus met him in a spectacular appearance and asked him, "Saul, Saul, why do you persecute me?" (Acts 9:4). That encounter with Jesus turned Saul's life around, and he became the apostle to the world, eventually writing one-third of the New Testament. He was a self-declared enemy of God, yet God came to him in a dramatic fashion. I have stood on that Damascus road quite a few times. I have seen the wall that still stands in the place it stood nearly two thousand years ago. Breathing threats against the followers of Jesus, Saul was brought to his knees in a moment, and history was changed. Sometimes change comes that spectacularly!

In the second instance of God's intervention, we find the apostle Peter in prison and the church in Jerusalem gathered to pray for his release. The book of Acts tells us that an angelic "visitor" came into the prison, freed him from his bonds, and led him past the guards and out into the streets (Acts 12:5 – 10). I have often wondered why the angel didn't lead him all the way to the prayer meeting, why he was left on his own to find his way there. He was the friend of Jesus, yet he was rescued from the prison and then left in the street to find his own way.

Does this "halfway" rescue sound familiar? How many times have we wished that God would take us all the way, not just half the way? But God has his plans and his ways, and he never violates the freedom of the person. Instead, he challenges us and invites us to trust him and surrender that lesser freedom to his greater call. Sometimes the miracle is dramatic; sometimes it is a halfway miracle.

Finally, we read of Jesus on the path to Calvary. At the last moment, when his pain is at its worst and humiliation at its highest, Jesus cries out, "My God, my God, why have you forsaken me?" (Matthew 27:46). He is the Son of God, left at the mercy of his enemies. This sense of abandonment by God seems to be repeated too often, and those who are the closest to him often appear to be least protected by him. Yet he still asks us to trust him, to believe that he is with us now as he works out his purpose in us and that he will be there for us at the end of the earthly journey. And I might add that at Jesus' worst moment, as he faced total abandonment by God — which because of him none of us will ever do — he was right in the center of the Father's will.

Some of us he meets in dramatic ways — often at the moment of our salvation. For others, it may seem that he is with us only halfway as we serve him in difficult circumstances. And still others of us may not be delivered from our trials, even to the point of death.

But in all of these there is one common thread. For everyone — except Jesus himself, who established the church by his death — the church is always near at hand to extend loving care in his name. For young Saul there was Ananias, who cared for him in the aftermath of his encounter with Jesus (Acts 9:17 – 19). Those very disciples whose lives Saul was seeking to destroy were there to lower him over an intimidating wall and enable his escape from the violent intentions of the religious zealots (verses 23 – 25). For Peter, the church was in prayer for him as he spent the night in prison, and they joyously welcomed him into their presence when he was set free in answer to their prayers (Acts 12:12, 16 – 17).

The mission of the church is not only to bring people to God but to take God to those who are wounded by the experiences of life, to touch those who are broken, to bring healing to those with damaged emotions. Those of us in the church recognize and accept our responsibility toward someone whose trust has been shattered, as evidenced by the schools, hospitals, rescue centers, and missions established by the church over the centuries.

But what about when the church is responsible for shattering a person's trust? What about the judgment we too often exhibit toward fellow believers who have failed to live up to their own beliefs? What about the collective behavior of the church that leaves a person with no place to go for acceptance, for forgiveness, for love? What about when the response of members of the body of Christ to those whose trust has already been shattered is far from the way Christ responded to those who had failed or sinned or been failed by someone? What about when that person whose trust has been shattered because of us turns his or her back on the Christ we claim to represent and walks away not just from the church but from God? What then? Christianity will seem to have betrayed those who turned to the church (made up of individual Christians) to receive a healing touch and found no help, no one to offer comfort. To the person who faces a dark night alone, feeling that Jesus has let him down and has not met him in the time of struggle, let me ask: *Is it the Jesus of the gospels that has failed you, or is it the church that bears his name that has failed you?*

In this physical world, the church is meant to be the hands, the arms, the heart of God. To those inside the church, let me change the phrase "Ask not what your country can do for you but what you can do for your country" to "Ask not what God can do for you but what you can do on behalf of God." Pain can best be mitigated by the touch of another person.

Sometimes the touch of a Christian comes early, unmistakably, and with great effectiveness. At other times the Christian in our lives can carry us only halfway, and we are responsible to trust God to take us the rest of the way. And at still other times this touch comes at the last moment and proves that, though it seems often defeated, true faith will survive all the assaults of its opponents.

The man looking for a new arm may find that the love and care of the church brings him an even greater miracle — the miracle of new life in Christ.

Sexual Fulfillment

There are both legitimate and illegitimate expressions of sexual desire. I want to first discuss the illegitimate expressions before turning to the legitimate expressions in the last section of this chapter.

Illegitimate Expressions

As we begin to address the tension of the sensual, I don't need to belabor how many stumble in this area. The impulses of the physical, especially during one's youth or when one senses the departure of youth, are so common to the human experience that we wonder why God has created such a drive within us without giving us the opportunity for fulfillment. And so we try to justify our mistakes. But have you ever thought it odd that we don't try to justify our illegitimate expressions of other passions or blame God for them? We might ask why God has allowed us to feel envious of people for the things that are not ours to have — but we don't. Or why God has allowed some people to experience racial tension when we know that racism is wrong — but we don't. Or why God hasn't made it easier to curb our appetites? In short, when it comes to sexual fulfillment, we try to excuse our indulgence because of desire and opportunity, but we will prosecute someone else who helps himself to our possessions by virtue of that same desire and opportunity.

Atheistic writers, such as Sam Harris, take religion to task for injecting guilt into the fulfillment of sexual desires. The sad truth is that they are partly right. These very days as I write, the news is filled with horrible pictures of a seventeen-year-old girl in Afghanistan who was flogged by a cleric for committing a supposedly immoral act — she was seen coming out of her home with a man who was not her husband. But as the real story was uncovered, it was discovered that she had been set up with this false charge by a spurned suitor who had taken offense at her rejection of his marriage proposal. Some critics of religion in general — sometimes of Christianity in particular — have made much of the guilt we encourage regarding sexual matters. Sometimes it is a valid criticism, for we often seem to reserve our loudest public condemnation from the pulpit for sexual issues.

The writers of Scripture, however, focus our attention on numerous other vices alongside inappropriate sexual behavior — injustice, pride, greed, malice, hatred, uncontrolled tongues, gluttony; the list goes on and on. Condemning sexual misconduct, we in the church have neglected to show *why* sexual deviations from God's prescribed way are so detrimental to an individual and to society. God has given us the gift of the intensity of passion within the context of the sacredness of love. Take away either the passion or the correct context, and you have something less than what God intended it to be. After all, sexual drives and fulfillments are God-given. It is the one sensation we experience that God himself is free of, because God is spirit and not flesh. Essentially, he has allowed us to experience the maximum pleasure that the body is made for until the spirit becomes the essence and substance of our existence and sexual drives no longer hold sway over us. This amazing gift to experience sexual love is built-in only as a transitory expression. To make it the pursuit of life is to take that which is intended to be temporary and make it the ultimate pursuit. It is taking that which is sacred and making it commonplace. It is taking that which is designed to be fulfilling only in a restrictive sense and trying to make it fulfilling in an unrestricted sense. Such deviation of purpose is destructive to the very act and to the intent of the gift.

In a 2009 article in a British medical journal, a demand was made that the pope retract a statement he had made about how the use of protection in sexual intercourse increases promiscuity and therefore the risk of AIDS.[6] In an effort to be objective, I will say that there may be more to what the pope said than was reported and that the journal may have some justification for its "outrage," but I want to pose a few questions: Would they have written an article taking any responsibility for a victim of AIDS who said he used the protections they endorsed and yet contracted it? Would they have written an article decrying promiscuity and its impact on the accepted values of society? Would they have written an article about the betrayals and broken hearts and broken homes that are the result of promiscuity? No, of course not! Some behaviors have become too politically volatile to write about honestly, even though the ensuing damage is ruinous both to the body and to society.

While the empiricist looks at science as an exact science and the social theorist and psychologist is engaging in behavioral science (admittedly somewhat less exact), the one dealing with spiritual and moral decay in a society is treated as the least exact in his or her descriptions or prescriptions. Jesus says that the person who ignores the most important things to focus on lesser things is, in effect, "straining out a gnat but swallowing a camel" (see Matthew 23:24). Scientists conveniently state that they only deal in facts. Are not the shattered lives and the emotional toll of guilt and regret also facts? Who should sit by the side of a child and tell them that their father has led a debauched lifestyle and paid the ultimate price? If all is simply matter and the so-called facts of science are the only facts that are important, why do we hunger for significance, for answers to our deepest questions, for hope?

A recent conversation I had with a film producer turned to the subject of violence as an art form. In a remarkable comment, he said that in our society we think something is violent only if it causes physical injury. "The worst kind of violence," he said, "is that which destroys personal dignity, value, and worth while appearing to be benign because it is not causing bodily injury." He was right-on. This is precisely what happens when the sensual drives our motives and the worth of a human life is diminished with every indulgence.

Marriage and sexual expression were tied together in the teachings of Jesus. One may choose to challenge these teachings and even criticize them, but one can not deny that he taught them. To take sexual practices and denude them of their intended purpose is to create a society open to the risk of realities too numerous to mention. Just as love that is denied pleads for the touch of compassion, love that is abused destroys lives and ultimately destroys society. As G. K. Chesterton said, "They have invented a phrase, a phrase that is a black and white contradiction in two words — 'free-love' — as if a lover ever had been, or ever could be, free. It is the nature of love to bind itself."[7] So if we feel that Christianity has failed us in this area because it has imposed a standard on us that we find difficult to keep, perhaps we need to listen to Chesterton, who wrote, "The Christian ideal has not been tried and found wanting. It has been found difficult; and left untried."[8]

The words of Francis Thompson in that memorable poem, "The Hound of Heaven," sum up well what I have been saying:

> "All which I took from thee I did but take,
>   Not for thy harms,
> But just that thou might'st seek it in My arms.
>   All which thy child's mistake
> Fancies as lost, I have stored for thee at home:
>   Rise, clasp My hand and come....
>
> "Ah, fondest, blindest, weakest,
>   I am He Whom thou seekest!
> Thou dravest love from thee, who dravest Me."[9]

Too often we shun that which is meant for our good because we are afraid it will deprive us of what we think we really want. With incredible rancor and strong language, atheistic writers (Sam Harris, for example) castigate the church for standing in the way of sexual freedom, which really means personal inclination as justification for indulgence. Harris ought to at least be willing to draw a distinction between that which political and cultural freedom may illegitimately grant and that which religious freedom has the obligation to warn people about. The Bible does not mute its warning here. We are drawn like moths to the flame — toward that which often destroys. I do not know of anyone who died as a believer exercising self-control who wished he had been an atheist or had lived an indulgent life, but I have known many in the reverse situation.

Augustine said, "You [Lord God] have made us for yourself, and our heart is restless until it rests in you."[10] Perhaps that is why a well-known Canadian broadcaster who once claimed to be a Christian and then renounced his faith was asked in his latter years what he thought of Jesus. "I miss him," he said. "I miss him."

Legitimate Expressions, Yet Unfulfilled

Until now we have been reflecting on illegitimate expressions of sexual desire. But there are many who yearn for legitimate sexual expression in marriage, and it has been denied to them. They are not wrestling against unsanctioned passions; rather, they deal with the natural God-given longing for touch and intimacy — a longing that remains unmet because they have not found that soul mate in life and face each day without the intimate touch that is part of marriage. This kind of longing, though often borne gracefully in silence, carries with it a deep sense of loss. A similar yet distinctive feeling is often present in a couple that longs to have a child but cannot have one, or in a marriage relationship where one partner has experienced a physical affliction that makes sexual love impossible.

I readily concede this is not my area of expertise, but I would be remiss if I did not at least seek to provide some helpful reflections. The simplest — almost escapist — answer is the possibility that this person is better off unmarried. I know that to most people in this situation, this seems like a nonanswer, a cop-out. But it also may be true. Let me use an illustration to contrast their situation with a hypothetical scenario that could have been painful.

Some years ago, I remember sitting in a plane for hours, waiting for a snowstorm to pass before we could take off. Passengers started to complain and to get restless and even a bit unruly. Finally the captain's voice came over the public address system, saying, "Ladies and gentlemen, would you rather be down here wishing you were up there or up there wishing you were down here?" Suddenly everyone became more relaxed and waited out the storm patiently.

It may be that for some, the experience of marriage has been so painful that they would find themselves advising a single person that it is better to have not loved than to have loved and been betrayed. There is certainly some truth to that. But it doesn't alleviate the pain of being denied the legitimate sexual expression of love, and the question remains: How does one deal with such legitimate longings that are unfulfilled?

The story of God's plan for marriage is introduced by God's own assessment that it is not good to be alone (Genesis 2:18). The complementariness of man and woman in God's design is clear and unmistakable. The physical, emotional, and psychological makeup of men and women is quite distinctive. This is not to say that one is better than the other — smarter, emotionally stronger — but that by design, each is brought to their sublime distinction and greatest potential by the other, with womanhood drawing out the strength of manhood, manhood drawing out the charm of womanhood. Men and women each have a unique touch and desire to bring to their mutual relationship.

In the days of their pristine relationship before the fall, Adam and Eve were both unclothed. There was no sense of shame but a sense of sacred expression. Then they rejected God's decrees as the desire for autonomy overrode God's warnings of its ramifications. They experienced shame for the first time, in response to a violation not of their marriage relationship but of God's authority. The incredible thing seldom expressed in this context is that by their rejection of God's law in their quest for autonomy, the very design of marriage was thwarted, and autonomy became an enslavement to the wrong desires.

So let us look at what is essential to marriage. In marriage, the most important things that are surrendered are autonomy and the isolation of fulfillment. This new relationship of two becoming one is no longer defined by what *I* want but what *we* want; it is no longer what is good for *me* but what is good for *us*. There is submission to one another and a lack of embarrassment with the unclad body, because it symbolizes that there is nothing between the husband and wife, nothing "hidden" — that there is, rather, total acceptance of each by the other. Inherent in the desire for each other is an unbreakable commitment to each other. You simply cannot have the love of the other without your commitment to the other. And this surrender of autonomy is accompanied by the exclusive expression of sensual touch.

But the price of rejecting God's law is that marriage is no longer the beautiful thing it had been intended to be. Instead, it has become a continual struggle of surrender, of trying to win the love of the one to whom that promise has been made. The direct result of throwing aside God's way in favor of our own way is that as a culture we are exactly the opposite of what marriage requires, if it is to be a perpetual state of delight as God intended. The sacrificing of autonomy and the exclusivity of commitment are the missing elements in human nature in virtually every area in which it is required for the sake of attaining something greater. Marriage has been redefined because God's place has been redefined. Commitment in marriage has suffered because our commitments to God have suffered. Marriage has become hard work, and that which has the potential to bring the greatest joy in life too often brings the greatest pain.

The church is supposed to be the bride of Christ. One look at that bride today and we have a glimpse at how the Lord himself grieves. Great change must take place if the bride is to be presented to her heavenly Bridegroom without spot or wrinkle and consummately surrendered to him.

In the old English usage, the marriage vow made by each partner was "With my body, I thee worship." In the temptation encounter between Jesus and Satan, Satan offered Jesus all the kingdoms of the world if Jesus would bow down and worship him (Matthew 4:8 – 9). If marital consummation is an act of worship, and if the ultimate seduction is false worship, I would dare suggest that those who are longing for a relationship of touch and intimacy — that lesser act of worship which is marriage — seek the greater form of worship until the day they can legitimately participate in sexual love. Perhaps this is why the women who came to Jesus with shattered marriages or profane entanglements fell at his feet to worship him. Their bodies had experienced the betrayal of false worship, and now they brought their temples in true worship before the living God.

There is no answer I can give to those who find themselves in this position that will take away their longing for legitimate sexual expression. But maybe, just maybe, the greater pursuit will be devoting oneself to the worship of our Lord in spirit and in truth while not totally abandoning the hope that the temple of earthly habitation will one day experience this lesser worship. Until then, one can be sure that, though marriage offers the promise and potential of unparalleled bliss and fulfillment this side of heaven, the promises and dues of a sacred marriage are so immense and encompassing that they are hard to fulfill in completeness, and there are many marriages that should not have taken place.

Denied the full touch of exclusive love, these who live with disappointment in this area may well be the most Christlike people in the world today, people who desire, yet do not see immediate fulfillment but who know the touch of the Master as they, with him, await the consummation at the marriage supper of the Lamb. More than anyone else, he understands the longing that is as yet unrequited. He must hold very dear those who grieve as he does, enduring the present sense of being incomplete in anticipation of the greater day of being totally fulfilled in his presence.

We may think that Christianity has disappointed us by making us wish we could feel God's touch or presence when we need it. We may be disappointed when we want to have what is not ours to have. But the reality is that the hands of God touch us through the lives of others he has made for that purpose, and the touch of God cautions us not to profane that which God has made sacred.

In Psalm 119:96, the psalmist says something quite profound: "To all perfection I see a limit; but your commands are boundless." At first reading, one might think it should be reversed — that to all laws there is a limit and that perfection is boundless. But a true understanding of the words of the psalmist reveals that when I do things God's way, even when it is hard, the delight I receive in return is limitless. When I do things my way, I exhaust pleasure very quickly. It is not that Christianity has failed to teach me how to delight in God's presence; it is that I have failed by seeking pleasure through godless ways or by resisting God's provision for me because it is not what I want.

C. S. Lewis's comment is appropriate: "You don't have a soul. You *are* a soul. You have a body."[11]

Ponder that.

4

LOOKING INCOHERENCE
IN THE EYE

One significant point of tension causing a sense of incoherence in the life of many Christians is the issue of pain. It is from this vantage point that we may find ourselves constantly questioning God. This problem is not only real; it is vast. Let me begin by telling two very different stories from two very different cultures.

The man walked into my office courteously. Somewhat apprehensive of where this conversation might go, I invited him to sit down and waited a moment before we began our pleasantries. I had never met him before; I only knew of him through one of my colleagues. I had been told that he had been brought up in a Christian home, had attended a Christian school, and had concluded that the faith he once held no longer met the challenges of his mind. He had married a follower of Christ without telling her that he was struggling with his faith, and they now had a young family. He had kept his agnosticism to himself, trying not to influence his family in that direction. He went to church with the family every week so that his children were not made vulnerable to his struggle. He was a successful businessman.

As we talked, he explained that his skepticism had grown with each passing year of his highly legalistic education at his Christian school. His story was not atypical for that kind of institution. Those who go through authoritarian, legalistic training often end up either unable to think for themselves or prone to rebellion, tossing away everything they had been taught was true.

"They brainwash you and control your thinking. They don't allow you to think for yourself," he said. "In many ways their graduates have lost their ability to reason or to raise the right questions."

I could tell there was something different about this gentleman. To all appearances, he had not given up his faith in order to justify a freewheeling lifestyle. He lived his life according to conservative family values, believing there were norms by which he ought to live and lead his family. But just as he was solidly convinced that society had its "dues to pay" if it were to survive, he did not believe that those truths by which he lived needed to be rooted in God. In fact, he stated that in his view, this world is totally incoherent if the Christian God is the creator of the universe.

His political leanings made him believe in the philosophy that teaches there is only one law by which humanity should abide: one must not initiate fraud or deceit. According to this political theory, we do not need laws, and we do not need government encroaching on our liberties. As long as we do not initiate fraud or deceit, we should have absolute liberty to do anything else.

He was a fine man, and I do not wish to impugn either his motives or his intelligence. Nor do I wish to challenge his sincerity. But as I sat and considered the reason he had given for walking away from God, I couldn't help but wonder how it was possible to be so resolutely irrational — in the name of reason.

Here was his problem: If he believed in God, he would have to believe in good and evil. But the presence of evil made the world incoherent to him, because he could not reconcile the reality of evil with an all-powerful, all-loving God. Therefore he could not believe in God. So how did he make sense out of a world that he had determined was incoherent if both evil and God were real? By denying both and buying into a political theory that assured him that all it would take to create a society of trust and respect was that everyone follow the single dictum not to initiate fraud or deceit.

But, I pointed out to him, he had violated his own inviolable first principle and introduced the reality of evil into the paradigm of his life by deceiving his wife about his Christian commitment while he denied the existence of evil. He was attempting to live rationally, logically, and morally in a world that he believed was irrational, illogical, and amoral. In doing so, he had violated his own first principle and ended up thinking he was superior to God — certainly, the God of the Bible. Such self-incriminations are hard to admit, and so silence is the response.

Thousands of miles from this scene, I sat across the table from a young woman who had been running from a memory for several years. Success had been within her sights when she had fallen in love with a young man and decided to marry him. In her culture, marriages based on love are viewed with societal disapproval — or at the very least with suspicion, at a generational level. Not only was it a "love match," but he had come from a lower rung of society's ladder, which made marriage to him an unthinkable thing to even contemplate. Her parents had refused to grant their permission for the couple to marry, so she had chosen to elope with the love of her life, and together they moved to another city, where no one would know them and where they could build a life together.

At first, things had gone quite well, even though both were totally alienated from their families. But one day, while on a business assignment for an extended period, miles away from her husband, she met another man and found that the lure of her growing feelings for him challenged the love she thought she had for her husband. After a few months, she told her husband she wanted a divorce from him. Across the miles, he begged her to change her mind, but she was determined to follow through with her decision. Her husband traveled to talk to her, but she spurned his pleas. Finally, one evening as they were arguing, he excused himself and went into another room for a few minutes. When he returned, he told her he had decided he would grant her wish if it was what she wanted. But he had one request — that she allow him to lay his head in her lap for a few minutes before he would go away, never to bother her again. Seeing his sadness and his love for her in his eyes, she agreed, and he lay down with his head in her lap. He closed his eyes, and within a few minutes she sensed something was wrong. She couldn't get him to wake up. He had lapsed into unconsciousness and within minutes was dead. He had ingested poison and taken his own life.

Years had gone by, and the memory continued to haunt her. Torn by guilt and confusion, more alone than she ever thought she could be, she visited a priest. After going through some ceremonial rituals and meditation, she was comforted as he told her that by his divinations he had determined she had no responsibility in what had happened — that she was free from any guilt in the matter — because in her husband's previous life he had raped her, and what had happened to him was payback time. She could rest in the knowledge that he had received his just reward and that she had played no part whatsoever in what had happened. This was the justification she needed to be freed from the guilt she had been carrying for her role in his death. The priest had accomplished his task. She found a new life, and her life could be lived happily ever after.

Or not. Was this true, or was it nothing more than a charade to bury the reality of what had happened under the weight of some mystical belief in order to ease her guilty conscience? The face across the table from me looked poised, successful, self-respecting — everything you would expect from a young professional. But it was evident that her past continued to tear at her heart, even as it did mine as I listened.

Only in an abstractly moral, systemically illogical, and personally cyclical world can one live free from guilt if consolation can be found by explaining away the pain as the payback from a previous life. In such a world, one must live with an impersonal morality and contradictory logic in order to escape reality.

I point to these two stories to show the extent to which we humans will go to rationalize evil or explain it away. In the first story, the naturalist's method of escaping evil was to dismiss it as incoherent to believe, in the face of evil, that someone was in control of this universe, because if nobody is in control, then evil is reduced to nothing more than a perversion of cultural norms. However, even if there is no personal, moral First Cause of the universe, some ethic is still needed to ensure the survival of society, though the purpose of survival to the naturalist remains unknown. Intuitively, we all feel that survival is better than extinction.

In the second story, attributing evil to the payback for something done in a previous life balances the ledger of good and bad and makes life more livable for the pantheist, who lives with the benefits of moral categories without having a personal God to whom he or she is accountable. Moral categories do exist, but only as an abstraction; there is a cause, but not a first cause; there is a judgment, but not a judge; there is accountability to a system, but no one to whom you are accountable; it is possible to find exoneration for flouting the moral categories, but there is no one who can pronounce pardon; there is a law, but no lawgiver. The amazing irony about this paradigm is that even though life at its core is not personal, all questions about evil and suffering are raised either *by* a person or *about* a person. Personhood then becomes a knife wound to the heart of pantheism, its impact mitigated by a mystical imagination.

There are some similarities between these two worldviews. In both, the realities of life are quite different from what the worldview holders want them to be, and in both, soothing words, spiritualized philosophies, and secular self-sufficiency weigh in, vying for allegiance.

STRANGE ESCAPES TO WHICH THE BIBLE IS NO STRANGER

There is a story in the Bible that raises this question of pain and suffering within the context of both worldviews above — the irrelevancy of sin in this life and generational sin from a past life. The question posed by the early disciples (John 9:2) was prompted by different reasons from those prompting the question for the typical Westerner today. The disciples believed it was impossible to escape from the consequences of sin against God, and therefore they questioned who was directly to blame. The Western skeptic today does away with God because of the inescapable presence of suffering. Jesus rejects both responses in this incident. So how does an all-powerful, loving God justify pain?

In John 9, we are told that in their travels, Jesus and his disciples came upon a man who had been blind from birth. Believing that blindness was a penalty for sin, the disciples were curious to know how a person could be blind from birth before he had had the opportunity to choose for good or evil. So they asked Jesus if the man was blind because of his own sin or because of someone else's. Behind their question were other questions that led to what they were really asking Jesus: How would a man be born blind? Is this a judgment caused directly by his sin? But how could that be? Can a child sin in the womb? But that didn't make sense, so they concluded it must be a judgment on the parents for *their* sin.

Jesus' answer surprised them, probably confused them, and eventually — when they looked back on the incident — enlightened them. This blindness was not the result of sin on the part of either the man or his parents, he said, but it happened so that the work of God in the man's life, and ultimately in human history, could be clearly seen.

In one sense, the text doesn't really answer the question, because it is given within the framework of a larger context. What is "the work of God"? If the work of God was the reason for the man's blindness, it is advantageous to discover what that work of God is, especially since Jesus adds that this event was taking place in the daylight of man's history on earth, before the night came and no such work could be done.

WHO IS ASKING THE QUESTION?

There are several things here that lead us to see the tension within us of pain, its reasons and remedy, and why the answers that Christianity puts forth are so great.

Four groups of people ask the question: What is the work of God being displayed? First is the man himself — the object of the disciples' question and the subject of the healing. Second are the disciples, who are asking for a resolution to the problem of pain. Third are those who recognize that the man's healing is supernatural but who have no way to explain it. And fourth are the religious and political leaders, who don't want to accept the explanation for the man's suffering and healing and its implication about who Jesus is.

The Man Born Blind

Let's first look at the man himself. He gives a simple testimony to the fact that all he knows about what has happened is that he was born blind and now he can see (John 9:25). Jesus points out that the greater blindness is to believe that one is seeing reality when, in fact, one is blind to the truth. When a person's false perspective on what is real is turned upside down, that is indeed a greater miracle than physical healing.

The man who was healed is ironically, perhaps, the weakest witness to Jesus' miracle of healing. Why? How often have you heard someone's testimony to the transforming touch of Jesus Christ in his or her life completely dismissed by someone who is skeptical? When one looks at the writings of skeptics such as Richard Dawkins and Christopher Hitchens, one can't help but wonder how much they really know about the Christian faith. How much have they really seen of Christianity at work? During the course of nearly forty years, I have traveled to virtually every continent and seen or heard some of the most amazing testimonies of God's intervention in the most extreme circumstances. I have seen the most hardened criminals touched by the message of Jesus Christ and their hearts turned toward good in a way that no amount of rehabilitation could have accomplished. I have seen ardent followers of radical belief systems turned from being violent, brutal terrorists to becoming mild, tenderhearted followers of Jesus Christ. I have seen nations where the gospel, banned and silenced by governments, has nevertheless conquered the ethos and mind-set of an entire culture.

I think, for example, of the church in China. In the middle of the twentieth century, after destroying all of the Christian seminary libraries in the country, Chairman Mao declared that the last vestiges of Christianity had been permanently removed from China, never to make a return. On Easter Sunday in 2009, close to half a century later, the leading English language newspaper in Hong Kong published a picture of Tiananmen Square on page 1, with Jesus replacing Chairman Mao's picture on the gigantic banner, and the words "Christ Is Risen" below it. It is estimated that the church in China is the fastest-growing church in the world. I have had conversations with young students in one of China's most prestigious universities who were eagerly asking their questions about Christ, some confessing that their faith in Christ is now the most remarkable thing about their lives.

I have also been in the Middle East and marveled at the commitment of young people who have risked their lives to attend a Bible study under cover of darkness, some having traveled from staunchly Muslim countries just to learn more about Jesus. I have talked to CEOs of large companies in Islamic nations who testify to seeing Jesus in visions and dreams and wonder what it all means. Granted, there may be individual experiences that, subjected to rigorous questioning, could be shown to be false, but to hear variations of this story repeated in the lives of thousands, if not millions, of people across the globe is to at least make it reasonable for anyone with a rational mind to legitimately ask the question: Who is Jesus, and what is happening?

To the person who argues that these things happen all the time in religious and superstitious countries because of the force of culture and therefore mean little, I could say much in response. But even as I write this, the newswires are abuzz with the dramatic turnaround of the British author A. N. Wilson, who only a few years ago was known for his scathing attacks on Christianity and his mockery of its sacred truths. This year, Wilson celebrated Easter at church with a group of other church members, proclaiming that the Jesus of the gospels is the only story that makes sense out of life and its challenges. Here is Wilson in his own words.

> Why did I, along with so many others, become so dismissive of Christianity?
>
> Like most educated people in Britain and Northern Europe (I was born in 1950), I have grown up in a culture that is overwhelmingly secular and anti-religious. The universities, broadcasters, and media generally are not merely nonreligious, they are positively anti.
>
> To my shame, I believe it was this that made me lose faith and heart in my youth. It felt so uncool to be religious. With the mentality of a child in the playground, I felt at some visceral level that being religious was unsexy, like having spots or wearing specs.

This playground attitude accounts for much of the attitude toward Christianity that you pick up, say, from the alternative comedians, and the casual light blasphemy of jokes on TV or radio.

It also lends weight to the fervor of the anti-God fanatics, such as the writer Christopher Hitchens and the geneticist Richard Dawkins, who think all the evil in the world is actually caused by religion....

My own return to faith has surprised no one more than myself. Why did I return to it? Partially, perhaps it is no more than the confidence I have gained with age.

Rather than being cowed by them, I relish the notion that, by asserting a belief in the risen Christ, I am defying all the liberal clever-clogs on the block: cutting-edge novelists such as Martin Amis; foul-mouthed, self-satisfied TV presenters such as Jonathan Ross and Jo Brand; and the smug, tieless architects of so much television output.

But there is more to it than that. My belief has come about in large measure because of the lives and examples of people I have known — not the famous, not saints, but friends and relations who have lived, and faced death, in the light of the resurrection story, or in the quiet acceptance that they have a future after they die.[1]

What do we make of all of this? When your life has been touched by the supernatural work of Jesus Christ, can you just dismiss it as nothing more than psychological aberration? Growing up in India with religions of every stripe around me, I struggled as a teenager to find meaning in my life and a way out of the complexity of religion. It was on a hospital bed in New Delhi, after I had attempted suicide, that Jesus Christ tracked me down, the last person I expected to meet in that situation. Out of the sheer emptiness of my life and my sense of failure, I had tried to end my life. I had not the slightest intention of "getting religious." Yet in that desolate moment, unexpectedly a Bible was brought to me. There in that hospital room, as the Word of God was read to me, something within me cried out that this was not just what I needed; it was the truth.

I am fully aware that most skeptics would not only find this pathetic; they would also find it irrational. But I ask the skeptic in return, "Why do you *not* believe?" I am aware that the arguments against belief will run the gamut from the experiences of other people who have not had this encounter with Christ to points of reason and logic — to which I have counterarguments. But now I want to focus on the experiential side of the issue. If the experience of someone in suffering and pain is valid as a counterpoint to the gospel, why isn't the experience of someone else who has known God's presence in suffering and pain just as valid? From the point of view of argument, I will go so far as to say that while the skeptic may score points in that it is not possible to scientifically verify someone else's experience of God in their lives, nothing can change my mind about what I have experienced with Jesus Christ. My transformation is as solid as the very act of writing this book. There is clearly implicit power in the gospel to change hearts. Jesus made this clear.

Likewise, the man who was healed of his blindness said, "Look, whatever you may make of Jesus, I just want you to know this. I was blind, and because of his touch, I now can see." That was the bottom line — and it was what he wanted the critics to understand.

Surprised by Suffering

The second group is the disciples who, having seen and heard what had happened, still needed an explanation. Let me specifically respond to two of the witnesses to Jesus' life and works who have recorded this story — John and Luke.

It is interesting to note the focus that the physician Luke brings to his narrative. From the beginning to the end of his gospel, his focus is on the women who were followers of Jesus and who believed the story with an exemplary depth of commitment. One need only remember how weak a woman's testimony was in court in those days. Yet Luke follows the women of the story in his narration from the virgin birth to the Garden Tomb on Easter Sunday as the women arrived to anoint Jesus' body and found him gone. He does so with such boldness that he could easily have run the risk of being totally discredited as a doctor and disrespected as a man for believing their testimony. Then he writes the book of Acts for his friend Theophilus, and there the testimony is rigorously masculine as he follows two main characters, the apostle Peter up to chapter 9, and then the conversion and ministry of Saul of Tarsus — who became Paul the apostle and carried the message to the Roman world and on into Europe. Luke accompanied Paul on many of these journeys and tells the story as a firsthand witness.

Luke states quite clearly in his gospel and in Acts that the disciples were eyewitnesses to Jesus' majesty. What does all this mean? They were able to tell of Jesus' birth, his life, the miracles, the prophecies, his death and res- urrection because they were there. Now how do the death and resurrection of Jesus fit into the "work of God" that we seek to define?

For most of us, death is the thing we fear most. We think about it. We may seek to explain it, and when it comes, we may sometimes try to confront it cavalierly. Yet it is the one event that most of humanity does everything it can to postpone or eliminate. Even if we are willing to face it ourselves, we do not wish to lose to death those we love. But it was the one event that Jesus prophesied about himself, including the specific manner in which he would die.

The cornerstone of each of the four gospels is clearly the last week of Jesus' life. Matthew and Luke begin with the birth narrative, both for particular reasons. Matthew, with his distinctively Jewish focus, wanted to highlight Jesus' royal lineage from David; Luke, as a physician, would undoubtedly have been especially interested in the virgin birth. Mark and John do not include any narration of the birth. John, writing to the philo- sophical Greek mind, goes directly to the idea of the *Logos* — the Word. But all give a great deal of space and attention to the death and resurrection of Jesus. John devotes half of his space to it; in the others, the death and resur- rection of Jesus take up from one-fourth to one-third of their manuscripts. There is absolutely no doubt that the death and resurrection of Jesus is *the* point of reference for them. It is clearly and unequivocally essential to the gospel story as they saw it. This has been reflected in Christian music throughout the centuries, including the great cantatas and compositions of Handel, Bach, Mendelssohn, Stainer, and others.

None of the writers of the gospels were expecting Jesus' death and resurrection, even though he had repeatedly tried to prepare them for it. Even the miracle of the virgin birth, as dramatic as it was, did not throw them and demand the attention of Mark and John; they were able to connect the dots of his birth to the prophecies in the Old Testament. But they simply could not fully comprehend the death narrative. John was captivated by two things, the very things that lend coherence to the story. I will return to this point later, but for now I want us to consider the incoherent side of the story — the issue of pain — and its impact on us and perhaps its incompatibility with our idea of God.

More than half of John's gospel is given over to what is referred to as the passion of Christ — his suffering and his purpose in coming to earth in the first place. When we have the joy of bringing children into the world, we wish them prosperity, health, and success. None of us would wish them pain and suffering. When God sent his Son into this world, there was every intention and assurance of success, but it came with full knowledge of the path of pain and suffering that Jesus would walk in order to fulfill his purpose. For us to truly fathom this is to move into a completely different paradigm of thinking.

We resist pain because pain debilitates and forces limitations on us; Jesus, however, willingly followed the path of pain because it would bring us healing and open new horizons for us. We resist pain because we think of the "now" rather than of life's ultimate purpose; Jesus endured pain in order to restore ultimate purpose to us and to our existence. We resist pain because we are drawn toward that which brings us comfort and a sense of well-being; Jesus experienced pain so that we would find our ultimate comfort and well-being in God and in doing his will.

Earlier we focused on the suffering of the cross in its real reflection of separation from God. I want to focus here on the Son who experienced that suffering and how pertinent his suffering is in the context of the revelation of the gospel to that time in history. I believe this is a context that is often ignored.

If we had to choose between inflicting pain on someone else or bearing it ourselves, most of us would not hesitate to inflict pain on the other person because we deny them the same rank or privilege as ourselves, except in the case of a parent and child. This is even more so in the Middle East, where scores are settled and resettled generation after generation, ad infinitum. Jesus took our pain in order to give us the greatest of all privileges — becoming the children of God — and to finally settle the score with God for violating his law.

In a recent newspaper article, I read something that struck a chord. A federal judge in India had been accused of malpractice, and he had been caught on videotape, manipulating the legal system. But when he was questioned by the newspaper, he said, "I swear by God and my two children that I have not done anything wrong."

As I read that line over a few times, I thought how odd it was to take an oath on God and his two children. Then it dawned on me. In our most vulnerable moments we grasp that which is the most inviolable and sacred and measure ourselves against that reality. The judge was actually saying, "If I am lying, I put myself in the hands of God to be my judge, and may he inflict on my children the penalty for that which I have violated." Does this remind you of the cries of the crowd at Jesus' sentencing: "Let his blood be on us and on our children!" (Matthew 27:25)?

Now come with me to the story of Abraham, for there are two defining moments in Abraham's life. The first is in Genesis 15, and it is important that we understand what is happening. Abraham is asked by God to sacrifice certain animals specified by God. After the animals are killed, their bodies are cut into pieces and the pieces are laid on the ground. "When the sun had set and darkness had fallen, a smoking firepot with a blazing torch appeared and passed between the pieces. On that day the LORD made a covenant with Abram" (verses 17 – 18).

The presence of God, demonstrated by the firepot with the blazing torch, moved among the pieces of the animals, and God's implication is this: If I fail to do my part, may the same thing be done to me that was done to this animal. In other words, may I cease to be if I break my word to you. God's pledge with Abraham is the ultimate and unbreakable guarantee, because it was based on the surety of his own existence. In effect, God is saying, "May I cease to be if I do not do my part." It is impossible for God not to be, and therefore it is impossible for God not to keep his promise. That's how certain it was.

The second pivotal incident in Abraham's life comes as God tells him to take his son up a mountain that God chose, and sacrifice him there to demonstrate that his first allegiance is to God (Genesis 22). Sorrowfully, Abraham obeys and everything is readied for the sacrifice. In the previous instance, the sacrifice is the demonstration of the consequences for the future if God were to fail to keep his pledge. In this instance, however, the sacrifice of Abraham's son demonstrates not only Abraham's allegiance to God but also his faith in the future, because even though this is his only son he still has faith to believe that God will fulfill his promise to multiply his descendants on the earth.

In every culture I know of, the lives of its children have more value than the adults' lives. Every parent I know of would gladly accept suffering herself if it would spare her child from having to suffer. To be willing, therefore, to risk one's children is the ultimate test of one's love, which is what gives children their value.

Let me put this in its most pragmatic setting. No part of the world has seen more pain and suffering and war than the Middle East. Just visiting the region, one feels the tension, consciously or unconsciously, and realizes that everything that takes place there is seen within the context of the conflict. It is interesting that, years ago, when Golda Meier was asked when the killing would stop in that region, she is reported to have said, "When they love their children more than they hate us." Only a mother would have said that, and only an Easterner would have taken such an approach on a matter so politically charged.

But there is irony in her answer because the whole question in the area is whose sons have the right to own and live in the land in that region. Both sides would argue that they do love their sons and that it is for the love of their sons that they fight for the land.

The question then is this: *Which* passion wins the day — love of one's own children or hatred of the other's? When the issue is distilled down, these are the two tensions at work, aren't they: my love for my children and my hatred for the enemy I perceive to be standing in their way. This is precisely where, I propose, the cross brings coherence to the question.

The best illustration I know is a conversation I had with one of the leaders of Hamas, the Islamic resistance movement that tries to create enough unrest in the region to accomplish its own goals. A few years ago, I along with other Western religious leaders engaged in a peace mission were invited to the home of the sheikh for lunch and conversation. We were profoundly aware of how deep the passions ran in that region as we listened to him and heard about all the suffering he and his family had endured and about how much death his people had witnessed.

We were each allowed to ask one question of the sheikh in response to what he told us. After I asked my question, to which I received an unsatisfactory answer, I said to him, "Sheikh, you and I may never meet again, but I have something I want to share with you. Five thousand years ago, on a hill not far from where we are sitting, Abraham took his son to offer him as a sacrifice. Do you remember that story?"

"Yes," he said.

"Abraham readied everything for the sacrifice. As Abraham raised his hand with his knife poised to sacrifice his son, God stopped him and said something. Do you remember what God said?"

Unsure of where I was going, the sheikh waited for me to continue. " 'Stop!' God commanded. 'Stop, do not lay a hand on the boy. I will provide.' "

"Sheikh, even closer to where you and I are seated today is another hill. And nearly two thousand years ago, God kept that promise when he took his own Son up that hill, and this time, God let the blade do its work."

The sheikh and others in the room remained silent. Then I said the words I wanted him to always remember: "Sheikh, until you and I receive the Son whom God has provided, we will always be offering our own sons and daughters on the battlefields of this world for land and power and ownership."

To say that one could have heard a pin drop would be an understatement.

The afternoon came to an end, and we descended the stairs to be ushered to our cars. The sheikh came over to my side, embraced me, kissed me on both sides of the face, and said, "You are a good man. I hope I shall see you again some day."

In that simple conversation, under the tensest of circumstances, a truth dawned on me. For most of us, everything we do or accrue in life — our jobs, our homes, the laws we support — are inevitably for one purpose: to give our sons and daughters a better chance at life and success than we had. I have heard this all over the world. If one is negligent in his or her family relationships or responsibilities and yet succeeds everywhere else, the sense of failure is hard to overcome. Any success is marred. But God offered up his own Son to pain and death because of his love for the world. This is the amazing story of the gospel. Only in the gospel is there ultimate triumph over pain, death, and sin because our pain, our death, and our sin were borne by God's Son.

This is the answer for the blindness and the pain of the world. This is the hope that God alone can offer. This is the defining distinction. For evil to continue, hatred has to exist side by side with love. In the gospel, the God who loves his Son also loves the world and as an act of love gave his Son over to pain, suffering, and death so that he would triumph over death and provide eternal love and life for us, ensuring the ultimate elimination of evil and pain. Both the means of the salvation that God offers to us and the object of his salvation is love. This is what the disciples discovered was the work of God to be displayed — and this was the reason the man in the story had been born blind.

So profound and spiritually laden is this truth that it points to the ultimate paradigm shift from the temporal things of the earth to the eternal things of heaven and eternity. This is the work that God displayed on the cross, and this is the defining lens that determines our blindness or sight. To the one who sees this and accepts the work that God has done, the Light of the world illuminates the darkness and dispels the shadows of fear. To the one who refuses to see this and rejects God's work, darkness shrouds the light, and everything appears indistinct or distorted.

Family, Friends, and Neighbors

The third group — the man's family, friends, and neighbors — found it hard to deny that something life transforming had taken place, but they couldn't explain it. They all knew he had been born blind and could now see, but they couldn't explain what had happened. The visible results were hard to deny. The question was: What had caused this change?

The answer begins with the nature of good and evil. Let us for now grant the basic idea that good is that which seeks the rightful and essential worth of humanity, while evil is that which puts self over every other person's right and essential worth. Much can be said to enhance each part of the statement, but for now we'll consider the basic ideas of worth and essence through the lens of history and culture.

Two of humanity's greatest needs over time have been the need for knowledge and the need to keep healthy. We take our health for granted until it's jeopardized. Look across history and see the deeds of Christians on behalf of the well-being of humanity: hospitals, doctors, medicines, food, schools. It is easy to demonstrate that anyone who has called himself a Christian and yet has victimized people and abused their rights has violated the precepts of the gospel while pretending to be living the gospel. But the record of Christians responding to their call to care for humanity is undeniable, and the message that Christ cares for and loves people is being acted out all over the world. Skeptics, such as the modern-day atheist Matthew Parris, have been candid enough to admit the impact of the gospel imperative in such matters. After returning from a visit to Malawi, where he had spent his childhood, Parris wrote an article titled "As an atheist, I truly believe Africa needs God." The subtitle was this: "Missionaries, not aid money, are the solutions to Africa's biggest problem — the crushing passivity of the people's mind-set."

> [Seeing the work of a small British charity there] inspired me, renewing my flagging faith in developing charities. But traveling in Malawi refreshed another belief, too: one I've been trying to banish all my life, but an observation I've been unable to avoid since my African

childhood. It confounds my ideological beliefs, stubbornly refuses to fit my worldview, and has embarrassed my growing belief that there is no God.

Now a confirmed atheist, I've become convinced of the enormous contribution that Christian evangelism makes in Africa.…

I used to avoid this truth by applauding — as you can — the practical work of mission churches in Africa. It's a pity, I would say, that salvation is part of the package, but Christians black and white, working in Africa, do heal the sick, do teach people to read and write; and only the severest kind of secularist could see a mission hospital or school and say the world would be better without it. I would allow that if faith was needed to motivate missionaries to help, then, fine: but what counted was that help, not faith.

But this doesn't fit the facts. Faith does more than support the missionary; it is also transferred to his flock. This is the effect that matters so immensely, and which I cannot help observing.[2]

Coming from Parris this is nothing short of astounding. I cannot help but think of Bertrand Russell's comment in *Why I Am Not a Christian*:

I regard [religion] as a disease born of fear and as a source of untold misery to the human race. I cannot, however, deny that it has made some contributions to civilization. It helped in early days to fix the calendar, and it caused Egyptian priests to chronicle eclipses with such care that in time they became able to predict them. These two services I am prepared to acknowledge, but I do not know of any others.[3]

This comment defies reason and betrays a hostility that blinds one even from common sense. It would have been better for Russell to argue that many without belief in God have done good things too, not just Christians. I would not deny this. But the skeptic must admit that he has no necessary rational grounds on which to determine the nature of good and evil, and therefore he has no imperative for doing good. The pantheist need not explain good and evil apart from cyclical repetition, and in the theism of Islam, love and grace are far from imperatives in their core teaching. Only in the Judeo-Christian worldview do we see good and evil operating in tandem. To focus only on the reality of pain and suffering and ignore the parallel reality of goodness and the basis for doing good is to render the world incoherent.

Religious and Political Leaders

We turn now to the last group — those who were politically and religiously driven, the people who denied the entire episode because they wanted to deny who Jesus was. Religiously speaking, this would translate into alternative interpretations for the work of God; politically, the belief that leadership has absolute and total autonomy over those it leads stands in the way of their religious freedom. Politics, of course, never has had and never will have the answers to ensuring the perpetuity of a nation. Look at history, and the facts are clear. From the feudal warlords of ancient Mesopotamia to the divine status of kings in Babylon and Persia, from the democratic ideas of Greece to the empire building of Rome, from the theocracies of Islam and the state church of Europe to flirtation with the idea of freedom without responsibility in postmodern America and the materialism of Communism, what has remained?

Political theories come and go. Nations and empires rise and fall. Civilizations wax and wane. For this very reason, Jesus resisted all efforts to make him an earthly king. The ultimate allegiance he wants is that of the heart, for the ultimate universal battle is that of the will against God. The truth of God's work that abides forever and results in coherence is first lodged in the heart of a person and then in society. To look at the world and to deny God is to open the door into that resulting vacuum for the myriad philosophies and pseudoreligious fancies that may help us run from the past — but only into the arms of an incoherent future.

The book of Job is known even by those who have no respect for God and his Word as that which best symbolizes the struggle of pain. Yet few have taken to heart what Job really says. I remember debating an atheist in which he quoted from Job and said that the answers given to Job were insufficient. I surprised him by telling him that Job would agree with him.

Then I asked him if he knew what Job's answer was to that insufficiency he was offered? The man was silent.

Job finds his answer in stages. He refuses to let one diagnosis or a great one-liner provide the satisfactory explanation for his situation. He starts his journey toward finding his answer for suffering and pain from the assumption of God as the Creator and Designer to seeing God as the Revealer of Truth, to recognizing him as Redeemer and Savior, and finally to experiencing him as the Restorer and Comforter.

How fascinating, for here the three aspects of the Trinity emerge — God the Father as Creator, God the Son as Redeemer, and God the Holy Spirit as Comforter. This triune God is a Being within whom there is a relationship. For Job, the overwhelming answer to his questions was not found in an argument. It was not found in a theological, philosophical, or scientific proposition. It was not even found in his relationships with his friends or his family, or in the truth or falsehood of their analyses of Job's problems. Job ultimately found the answer to his questions and his fear — to his pain and his grief — in the voice of God and his divine encounter with him. The answer to his questions was a Person.

In an amazing way, all arguments die in the face of a thousand other questions. This is principally God's answer to Job. In fact, when God first began to respond to Job, he raised over sixty questions for which Job had no answers. There is no limit to argument and counterargument. Arguments are like weapons. Each time a new weapon is designed, a defense or a counteroffensive against it is designed — which is why the arms race, like the argument race, is never ending.

When all the words had died down, Job began his response to God with these humble words found in Job 42:2 – 5:

> "I know that you can do all things;
>   no plan of yours can be thwarted.
> You asked, 'Who is this that obscures my counsel
>   without knowledge?'
> Surely I spoke of things I did not understand,
>   things too wonderful for me to know.

"You said, 'Listen now, and I will speak;
I will question you,
and you shall answer me.'
My ears had heard of you
but now my eyes have seen you."

There lay Job's answer — in his experience of the voice and presence of God. It is not surprising that the book of Job ends with Job praying for his friends that they, too, might find the answer to his and their questions regarding pain and suffering in the person and presence of God. A friend of mine in India, who lives in a meager little place, once told me he always prays for America because "it must be so hard to trust in God when you already have so much."

For the many I know who have drawn closer to God through pain, I know of countless others who have turned away from him for the same reason. Perhaps that's why a verse from Job is engraved in Latin on the tomb of Oscar Wilde, a man who lived for pleasure and lost — the quintessential hedonist — and who in his closing moments suffered much and asked to be prayed with before he breathed his last.

To be sure, the problem of evil *is* a problem. But to reject the only One who can change the natural proclivities of my heart so that I learn to live and think and work like him is to perpetuate evil, not eliminate it. For Job, and the others mentioned in this chapter, the incoherence they struggled with was not so much the incoherence of suffering in a world where God was in control but the incoherence of trying to explain the world if there is no God. To walk away from one's faith because of unanswered questions about evil is to walk into a storm of unanswered questions about good.

5

PURPOSE DRIVEN OR REASON DRIVEN?

Some time ago, I was invited on a radio program to discuss the book *The Reason-Driven Life* by Robert M. Price, professor of theology and scriptural studies at the Johnnie Colemon Theological Seminary. Price had once been a leader in one of the chapters of InterVarsity Christian Fellowship and had studied at Gordon-Conwell Theological Seminary. He specifically mentions on his website that Billy Graham was the commencement speaker at his graduation. Yet in his early twenties, he began to reassess his faith and to suspect that Christianity did not have either the historical credentials or the intellectual cogency its defenders claimed. After doing doctoral work in theology at Drew University, he pastored a church for some time before enrolling in another PhD program at Drew, this time in New Testament studies. He read scholars such as Jacques Derrida, Don Cupitt, and others like them. Finally, he resigned his pastorate. One of his biographical information sheets states he now attends an Episcopal church "and keeps his mouth shut." Those who know him describe him as a quick-witted, funny, and brilliant individual, and these descriptions seem to be supported by his writings.

I had not previously read much by him, except for a few debate transcripts and some papers he had written. But I picked up his book because I wondered what it was that made it so persuasive to the two hosts of the radio program. I read the book from cover to cover, trying hard not to be too surprised by what I was reading — but indeed I was. Surprised not once, not twice, but repeatedly.

My principal surprise lay in the fact that I can't think of a single substantive argument in his book that I have not either read or heard in my dialogues with various people. In fact, Winston Churchill's statement to his research assistant, Ashley, kept coming to mind as I read it: "Give me the facts, Ashley, and I will twist them the way I want to suit my argument."[1]

I realize that one cannot judge another's motives with any certainty. But I have to admit that it appears to me that in the throes of Price's skepticism, he pursued the very disciplines he would need in order to attack the story of the gospel. How impressive it is that "unbelievers" can find a following and still make a good living from the belief they once held. After all, I don't find such passionate books written against the existence of the tooth fairy. I am tempted to say sarcastically that the ultimate proof of God's omnipotence may well be that he doesn't even have to exist in order to make a materially abundant life for his detractors. In the days of my graduate studies, I had a classmate who was a convinced atheist. I asked him what on earth drove him to study theology when he held the Scriptures in such low esteem. "There are big bucks in the God racket," he replied.

For someone to be a professor of theo-log-y when he doesn't believe in either *Theos* (Greek for "God") or the *Logos* ("the word") leaves one rather mystified. It would be tantamount to asking President Mahmoud Ahmadinejad of Iran to hold the chair of American cultural studies at a university. Perhaps all the years of study and preparation have to provide some sort of living, even if the subject matter being taught is demeaned more and more with each passing year. I, for one, can't imagine spending my time in such a venture of unbelief, but I suppose rationalization is the handmaiden of personal passion.

Price writes purportedly to take to task *The Purpose Driven Life* by Rick Warren. First and foremost, he tries to demonstrate that belief in God is based in nothing more than fiction. "So grow up, Christian, and smell the roses of reason rather than be shackled by the hollow unreason of spiritual doublespeak," he says, so to speak. He attacks Warren's ideas as nothing more than the use and abuse of Scripture. Even its cover design of Price's book matches the design of Warren's book — but as is already evident, it will not sell as many copies, not by any stretch of imagination.

However, it is important to underscore that Price's book is not simply a response to Warren. And I want to make absolutely clear that it is not my purpose to defend one book against another. But in very clear terms, Price shows that his attack is not primarily against Rick Warren's book but unequivocally against *all Christian belief that subscribes to the person of Jesus Christ as Lord and Savior.* He has simply used Warren's book as his means, because he says it lends itself to the hostility he feels against what he says he once believed.

Any author knows that nothing is easier than taking one chapter at a time from a book and writing a response to each chapter because half the work has already been done for you. All one needs to do is vent on each chapter, sometimes handing out a token bouquet to soften the attack and then go for the sting.

Price sets the stage early. He makes a valiant attempt to disavow any hatred or hostility — a rather humorous attempt that reminds me of the old adage, "When someone says it's not about the money, you can be sure it is about the money." So whether or not Price has a hostile mind-set, the reader can decide.

These are some of Price's early thoughts in his book:

Price writes, "I view myself as a would-be philosopher, with leanings toward Friedrich Nietzsche and Jacques Derrida. I'm not in a hurry to find a label that will fit just right...."[2] These words of such irenic splendor and kindness follow what was written a few pages before: "I fear Freud was right about born-again Christianity: it is at least highly conducive of 'obsessional neurosis.'"[3]

He saves his most appreciative words for those Christians who do not take their Christianity seriously, not surprisingly, as he feels they are the truly rational ones. He makes me think of a gynecologist who tells his patient, "Yes, you have all the signs of pregnancy, but, thank God, you aren't. Because if you were pregnant, I would have to change my original diagnosis, and if you weren't under the impression that you were pregnant, I wouldn't be able to make a living."

I had to chuckle at the comment of a psychologist when I shared some of Price's thoughts with her. She said, "I can tell you more about this man than he has told you about himself." I wondered what a comic scene it would be for two people, each believing the other had a neurosis, to be in a discussion. I am sure Monty Python could make a killing on an imaginary conversation like that. But that, I'm afraid, is what a discussion is reduced to by such hostile language — when one pretends to be beneficent while adding poison to the darts.

I read Price's book because I was asked to respond to it on a radio show hosted by two atheists. However, I read many such books. For every one book I read where the author may be sympathetic to my belief, I read a vast number written by those who are hostile to my belief. I have always taken my Christian faith seriously and make it a point to read any competing perspective carefully. When I studied at Cambridge, I chose to take every course offered by the former Anglican priest-turned-atheist Don Cupitt (mentioned earlier as an author Price enjoyed). It made for several uncomfortable classes, but I wanted to hear it right from a mouth of a man who had stood on both sides. Price is such a man. So let me give him the full benefit of belief when he says that he honestly couldn't square reason with his Christian commitment. But for those who, like Price, say that Christianity has failed to give them the intellectual confidence to believe it, let me start at the beginning, where he starts, and check out the philosophy behind *The Reason-Driven Life*.

I'll begin with a brief examination of a few statements that explain his rationale for writing. Then we'll look at the reasons he gives for why he walked away from the faith and, finally, I'll respond to his principal assertion that the reason-driven life is in contradiction to the Christian way of thinking.

ON BIDDING GOD
FAREWELL

First, I think it is important to quote parts of the foreword to *The Reason-Driven Life* by Julia Sweeney. Her credentials are that she is a comedienne on *Saturday Night Live* and has written a couple of books.

> I began to think that even Jesus, if he existed, would have to agree that the Bible itself was a house built on sand. Ultimately, I had to discard my faith.... I didn't take the time to go over the Christian viewpoint again and decipher what made those religious ideas so compelling, so insidious, and so seductive. I didn't have the scholarly background or the patience to look into each seemingly harmless evangelical belief and find out where it came from and why it deserves to be thoroughly trashed! But Bob Price has that background![4]

That gives the reader just enough insight to know how the reason-driven life of this stripe works, at least for some. A bitter experience left this "follower" feeling abandoned. So there was a departure from the faith. Years later, a scholar comes along and takes Christianity apart, and there is a shout in the gallery from those who had already jumped ship, "Hurray! I knew I was right and that those who continue to believe are the fools!" Read Sweeney's words again. It's ironic isn't it, that the very metaphor she borrowed for an unfounded belief comes from the person she doesn't believe in? Had she carried Jesus' parable of building one's house on the sand (Matthew 7:24 – 27) to the full extent of what he is teaching, she would have found that he knew that people like her existed, people who doubt what he says and foolishly build their houses on nothing, houses that cannot withstand the storms of life because they have no foundation.

I sincerely ask you to be the judge of whether this pathetically simplistic approach is reasonable. It is actually a will in search of a reason to support it. Does she really assume that just because *she* didn't scrutinize the Bible's teaching, nobody else has? Does she think that if any rational person did examine it, he or she wouldn't maintain faith? And any time someone suggests that Jesus might never have existed, you can be certain that this is what they want to believe rather than what the historical data indicates. Price and Sweeney would do well to save their cheering until they have talked to some of the people whose cultures have reaped the reason-driven implications that follow from the belief that man is the measure of all things.

I want to say also that there is something quite remarkable about such iconoclasts who mock the Christian faith. In contrast to their disrespect for Christianity, their deference to any other belief, especially one that has an Eastern sound to it, is very much evident. How reverential they are when quoting from the Vedas or the Buddhist scriptures, almost fawning at their beauty, while trying to make the Bible look absurd. This duplicity — ignoring the fanciful and sometimes bizarre tales that are so replete in Eastern texts that even Gandhi once said he was embarrassed by them — is in itself a revelation of distorted reasoning. But before I move too far ahead, let me discuss the basics on which thinkers such as Price empty out their ammunition.

THE UNREASON
OF OVERGENERALIZATION

Repeatedly you will find that those who attack the theist utterly fail to distinguish between the specifics of belief, making all belief sound stupid. Here, for example, are a few lines from Price:

> The great danger of ... fundamentalist Christianity ... is an alien imposition of a self-concept and life agenda *from without*, no different in principle than the discredited Communist attempt to mint a new species of "Soviet Man.". . .
>
> Fundamentalists or evangelicals ... are afraid of being damned to hell. That's why many of them embraced the faith in the first place.... Such dear souls, terrorized into belief, heave a sigh of relief once they believe themselves safely within the fold.[5]

Unfortunately, I must admit that this caricature of some Christians and of some of what passes for Christian worship is not completely off the mark. But are such gibes, where the extremes of some are portrayed as a realistic description of all evangelicals, really intended to bring reason into the discussion or just to be disrespectful to evangelical believers and to their beliefs? Price cleverly makes use of his past to convince the reader that he had a front-row seat and an inner-sanctum experience, so now he can hang it all out to dry.

I have news for such a critic. I could tell even more pathetic stories than these, having seen the "underbelly" of Christendom in numerous cultures. I have seen the abuse of power, money, ego, sexuality, and much more on the front lines of Christianity. But by the same token, would I be fair to refer to atheists such as Nazis, Maoists, Stalinists, and Pol Potists in one breath because they have all had atheism as their worldview? What does such overgeneralization accomplish, other than to show unreason at work in the name of reason? It is a vacuum cleaner mentality that sucks up everything in sight without distinction.

Price is also clever in denying that he himself is an atheist. He doesn't know what tag to give himself. Why so? Here's how he says it: "'Atheist,' though I do not disclaim it, is not my description of first choice because it merely indicates what I no longer believe, not what *else* I have since come to believe. It says what I don't stand for anymore. But I would rather be known for what I do stand for."[6]

To quote Churchill again, referring to Germany's attack on Russia, "We are in the presence of a crime without a name."[7] Perhaps we do not have a crime here, but we certainly have verbal guns blazing and a full-fledged attack explicitly on Christian theism and implicitly on any belief in a personal, moral, transcendent first cause, an attack that is still searching for a tag to give itself. (This ought not to surprise us. Sam Harris doesn't like the tag "atheist" either.) But Harris does organize and attend atheist conferences. Existentialists didn't like their tag, and postmodernists don't like their tag. This is a brilliant strategy, because when there is no category, the position can't be critiqued. This is the metaphysical version of quantum:

If you know where a particle of reason is, you don't know what it is doing; and if you know what it is doing, you don't know where it is.

I want to come back now to Price's caricature of the reason that most people respond to the gospel. In my case, I do not recall a single thought of hell as an eternal destiny awaiting me. What is more, I do not recall that any of my friends, of whatever background, came to Christ because of the mention of hell. Among the many with whom I shared Christ in India as a young believer were those diametrically different in their thinking. The first, from a high Brahmin background, was a President's Gold Medal winner in one of India's most prestigious Institutes of Technology. He went on to do his postgraduate work at the Massachusetts Institute of Technology. Later, he joined Atomic Energy of Canada. Very few could match the brilliance of this man, especially in the pure sciences. Nor would many stand today in biblical knowledge against this man. Never once, after I saw him give his life to Christ, have he and I discussed hell as a motivation in our salvation. Not even once.

Another was an accomplished musician who entertained in the nightclubs of India's major cities. He had taken the road to drugs and all that such a world brings with it. Even as he came to one of our Bible studies at my invitation, he saw in the gospel what his heart and mind yearned for, and he began his journey of following Christ.

I mention these two because today both are in Christian ministry, one in Canada and the other in India. It was not the fear of hell that brought either them or me to Christ. In my case it was the hell I had made out of my own life without the help of any spiritual inclination whatsoever that made me commit my life to Christ. Those who either accuse others of coming to Christ only because they live in the narrow world of Western commercialized evangelism or use the dark days of a politicized Christianity as an excuse to deny the gospel simply don't understand it or its work in history.

Many could tell stories of their own here, and I'm quite certain that some *have* come to Christ initially out of fear for their eternal souls. But it is wrong to generalize conversion and claim that all who belong to Christ do so out of fear for their immortal souls.

I also find it amazing that Price compares Soviet-style "man making" and mass evangelism. Does anyone need to remind him that the entire Soviet experiment was given impetus by Stalin's absolute disavowal of God and his self-determined "right" to define man in his own terms? Stalin logically deduced that if there were no God, man became God, and rather than allow Western capitalism to define man, he would make certain it would be Russian-style Communism (according to his interpretation) that would do the defining. Stalin's last gesture before he died was to shake a clenched fist toward the heavens as he hallucinated and then fall back on his pillow. Like Price, he too believed that man was the measure of all things. He was The Man. That was the reason-driven life as his reason drove him to believe.

TAKING REASON
TO THE LAWS THAT BIND IT

What are the laws of logic? Simply put, there are four basic laws, each with many subdivisions that address many more formal and informal fallacies that are footnotes to a discussion of logic.

1. the law of identity: If A, then not B.
2. the law of noncontradiction: A and B must exclude each other unless there are qualifiers.
3. the law of rational inference: If A, then what necessarily follows.
4. the law of the undistributed middle: Just because two things have one thing in common does not mean they therefore have everything in common.

Please note that by their definition, even the laws of logic must have transcendent reality — that is, they must be based in reality and recognized as unassailably true, regardless of who believes it or doesn't or of their cultural perspective — as their logical starting points; otherwise, the arguments that stem from them cannot be logical, and there can be no true basis or beginning point for any argument, leaving us, as the ancient philosopher Heraclitus taught, with "flux, nothing but flux." Alfred North

Whitehead, Michael Polanyi, Stanley Jaki — all philosophers of science — held to some form of theism as the assumed framework for law and order and for the predictability of cause and effect in the universe. Whitehead's comment in which he refers to the great progress within the sciences in medieval times is worth noting:

> It must come from the medieval insistence on the rationality of God, conceived as with the personal energy of Jehovah and with the rationality of a Greek philosopher. Every detail was supervised and ordered: the search into nature could only result in the vindication of the faith in rationality. Remember that I am not talking of the explicit belief of a few individuals. What I mean is the impress on the European mind arising from the unquestioned faith of centuries.[8]

The atheist Frederick Nietzsche, one of Price's mentors, said that if there is no transcending reality, words are nothing more than manufactured ideas, endlessly reflecting themselves and each other within a hall of mirrors, becoming more distorted with each reflection. Recognizing this, he came to admit that he was pious enough that "even he still worships at the altar where God's name is 'truth.' "[9]

Nietzsche and the existentialists/nihilists were far more honest about where their atheism led than the doublespeak of Price and Sweeney, who want to have total finitude while granting themselves transcending privileges. It is for this very reason that the sciences have been denied any prerogative on ethics, even though some scientists desperately seek to bring it under their purview.

If the opinions and beliefs espoused in *The Reason-Driven Life* are evaluated against the laws of logic, the law of rational inference (that if something is true, what must necessarily follow) kills any discussion of morality other than from the perspective of its various humanistic coverings, each of which has its own "reason" and qualifiers. Here is Price on ethics and meaning:

> I believe we live in a morally neutral universe, that the moral laws

and grids of meaning through which we see it are artificial impositions by our various ancestors....

There is no already-determined meaning somewhere else, in the mind of some God viewed as a kind of heavenly Bureau of Weights and Standards. Where else could meaning be but in the eye of the beholder? And that is in you. That is in me.[10]

To pass off this paragraph as reason driven strains credulity. Note the consummate contradiction in just this one paragraph:

It is the great privilege and challenge of the human race to work out the best rules we can, the best standards of good and evil we can muster, and to strive to impose them upon the universe.... But we must carve out a moral space where our culture and civilization can live. We are part of Chaos, and we begin, little by little, to impose our own order and meaning upon it.[11]

Is he serious? Is this his logic of escape — from the totalitarianism of religion to the totalitarianism of secularism? Can he really mean what he says — that he did not write this book with any intention of changing the minds of his readers, when he holds to this methodological plan of morality? The sheer lunacy of the moral reasoning here is so terrifying that even secular philosophers must groan.

It was no one less than the philosopher Iris Murdoch who wrote of this vortex of self aggrandizement and its destiny:

How recognizable, how familiar to us, is the man so beautifully portrayed in the *Grundlegung*, who confronted even with Christ turns away to consider the judgment of his own conscience and to hear the voice of his own reason.... This man is with us still, free, independent, lonely, powerful, rational, responsible, brave, the hero of so many novels and books of moral philosophy. The *raison d'être* of this attractive but misleading creature is not far to seek. He is the offspring of the age of science, confidently rational and yet increasingly aware of his alienation from the material universe which his discoveries reveal.... His alienation is without cure.... It is not such a very long step from Kant to Nietzsche, and from Nietzsche to existentialism and the Anglo-Saxon ethical doctrines which in some ways closely resemble it. In fact, Kant's man had already received a glorious incarnation nearly a century earlier in the work of Milton: his proper name is Lucifer.[12]

Make no mistake, Price's desire to live not by negations but only by affirmations is a pipe dream that has resulted in nightmares for humanity. The problem with this philosophy is not that individuals may choose the noble and the virtuous but that there is no compelling reason for them to do so if their only desire is to be the last one left standing. Any doubt on this point is to live in denial of reason, not in support of it.

THE UNREASON
OF MISINTERPRETATION

To take every argument of Robert Price's hermeneutic to task would require a book of its own. And yet, nothing would ultimately be accomplished because the philosophical underpinnings in his arguments on the nature of interpretation reveal such a deep prejudice on his part. I could imagine conversing with C. S. Lewis about Price's kind of Bible bashing. I suspect Lewis would blow smoke rings from his pipe and with a wry smile say, "Write children's stories instead — you will meet a more honest heart in search of truth." Chesterton insisted that he learned more from observing a nursery than he ever did in studying philosophy. Jesus shocked his audience when he said that a child was a better representative of the kingdom of heaven than any one of his learned skeptics. Why is this so? Is it because children are gullible and unsophisticated in understanding? Not so, for I have been asked tougher, more honest questions by children than by most adults. It is because children are open to the truth and are not looking for reasons to believe a lie.

So let me get to the substantive part of Price's criticism of the Bible, pointing out that none of his arguments are new. Commentators and scholars have wrestled for centuries with teachings in the Bible that may seem at odds, numbers that sometimes do not seem to add up, and other objections to the biblical text. One need only read books introducing the Old and New Testaments to find page after page dealing with challenges to the text that higher or lower critics have brought to its study.

Coming from the East, I have often thought it strange that Western-trained, Western-raised, Western-bathed thinking has been responsible for volumes of books evaluating what is principally an Eastern book. For years I looked in vain for someone from the East who had dealt with the hermeneutics of the biblical text. In recent times, one or two have surfaced, but, by and large, dismantling the texts of the Bible has been a Western preoccupation. So it is not at all surprising that the attack on conservative theology has been followed by an attack on almost anything conservative here in the West.

In contrast, because the measuring line for "conservative" in the East is an authoritarian line drawn by "interpreters of the law," vitriolic language there is usually reserved for expressing strong resistance to those who sanction any *scrutiny* of the indigenous texts rather than aimed at those who *support* the text. People like Price understand very well the difference between the response he can expect from Christians to higher critical theories and the response he will get from Islamic scholars to any challenge to the Qur'an. Even more to the point, the tactics employed by the radical conservatives in Eastern thought are no different from the tactics of the radical liberals in the West. Islamic radicals silence the opposition with the threat of ostracism, personal injury, and death. While radical liberals in the West don't resort to death threats or personal injury, they do threaten ostracism and loss of public respect and acceptance in the ranks of their sophisticated schools, journals, and — increasingly — job opportunities. It is a different kind of violence.

I know of a fine school in Atlanta, for years a bastion of Christian education at the highest academic level, where one person of liberal thinking was appointed to the board and immediately began to demand a liberalization process in the school. The trustees resisted his demands, wanting to retain the Christian worldview that was the foundation of the school. So he contacted the Ivy League schools to which the majority of the school's graduates applied for their college education, and they, in turn, threatened that they would not admit future graduates unless the school changed its worldview and policies.

No, it is not a death threat, but it is death to the Christian or conservative aspirations and pursuits of higher education for many young lives. Some of the brightest, smartest kids happen to be Christians as well. There is compulsion in the extreme forms of both conservative and liberal thinking. While the nonextremist liberal may describe all conservatives as bearing out a psychologized, Freudian diagnosis on religion, the extreme liberal treats his ideology as sacrosanct to the point of hostility toward all who do not share that view. They also play God, but with rabid secular extremes.

I mention this to point out something basic. Resistance in the West toward the supernatural in general and the Christian faith in particular has taken a bigoted turn, accompanied by irrational responses. Francis Crick's postulation that a spaceship from another planet may have brought spores to seed the earth is accepted as a more scientifically satisfying explanation for the origin of the universe than the words "In the beginning God created the heavens and the earth." The attack on the Bible is not primarily for scholarly reasons but for ideological reasons, and the ramifications of reading the Bible apart from an understanding of the culture within which it was written can easily lead to misinterpretation.

It would be easier to respond to Price's allegations point by point, the same way he has attacked the Scriptures, but I will restrict myself to a few philosophical points. To those who wish to go further with the arguments, I point you to the books and blogs of scholars such as Ben Witherington and Darrell Bock. There you will be able to read their specific responses to those who have attacked the gospel narrative. (Chief among the names making the news in this regard is Bart Ehrman, another former evangelical who has taken to attacking the Scriptures and appearing on talk shows where gleeful humorists or skeptics cheer him on, thinking they have heard the truth.)

THE BIBLE
THROUGH EASTERN EYES

The Old and New Testaments, with their many writers and single focus, stand unique with respect to any other texts that claim to be revealed and authoritative. For example, the Qur'an has a single author and claims to be perfect in every word, never altered and never needing correction. It asserts itself as the sole and sufficient miracle of Muhammad. It is verbally inspired, verbally transmitted, and verbally preserved in the original text. That is the claim of Islam. Muhammad is considered to supersede every other prophet or authority in regard to any claim to divine revelation — the last, the greatest, and the ultimate revelator of Allah.

Yet when scholars in the field of textual origins and language examine these claims, they discover that numerous variant readings have existed over the years but were dismissed as flawed and destroyed. Excavations at a mosque in Yemen in the 1990s uncovered numerous variants, but before any real study could be done, those who had raised questions about the texts were either silenced or had disappeared. This is how Islam deals with questions. Why doesn't Robert Price write the same kind of books about Muslims and the Qur'an that he writes about Christians and the Bible? Why doesn't he deliver robust, animated talks to university audiences about the fallacies of Islam? Why doesn't he plan a tour in the Middle East to debunk the Qur'an? We all know the answer: rabid Islamists would have him silenced.

Price quotes the Mahabharata, part of the Hindu sacred texts, *The Iliad*, and the Bible in the same sentence because all three tell a story about two brothers. But he betrays how Western and restricted his context is because he doesn't seem to understand how very different each of these stories are culturally. He dismissively mentions the story in the Bible of the prodigal son saying, "Like all ancient stories of two estranged brothers, [it] can be read as a psychological allegory for the two estranged sides of a single personality."[13] I had to read this line several times, thinking he couldn't be serious. But then he footnoted it with the Freudian psychologist Bruno

Bettelheim's book *The Uses of Enchantment: The Meaning and Importance of Fairy Tales*, drawing from the section titled "Tales of Two Brothers."

Anyone who interprets the story of the prodigal son within such a framework defies a response. Of course this framework can be applied in a helpful manner to certain situations, and that is a different manner. But I am absolutely sure that Jesus' intention when he told the story was not as Price has inferred by his interpretation. I urge any who are interested to read the discussion of the parable in *The Cross and the Prodigal* by Kenneth E. Bailey, a brilliant scholar in Middle Eastern Studies. It was seeing Rembrandt's painting "The Return of the Prodigal Son," first on a poster on a friend's door and then while visiting the Hermitage Museum in Saint Petersburg, Russia, that changed the life of the renowned Henri Nouwen. As he sat in front of the painting by Rembrandt and gazed at it for hours, he felt a strong confirmation of the decision he had made to leave Harvard Divinity School, where he was a highly respected professor, and move to Toronto, Canada, to work with mentally challenged young people at Daybreak, a L'Arche community.

At my office in Atlanta, we have a small chapel. Inside the chapel is a painting ("The Forgiving Father") by an artist from India, Frank Wesley. In my opinion, Wesley's painting is much more reflective of the reality of the story than the more famous painting by Rembrandt. In Wesley's painting, I am struck by the details of the boy's condition, terribly scorched by the fierce heat of the open spaces in a parched land. Reduced to little more than a skeleton by his circumstances, he is barely able to stand on his own. The father, wrapped in a clean, white dhothi (an Indian garment worn especially in the summer) is supporting the young lad in his arms. My wife pointed out that the horizontal position of the father's arms around his boy juxtaposed with their bodies forms a cross. Only an Easterner would have so subtly rendered that motif.

My wife and I met an amazingly talented sculptor of bronzes. One of his small works took him many years to complete and be able to share with others, as it was too close to a reflection of his own spiritual journey. It is the depiction of a man holding on to a bottle, lying on his side on the ground, desolate and lost. The sculptor said that to him, the most important words in the Bible came from the story of the prodigal son: "And when he had come to himself." He said his sculpture reflected his own life, because it wasn't until he had reached the bottom that he "came to himself," recognizing his own shortcomings and failures, and was able to get to his feet and begin his journey upward. His message to the world through this bronze sculpture is that it is not until one recognizes the spiritual and moral depravity of his own heart that he will turn his steps toward home and God.

For Price to resort to Bettelheim's theorizing on the prodigal son is as far afield from the truth as the prodigal was from his father and home. Helmut Thielicke may have captured the true focus of the story when he said it should really be called "The Waiting Father."

You can tell a man by his heroes, and so far we see the names of Freud, Nietzsche, and Derrida having great impact on Price. He should beware: the more you read what he has written, the more his own Freudian slip shows.

Not only does Price not understand the cultural contexts of these texts, he doesn't recognize the difference between the Code of Hammurabi and other "ethical documents of old" — all of which lay out a code of cultural existence — and the Ten Commandments of the Old Testament. The Mahabharatha is well loved in India and is the revered origin of the folktales from which India gleans its ethos. But a Hindu would not think of holding the Mahabharatha on the same level as the Vedas. In the same way, these other codes of conduct, acknowledged as rules written by men for other men to follow, cannot be compared with the Ten Commandments, which were written by God for men to follow. I have no doubt that Price knows this, but it doesn't serve his purpose to admit that he is comparing as equal in authority texts that are very different in origin.

This kind of dishonest use of facts or elimination of details that don't support his storyline reminds me of a lecture I took from Don Cupitt at Cambridge University, in which he was trying to establish that all theology is really anthropology. As an example of what he was saying, he railed against Hinduism where, he said, all power is patrilineal — through the male — which explained why India is a culture in which women were held to be inferior to men. When I raised my hand to interrupt him his expression revealed that he wished I were not in his class. I disagreed with the position he had taken and pointed out that the transference of divine power in Hinduism is actually matrilineal, through the female goddess Shakti. He paused, looked at me and said, "We have a problem then, don't we?" Then he moved on with his lecture.

Hindus differentiate between their two levels of authority, the Shruti and the Smriti. The Shruti is "that which was heard"; the Smriti is "that which is remembered." They are not concerned that every detail in a story is consistent (that in itself is consistent with the way they look at the world) — they are gleaning the deep lesson contained in each narrative, the true object of the recitation. The most beloved of the texts is the Bhagavad Gita or the "Sacred Song." Would Mr. Price consider going to India and ridiculing the stories of the Gita and its backdrop in the Mahabharatha? There are aspects to these texts that would lend themselves to such ridicule. But he couldn't do that, because he would not be permitted to execute such an affront to their beliefs.

Isn't it interesting that the only group of religious believers that can be openly attacked and mocked to the cheers of like-minded skeptics is evangelical Christianity? Doesn't that say something about the nobility of the evangelical Christian message that Christians will accept such a challenge without resorting to the extremes that all other faiths do when faced with a similar assault?

CONCLUSIONS
OF THE REASON-DRIVEN LIFE

Consider these three implications of *The Reason-Driven Life*:

Man Is Taken to Be God

In his chapter titled "You Are a Work of Art," Price writes the following:

But I say that you are nonetheless a work of art. And so am I....
Thanks to your parents and your position in time and space, you have

a palette of particular colors in your hand. It is up to you to create the life you will live. It is up to you to create your own meaning.... If there is a God, he may have his own opinion as to what your life ought to be used for, what it means. But your life can have no meaning for you other than what it means *to you*, not him. You have to create it!

I like what Albert Camus said about art and why it must be gratuitous, why it must serve no purpose, neither to educate nor to propagandize.... It serves no purpose, obeys no command, does not labor to convey a message.[14]

Please note that what Price affirms art must not do — not educate or propagandize — he takes the trouble to do in defending this view of art. And indeed, in accordance with what he believes about art, it has become a purely emotive expression, bound by no ideas of beauty or truth, invariably driven toward the sensuous and the profane. In his purposeless world, there is a purpose to his descriptions; he labors to convey a meaningful message in a world that he says is bereft of meaning. This is what happens when the reason-driven life attempts a rational explanation of life that it insists is irrational at its core. You are a work of art — but art has no objective purpose; by extension, *you* have no purpose and no meaning. He has rejected God as the Creator because he feels a creator is contradictory to making sense out of life. But when man becomes God, life at its core is contradictory.

This Life Is All There Is

According to Price and those he admires and seeks to emulate, "now" is all we have, and there is nothing beyond the grave. All injustice, all hope of justice, all closure, all possibility of relationship is brought to an end by death.

The Greeks thought that justice was the supreme virtue. Ethicists talk of love as the supreme ethic. Many assert that even in despair, with a little hope one can withstand the deepest of disappointments. Many a psychologist has asserted that with personal meaning many indignities can be endured. But if all hope for justice ends at death, it becomes incumbent on each of us to secure for ourselves what we see as justice before it is too late, no matter what this means for anyone else.

No worldview can exist without some degree of faith. Rationalism had its heyday in the middle of the last millennium and gave birth to existentialism, which ultimately produced postmodernism. Now we have a rationalism that is materialistic, existential, postmodern, positivistic, and relativistic — all of which are held with an absoluteness that defies reason — and Time becomes an unending sequence of events that have no ultimate purpose, either singly or as a whole, and inevitably we are brought to meaninglessness and ultimately to despair.

Man Is Only a Body

The third implication of *The Reason-Driven Life* is that you are only a body. You are, according to Price, a neurological-chemical quantity with a brush in hand to paint on your own canvas. He goes to great lengths to deny the resurrection, as taught in the gospels, saying that it is both contradictory and contrary to reason. I strongly recommend that the reader visit the website of William Lane Craig (*www.reasonablefaith.org*) to read his debate with Price on this issue. The position held by Craig is also held by many intelligent people who have come to different conclusions than Price has about the facts they see. For either of them (or for proponents of the worldviews they represent) to refuse to examine what is said by the other side is to betray nothing more than a deep prejudice.

The truth is that there are valid arguments for the existence of God. There are arguments raised by atheists that present serious challenges for those who believe in God. There are experiences that people have that demand explanation. There are struggles on both sides of the issue. So the bottom line becomes this: Which side of the argument best takes into consideration all of reality without amputating any of it?

The price is eternal if Price is not right, and I believe Price is dead wrong. The person of Jesus Christ stands tall among the ideas of the world because he is exactly who he claims to be — the Way and the Truth and the

Life. The words of C. S. Lewis as he reflected on his recognition of God as God are worth repeating because they capture the very thing Price wishes to deny:

> You must picture me alone in that room in Magdalen, night after night, feeling, whenever my mind lifted even for a second from my work, the steady, unrelenting approach of him whom I so earnestly desired not to meet. That which I greatly feared had at last come upon me. In the Trinity Term of 1929 I gave in, and admitted that God was God, and knelt and prayed: perhaps, that night, the most dejected and reluctant convert in all England. I did not then see what is now the most shining and obvious thing; the divine humility which will accept a convert even on such terms. The prodigal son at least walked home on his own feet. But who can duly adore that Love which will open the high gates to a prodigal who is brought in kicking, struggling, resentful, and darting his eyes in every direction for a chance of escape?... The hardness of God is kinder than the softness of men, and his compulsion is our liberation.[15]

In C. S. Lewis's fourth book in The Chronicles of Narnia, *The Silver Chair*, a little girl named Jill finds herself in a strange forest in the land of Aslan. Her pride and foolishness have brought her there all alone. She is intensely thirsty, but as she approaches a stream, she sees a huge lion lying down beside the stream. The lion coaxes her to come closer and have a drink. With a "heavy, golden voice" he invites her to come and drink. In her fear she asks the lion if he would mind going away so that she can take a drink, to which his only response is a low growl. The sound of the clear water trickling over the little stones in its path adds to her thirst, so she asks the lion if he will promise not to hurt her if she advances. He gives her no promise. In desperation she asks, "*Do* you eat girls?" To which the lion responds without boasting, apology, or anger that he has "swallowed up girls and boys, women and men, kings and emperors, cities and realms."

Now she is really frightened and suggests that perhaps she'll do without a drink after all, until the lion reminds her that without water, she will die.

"I suppose I must go and look for another stream then," Jill says. But the lion says, "There is no other stream."[16]

To all the searches of men and women, boys and girls, kings and emperors, cities and realms for another way to assuage their thirst for the eternal by any means other than what God has provided — digging their own streams or denying the existence of eternity and giving themselves full autonomy — the Lion of the tribe of Judah revealed in the Holy Scriptures of the Bible says, "There is no other stream."

G. K. Chesterton, whose book *Everlasting Man* had a great impact on Lewis in his conversion from atheism to Christ, had gone the same route. His poem on his own conversion is remarkable:

> After one moment when I bowed my head
> And the whole world turned over and came upright,
> And I came out where the old road shone white,
> I walked the ways and heard what all men said,
> Forests of tongues, like autumn leaves unshed,
> Being not unlovable but strange and light;
> Old riddles and new creeds, not in despite
> But softly, as men smile about the dead.
>
> The sages have a hundred maps to give
> That trace their crawling cosmos like a tree,
> They rattle reason out through many a sieve
> That stores the sand and lets the gold go free:
> And all these things are less than dust to me
> Because my name is Lazarus and I live.[17]

6

DOES PRAYER MAKE ANY DIFFERENCE?

There is an immense difference between a worldview that is not able to answer every question to complete satisfaction and one whose answers are consistently contradictory. There is an even greater difference between answers that contain paradoxes and those that are systemically irreconcilable. Once again, the Christian faith stands out as unique in this test, both as a system of thought and in the answers it gives. Christianity does not promise that you will have every question fully answered to your satisfaction before you die, but the answers it gives are consistently consistent. There may be paradoxes within Christian teaching and belief, but they are not irreconcilable. To those who feel that Christianity has failed them because of prayers that went unanswered, it is important to realize what I am saying here.

I sat with a man in my car, talking about a series of heartbreaks he had experienced. "There were just a few things I had wanted in life," he said. "None of them have turned out the way I had prayed. I wanted my parents to live until I was at least able to stand on my own and they could watch my children grow up. It didn't happen. I wanted my marriage to succeed, and it didn't. I wanted my children to grow up grateful for what God had given them. That didn't happen. I wanted my business to prosper, and it didn't. Not only have my prayers amounted to nothing; the exact opposite has happened. Don't even ask me if you can pray for me. I am left with no trust of any kind in such things."

I felt two emotions rising up within me as I listened. The first was one of genuine sorrow. He felt that he had tried, that he had done his part, but that God hadn't lived up to his end of the deal. The second emotion was one of helplessness, as I wondered where to begin trying to help him.

These are the sharp edges of faith in a transcendent, all-powerful, personal God. Most of us have a tendency to react with anger or withdrawal when we feel God has let us down by not giving us things we felt were legitimate to ask him for. We may feel guilty that our expectations toward God were too great. We may feel that God has not answered our prayers because of something lacking in ourselves. We may compare ourselves with others whose every wish seems to be granted by God, and wonder why he hasn't come through for us in the way he does for others. And sometimes we allow this disappointment in God to fester and eat away at our faith in him until the years go by and we find ourselves bereft of belief.

G. K. Chesterton surmised that when belief in God becomes difficult, the tendency is to turn away from him — but, in heaven's name, to what? To the skeptic or the one who has been disappointed in his faith, the obvious answer to Chesterton's question may be to give up believing that there's somebody out there, take charge of your own life, and live it out to the best of your own ability.

But Chesterton also wrote, "The real trouble with the world of ours is not that it is an unreasonable world, nor even that it is a reasonable one. The commonest kind of trouble is that it is nearly reasonable, but not quite."[1] He is right. Only so much about life can be understood by reason; so much falls far short of any reasonable explanation. Prayer then becomes the irrepressible cry of the heart at the times we most need it. For every person who feels that prayer has not "worked" for them and has therefore abandoned God, there is someone else for whom prayer remains a vital part of her life, sustaining her even when her prayers have gone unanswered, because her belief and trust is not only in the power of prayer but in the character and wisdom of God. God is the focus of such prayer, and that is what sustains such people and preserves their faith.

Prayer is far more complex than some make it out to be. There is much more involved than merely asking for something and receiving it. In this, as in other contexts, we too often succumb to believing that something is what it never was, even when we know it cannot be as simple as we would like to think it is.

The Irish poet Frances Brown framed a poem about a band of pilgrims sharing about their losses in life. One pilgrim spoke of a treasure lost on the high seas, another of a fortune, ravaged and plundered. A third spoke of a lost love, and a fourth of having buried a little child.

> But when their tales were done, there spake among them one,
> A stranger, seeming from all sorrow free:
> "Sad losses ye have met, but mine is heavier yet,
> For a believing heart hath gone from me."
>
> "Alas!" these pilgrims said, "for the living and the dead,
> For fortune's cruelty, for love's sure cross,
> For the wrecks of land and sea! but, however it came to thee,
> Thine, stranger, is life's last and heaviest loss!
> For the believing heart has gone from thee."[2]

I remember my mother, lying in bed, her life hanging in the balance after a stroke at the age of fifty-seven. A group of elders from the church came and prayed for her. Afterward, one of them told us that the Lord had told him that my mother would get well. My younger brother, especially, who was twenty-two at the time and a medical student, was greatly buoyed and encouraged by this assurance of God's promise to heal her. However, only a few days later, her condition deteriorated, and she passed away. Of course we were grief-stricken and bewildered. But even more devastating was the response of some in the group — that she had died because someone in the family had lacked sufficient faith for her healing. We were already reeling from our loss, and now we each found ourselves, like the disciples, examining his or her own heart, asking God, "Is it possible that I am responsible for her death, or was this always in your plan and purpose?"

You are not alone in your experience of prayer. One hears stories of unanswered prayer all the time. Adding insult to injury is hearing someone else's story, someone whose prayers seem to be always answered or even someone who never thought of praying and yet their loved one has recovered. Read the following thoughts of a prominent Christian author, which I have compiled from his various writings. I have changed some of the wording but retained his ideas.

- I have prayed long and hard for God to save my mother's life, but my prayers have gone unanswered.
- I wish so much that God would rescue me from this dreadful school, and I have prayed to no end. I am still here.
- I finish praying and then struggle with my conscience, wondering if I had concentrated through it at all.
- Prayer for me meant pain, defeat, and much lost sleep.
- It is this terrible burden of duty in prayer that has taken its toll.
- Every evening was so cloaked in gloom because I dreaded bedtime and the nightly struggle for supreme concentration.

His struggle over his problem with unanswered prayer caused him to turn away from his Christian faith at the age of thirteen, and it was not until some twenty years later that he knelt and prayed, "perhaps, that night, the most dejected and reluctant convert in all England."[3] Yes, these are the experiences and words of C. S. Lewis. Lewis stated clearly that it was his disillusionment with prayer that made him walk away from his Christian belief when he was only a young lad. Yet fifteen or so years after his conversion, Lewis said he found himself in "philosophically a rather embarrassing position" of praying and trusting this same God for the safety of his brother Warren, who was in Shanghai during a Japanese attack.[4]

If we are being honest, which of us has not sensed this frustration, dejection, and confusion over prayer? Scholars of great philosophical prowess have asked what sort of God this is who needs to be pleaded with, cajoled, and begged. Once again, they show their total ignorance of how people in the East relate to God and have no difficulty accepting the distinction and inequality between God and man. Some Western celebrity thinkers, on the other hand, not only don't accede to this difference; they suggest that, if anything, man's ethic is higher than God's. But leaving the philosophers, scholars, and celebrities out of the discussion for the moment and returning to the subject of our own experiences with prayer, we all fully understand Lewis's frustration and readily identify with him.

It is not always as easy for us to identify with the profound prayers of some who seem to know God so well, and we listen with rapt attention, wondering at just how foreign it seems, as if it originates from another planet. Years ago, I read about a notable Indian Christian by the name of Bakht Singh, truly a remarkable person. Born into a Sikh family in Punjab, he regularly attended Gurdwaras (Sikh temples). When he was presented with a Bible at school, he promptly tore it to shreds. Years later, he went to Kings College in London, and while an engineering student in Canada, in 1929 — the same year C. S. Lewis became a Christian — Bakht Singh surrendered his life to Jesus Christ. He became one of the most notable Christians in India's history and was highly respected and revered, dying in 2000 at the age of ninety-seven.

Stories abound of the power he wielded in prayer. On one occasion on a long walk across India, a stranger is said to have stopped him and challenged him to pray for relief from drought for the area he was passing through. Bakht Singh asked the man if he would believe in Christ, should his prayer be answered. The man hesitated and then consented. As Singh was about to get on his knees to pray, his traveling companion supposedly cautioned him, "Don't you think we should wait to pray for rain until we are within range of our stop for the night — we still have some way to go, and we don't have any umbrellas."

Fact or fable, I have never bothered to determine. There is precedent in Scripture, however, when Elijah prayed for rain during a time of severe drought and had to run for cover himself (1 Kings 18). The Bible is replete with such answers to prayer, and it is a fact that George Mueller of Bristol, England, was just such a man of prayer in the 1800s. Often he would have not enough food to feed the orphans and street kids in his charge, but would offer thanks for the food anyway, before it even arrived. Numerous eyewitnesses and biographers have testified to his prayers of faith.

Saint John Chrysostom wrote this about the power of prayer:

> Prayer is an all-efficient panoply, a treasure undiminished, a mine
> which is never exhausted, a sky unobscured by the clouds, a heaven
> unruffled by the storm. It is the root, the fountain, the mother of a
> thousand blessings....
>
> The potency of prayer hath subdued the strength of fire, it hath
> bridled the rage of lions, hushed anarchy to rest; extinguished wars,
> appeased the elements, expelled demons, burst the chains of death,
> expanded the gates of heaven, assuaged diseases, repelled frauds, res-
> cued cities from destruction, stayed the sun in its course, and arrested
> the progress of the thunderbolt.[5]

Who can read that and not be tempted to exclaim, "Is that mere rhetoric?" No, not so. Each of the instances referred to by Chrysostom is drawn
right out of the Scriptures. The Bible talks about the privilege of prayer
and cautions against insincere prayer. Whether we're talking about the
Welsh Revival or that in the Hebrides or the Second Evangelical Awakening in America, all had one thing in common — concerted prayer over a
protracted period of time. Often as a student I would read stories of those
revivals and their foundations of prayer, and I would think, *That's what I
want to build my life on — the solid footing of prayer.* My library is full of
books on prayer. One would think that with each passing year the discipline of prayer would get easier, but in fact it doesn't. Whether early in the
morning or late at night, it is always a challenge. But as God has proved
himself, I have had several different experiences in which I sensed God's
very clear answer within my spirit. There is no doubt in my heart that
prayer makes a difference in anyone's life.

IS ANYONE LISTENING?
DOES ANYONE CARE?

There is no getting around the fact that the answers to prayer that Bakht
Singh and George Mueller regularly experienced don't fit the common

experience. My daughter Naomi has experienced some tough situations, but, by God's grace, has kept her feet steady. She travels the globe, working on behalf of the neediest of the world. Whether in the rescue or rehabilitation of women enslaved by the sex-trafficking industry or help for children affected by AIDS — either through the loss of their parents or their own diagnosis of HIV positive — she is in the thick of situations where the need and pain are overwhelming. She often says that perhaps God intended her place to be among the broken people of the world, and in her own personal life she has endured much pain, disappointment, and betrayal. Every now and then I hear her say, "I wish God would answer some of my prayers in a way that would let me know he is even just listening."

She currently makes her home in a quiet neighborhood on the West Coast of the United States. Recently, after a visit with us in Atlanta, she returned home to be greeted by her energetic Golden Retriever, India, who insists that Naomi first make up for all the lost time with her before anything else is done. Her landlady also came running to welcome Naomi home. So she set her suitcase on the ground just outside her door and got down on the floor, greeting the dog with all the preoccupation of the one-way conversation that a person with an affectionate dog regularly engages in, and also responding to her landlady's conversation. Finally she turned back to grab her suitcase. Only ten minutes had elapsed from setting it down outside the door and returning to retrieve it, and when she opened the door it was not there. She began to wonder if she had left it in her car, although she was sure she remembered unloading it. But her landlady confirmed that the suitcase had been at the door, which is how she had known that Naomi was back. She searched the periphery of the house in case it had been moved, but there was no sign of either the suitcase or its contents. I was ten thousand miles away when she called home, quite upset. Some of her favorite things were in the suitcase, as well as a few new things she had bought while she was away. She reported the loss to the police, and after two days when it still hadn't been located, they didn't give her much hope that she would ever see it, or anything in it, again.

I wrote to her, encouraging her not to lose hope. This was a small thing for God, and we continued to earnestly pray that he would restore it to her. Her prayer was, "I know it isn't important in the grand scheme of things. It's just a suitcase. But there are things in it that are important to me. I've experienced so much of the pain of life and seem to have known so few answers to my prayers — couldn't you bring my suitcase back? It would mean so much to me to know that you are there and that you are listening."

The fourth morning after its disappearance, she got up and checked outside the door as she had for the last three mornings — only to find nothing. She spent the morning working, frequently asking the Lord for the return of her suitcase. At noon she again checked outside the door, finding nothing. In the early afternoon she went out to run an errand, and when she came back there was still no suitcase in front of her door. A few minutes later, she went to the door, and sitting in the exact spot where she had left it three days earlier was her suitcase! She couldn't believe her eyes. In great excitement she opened it up and found everything there. Not a single thing had been taken.

Now mystified but filled with gratitude to the Lord, she called me. "Dad! Dad, you won't believe this! My suitcase is back, and nothing has been taken!" Later that day, she wrote to me and said, "You know, it's a small thing, but I needed that little small thing from God right now. I needed that little gesture just to know that he cares when I'm a little down."

Someone once humorously quipped that if you really want your spouse to hang on to every word you say — to listen with rapt attention and remember every word — just talk in your sleep. Someone else told a story about a bishop who knelt before the altar and began praying, "Dear Lord …" And a voice came from heaven asking, "What is it?" They had to pick the bishop off the floor, as he had fainted. The reason these stories strike us as funny is that it is so important to us that someone care enough about us and love us enough to listen to what we say, to care about what we think. And when we pray, when we pour out our hearts and make ourselves vulnerable before God, we sometimes cannot help but wonder — even a little bit — if there really is anyone listening.

LITTLE THINGS
THAT MAKE A BIG DIFFERENCE

Prayer has wings. It can lift you beyond the dark clouds of the human struggle so that you are able to soar above. At the same time, prayer is a reminder that we are not God. Do you remember those lines by Robert Browning?

> Go on, you shall no more move my gravity
> Than, when I see boys ride a-cockhorse
> I find it in my heart to embarrass them
> By hinting that their stick's a mock horse,
> And they really carry what they say carries them.[6]

I have absolutely no doubt that if you are a praying Christian, your faith in God is what is carrying you, through both the good times and the hard times. However, if you are not a praying person, you are carrying your faith — you are trying to make your faith work for you apart from your source of power — and trying to carry the infinite is very exhausting.

The question of unanswered prayer is a haunting one. What if prayer doesn't make the difference it's supposed to make? In this chapter it is not my intention to deny the great disappointments of unanswered prayer or even to attempt to provide answers to why our prayers are not answered. Rather, I want us to take a good, hard look at what God intends prayer to be.

THE MYSTERIOUS IMPACT
OF PRAYER

The Bible has a lot to say about prayer, either directly or by inference, with respect to the effect of prayer both on a situation and in the life of the person praying. Nearly fifty quite lengthy prayers are recorded in the Scriptures, along with numerous short ones. If we want to understand prayer, it is critical to understand how the Bible views prayer.

In all of its expressions, whether halting and short or flowing in beautiful, well-structured phrases, prayer is simply a conversation with God.

If we turn prayer into a monologue or use it as a way to showcase our gift with words or as a venue for informing or instructing others who may be listening, we defeat the very purpose of prayer. The Bible makes it clear that prayer is intended as the line of connection from the heart of the praying person directly to the heart of God. Jesus himself practiced a lifestyle of prayer and urged his disciples to imitate him by making it part of their daily existence. His prayers represented prayer at its best and most sincere.

I marvel at the impact of praying with a hurting person. I have prayed many times with someone who has claimed to be a skeptic and is living in a manner that supports that claim, only to finish my prayer and open my eyes to see tears in his eyes. Although prayer remains a mystery to all of us but especially to one who lives apart from God, I have observed again and again that even the hardened heart retains a longing for the possibility of communicating with God.

For example, on a trip to Hungary, I spent an evening with a few colleagues as we discussed spiritual and philosophical issues and tried to answer the questions of our six Hungarian hosts. They included, among others, a member of the parliament, a theoretical physicist, and a successful businessman. None of them were followers of Jesus Christ. They were in the truest sense atheistic — with no belief in God or recognition of any need for God.

After hours of interaction, the evening came to an end. Before we separated, I asked if they would mind if I concluded our time together with prayer. They were a bit taken aback, but in a rather bemused manner they agreed that I should pray. I prayed briefly for their nation, their families, and their own lives. I prayed that God would show himself to them in some meaningful way and thanked him for the opportunity to meet them in their homeland and spend the evening with them. When I said Amen and lifted my eyes, I saw tears in the eyes of each of our hosts. There was a hushed silence. Everyone seemed peculiarly reluctant to disturb the sense of God's sudden, unexpected presence. We bid them good night.

The next morning, I stood to address an audience miles away from the dinner of the previous night and recognized some of the very people with whom we had spent the previous long evening. I was surprised, not only because of the distance they had traveled to be there, but also because this was a closed event, open only to registered delegates. But there they were.

When the session finished and the hall cleared, the businessman approached me and said, "Something happened last night." He went on to say that after the prayer the previous evening he had been so moved that he hadn't gone back to his hotel room. Instead he had walked most of the night until he had come to the place of accepting that Jesus Christ was who he claimed to be — the Son of God and the Savior of the world. And he had given his life into the keeping of that Savior. Prayer can accomplish amazing things, reaching into hearts in a way that all the correct answers to questions that are honestly asked sometimes cannot do.

Conversely, more certainly than anything else, sustained prayer that seems to bring nothing in response can result in a sense of futility with life and an erosion of faith. Like the myth of Sisyphus, who repeatedly rolled a huge rock up a mountain only to watch it roll down again, unanswered prayer may well be where most of those who have lost their faith began that journey into unbelief.

JESUS ON PRAYER

No one is a better instructor on prayer than Jesus himself. By simply observing the specific occasions in which the Scriptures tell us that Jesus spent time in prayer, it should be evident how very important prayer is: at his baptism (Luke 3:21); on the occasion of his transfiguration (Luke 9:29); at the selection of his twelve disciples (Luke 6:12); at the Last Supper with his disciples during the Passover Feast (John 17:1 – 26); before his arrest in Gethsemane (Matthew 26:36 – 46); and at his cruel execution on the cross (prayers that are recorded by all four gospel writers).

Reading these prayers and coming to terms with how Jesus prayed and why he prayed as he did provide all we need for a fascinating study. The most definitive passage on prayer is what is often called the Lord's Prayer or, as some scholars like to call it, the Disciples' Prayer. (More than once I have heard an audience asked to recite the Ten Commandments by memory, and few can do so. But most people who have attended church even for a short period of time or are over the age of fifty have learned the Lord's Prayer either in church or in school.) A mere sixty-five words, it is uttered thousands of times a day. In this simple prayer, we see what prayer, however expanded, should be.

The highly significant first words carry the weight of all of prayer: "Our Father in heaven." This is a uniquely Christian utterance. I have never heard a Hindu, Muslim, Buddhist, or anyone of any other faith ever begin prayer with those words. The conversion story of a wealthy socialite woman in Pakistan, Bilquis Sheikh, is appropriately titled *I Dared to Call Him Father*. In these two words alone — "Our Father" — we recognize, at least implicitly, two truths: the nearness of God as our heavenly Father, and the sovereignty of God as the one who controls everything. As soon as you cry out in prayer, "Heavenly Father," you are recognizing his sovereign rule over your life.

The great prayers of the Old Testament — even from Abraham, the friend of God, or from David, a man after God's own heart — do not begin this way. To address God in this way is distinctive. It was Jesus' way of introducing to his disciples that God was their heavenly Father. Can you imagine how new this must have been to the disciples — even shocking — to hear God addressed this way. In the Jewish faith, of which Christianity is the fulfillment, God was so revered, so distant, so holy — so "other" — that his name could not even be spoken. That attitude is still true among Jews today. To hear God addressed in such a familiar and intimate manner must have made an immediate impression on them of what Jesus was teaching about their relationship with God.

The prayer recorded by Matthew (6:9 – 13) is also recorded by Luke (11:2 – 4). Jesus gives the context in verses 5 – 10.

> Then [Jesus] said to them, "Suppose one of you has a friend, and he goes to him at midnight and says, 'Friend, lend me three loaves of bread, because a friend of mine on a journey has come to me, and I have nothing to set before him.'

"Then the one inside answers, 'Don't bother me. The door is already locked, and my children are with me in bed. I can't get up and give you anything.' I tell you, though he will not get up and give him the bread because he is his friend, yet because of the man's boldness he will get up and give him as much as he needs.

"So I say to you: Ask and it will be given to you; seek and you will find; knock and the door will be opened to you. For everyone who asks receives; he who seeks finds; and to him who knocks, the door will be opened."

The New Testament events took place in the Middle East, and in the East it is an absolute must to place food in front of a guest, without exception. You simply do not welcome anyone into your home without offering them food and drink. My first reaction when reading this story was to think that I knew exactly how the host felt: *What on earth is this friend thinking, arriving unexpectedly at midnight [it had to be unexpected, or the food would have been ready], and hungry at that?* But it happens all the time.

I had an uncle who, when an earthquake hit our city, moved his whole family of seven into our home for three months. Already a family of seven living in a small two-bedroom home, we had to feed and provide a place for them for all those months. Even then, I marveled at it. I remember asking my mother how my uncle felt he was safer living with us when his own home was a mere half mile away. Why was it necessary because of one earthquake for their family to move in with us for three months? There we were, fourteen of us in a four-room house — two bedrooms, a small kitchen, and a living room. Indeed, they actually did arrive at midnight, and all of a sudden we all had to vacate our beds and give them to the "guests." We were not happy. But there was absolutely no possibility, not even a thought on the part of my parents, of turning them away. Courtesy demanded that we open our home to them and share all that we had.

This is precisely the context of Jesus' story. It is one of those "how much more" passages. If through sheer pressure of culture a person yields to the needs of a friend because of his friend's persistence, "how much more will your heavenly Father do for you?" The man's neighbor was asleep; God doesn't sleep. The neighbor had locked his door against any intrusion; God is always available to us. The neighbor didn't know his friend; God knows every heart and every need. He knows the numbers of hairs on our heads. He knows the days each of us have been given for life on this earth. He sees every sparrow that falls. He knows our need before we even ask him to meet it.

Jesus then applied the lesson by saying, "Which of you fathers, if your son asks for a fish, will give him a snake instead? Or if he asks for an egg, will give him a scorpion?" (Luke 11:11 – 12). Then he gives the key to the whole passage that begins with his model prayer: "How much more will your Father in heaven give the Holy Spirit to those who ask him!" (verse 13).

On the heels of the Lord's Prayer and as his conclusion to it, Jesus tells us that God will give the Holy Spirit, his indwelling presence, to those who ask for it. That is the whole point of the prayer. It is not spoken in the form of a question — it ends with an exclamation point. God *will* give the gift of the indwelling presence of the holy God to any who ask for it — this is an absolute certainty! You can count on it!

We hear so little of this today. In its efforts to make God relevant to modern men and women, the emergent church seldom emphasizes to its audiences that the ultimate result of prayer is that Jesus intends to make his home within the life of the supplicant. We have turned prayer into a means to our ends and seldom wait on God's response long enough to think about what he wants for us in that very moment. By reducing the evidence of the indwelling of the Holy Spirit to one particular gift, we have robbed people of the Holy Presence that prompts us in prayer, prays for us when we don't have the words to pray for ourselves, and comforts us in our times of need.

The paramount need in the church today and in the individual Christian is the indwelling presence of God. In an incredible twist, this indwelling presence of God, the Holy Spirit, makes God both the enabler of our prayers and the provider of answers to those prayers.

This is precisely how a wise parent raises his or her child — teaching the child to train his or her hungers and longings so that in turn, the parent is able to provide for those hungers and longings. More than anything else, this is what prayer is about — training one's hungers and longings to correspond with God's will for us — and it is what the Christian faith is all about. Paul reminds us of this numerous times. Jesus talks of the prompting from within and the provision that comes from without, which is the work of the Holy Spirit within us and the provision of God from without.

A neighbor once came to our door, asking me to pray for a particular family need. I smiled at her and said, "I'm glad to pray for you, but you know, you have equal access to God and can come to him yourself at any time." I thought I had captured a nice, culturally relevant term for her. But she paused for a moment and said, "I know that, but you seem to have an 800 number for him; for me it's a long-distance call." I suppose if that had happened today, I could have replied by suggesting that she get a roaming package on her phone.

Humor aside, I think the reason we sometimes have the false sense that God is so far away is because that is where we have put him. We have kept him at a distance, and then when we are in need and call on him in prayer, we wonder where he is. He is exactly where we left him.

Calvin Miller makes a powerful point:

> The sermon and the Spirit always work in combination to pronounce liberation. Sometimes the Spirit and sermon do supply direct answers to human need, but most often they answer indirectly. Most problems are not solved by listening to sermons. The sermon, no matter how sincere, cannot solve these unsolvable problems. So if the sermon is not a problem solver, where shall we go for solutions? Together with the Spirit, the sermon exists to point out that having answers is not essential to living. What is essential is the sense of God's presence during dark seasons of questioning.... Our need for specific answers is dissolved in the greater issue of the lordship of Christ over all questions — those that have answers and those that don't."[7]

This is one of the most defining differences between an apologist who is merely interested in arguments and an apologist who knows God in a clear and personal walk with him. To the skeptic, to say that prayer is more about the lordship of Christ than it is about getting answers may seem at first blush to be evasive, but it is not. It is in keeping with the worldview that God's presence is a felt presence and must be pursued with diligence — and it is precisely what "ask, seek, and knock" means.

In his book *The Integrity of Worship*, Paul Waitman Hoon makes a powerful observation about how God works on us as individuals through prayer, molding us into what he wants us to be, teaching us to think as he wants us to think:

> How often have we craved light on our life in the world, only to be summoned to ponder our destiny in eternity. How often have we been preoccupied with the church local and instead found our vision turned to the church triumphant and universal. And how often have we asked that worship bless our souls with peace, only to hear the lesson for the day calling us to a holy warfare. How often have we desired strength to overcome the world, only to learn that we are to be stoned and sawn asunder in the world. How often have we sought comfort to our sorrows and instead found the sorrows of the world added to our own. Such reversals may be strange to men. But only such contradiction answers to realities both relevant and irrelevant that are at the heart of the church's worship.[8]

MORE ON THE LORD'S PRAYER

Let us now focus our thoughts on three other dimensions to the Lord's Prayer. They are obvious in one sense but not in another.

"Hallowed Be Your Name": From Nearness to Distance

The opening affirmation reveres the name of God as sacred and is the starting posture of prayer. God is our Father, but he is also holy in character. This alone should remind us that God's name in our lives and in our requests must be paramount. What's in a name? Who you are in your character is carried in your name. It is *because* of his name that numerous prayers are prayed. It is *in* his name that numerous prayers are prayed.

The failure to recognize that our prayers carry his name has brought much disaster to many Christians. His name is quite "unhallowed" in the way we see God in relation to ourselves, if the contemporary expressions of worship that we often engage in are any indication. This vacuous understanding of the sacred may be part of the reason for the collapsing foundation of Christianity in the West.

In Jeremiah 7, we find the people of God living with a false sense of security. They knew the northern portion of their divided kingdom had fallen to the Assyrians, but they lived with the false hope that the southern kingdom of Judah would never fall because the temple of the Lord, which symbolized the presence of God, was located there. God speaks to Jeremiah in clear terms:

> "Do not trust in deceptive words and say, 'This is the temple of the Lord, the temple of the Lord, the temple of the Lord!' ...
>
> "Go now to the place in Shiloh where I first made a dwelling for my Name, and see what I did to it because of the wickedness of my people Israel."
>
> JEREMIAH 7:4, 12

The citizens of the southern kingdom rested in the false hope that because Jerusalem was special to God, he would never let it fall to the enemy. God shocked them by reminding them that Shiloh had preceded Jerusalem chronologically in God's affections — and yet Shiloh had become a byword, a topic of conversation in the region because of its devastation — and that Jerusalem's turn was coming. In the end, God will always protect his name, but when we disrespect that name — when we imply by our speech and by the way we live that the character of God is not revered — and when we live with the illusion that God will not call us to task for what we are doing to his name, he will act drastically to disassociate himself from the desecration of his name. To be reverenced is the very least that God expects from every human being.

The name of God must always be treated as sacred, and history brings staggering reminders of how much we need to keep this in mind. There is nothing more memorable in the history of Russia than Czar Alexander I, a totally profane man, falling on his face before God in a church in Saint Petersburg, asking God for the deliverance of his nation, even as Napoleon's army was preparing to torch the spires of Moscow. God responded by sending a minor prophet — the winter. How ironic that the very church in which he prayed was later converted into the Museum of Atheism during the high noon of Marxism. Success seems to bring with it short memories of divine intervention, and prayer is a ready casualty.

The sacred is that which cannot be made commonplace. We have to ask ourselves as individuals and as a culture if we really think we can desacralize God's name with impunity. It is telling that throughout the world it is the name of Jesus that is used profanely — not Buddha, not Muhammad, not Krishna. Even the profane in those cultures have enough reverence for the names of their own prophets or deities. We in the West are the only ones who use the name of our God more as a punctuation mark that reveals our irreverence than as a name that speaks to us of the sacred. This applies to nations, to communities, and to individuals. No prayer is sincere if his name is unhallowed. The reason is straightforward and of enormous significance. In the end, how we see his name is how we will see ourselves. This is the logical connection in prayer.

But whether our prayer meets with "success" or "failure," we are far too inclined to think of God either as a magician, answering all our demands or needs as we see them, or as distant and uncaring when our prayers aren't answered and we don't get what we asked for. The first mistake we make is to turn prayer into merely a wish list because when those wishes aren't granted, we struggle to believe in God and feel that he has disappointed or failed us.

Some years ago, Steve Martin starred in a movie called *Leap of Faith*. It told the story of a faith healer with the memorable name, Jonas Nightingale. Jonas works a circuit, setting up his tent in various small towns for his revivals. He uses all the crooked and perverted terms for faith associated with a glamorized version of Christianity that is too often displayed on Christian telecasts. He had created a system that informed him of who in the audience was suffering from what and where they were seated. Then, in the climax of a "healing service" and with the grandiloquence of a circus ringmaster, he would call his "would-be victim" to the front to be healed.

Because his bus breaks down, he ends up in a simple agrarian community in the Midwest, in the throes of a dreadful drought. The entire community had pitched their tents in small family units, spending nightlong vigils in prayer for rain when Brother Jonas arrives and finds a ready-made audience for his exploitation. He befriends a waitress who is earnestly in need of the touch of God in her family, especially for her brother, who cannot walk. Believing Jonas, she asks him to heal her brother. He realizes this is serious stuff to the "simpleminded" believing community in a town where people grow up depending on the elements for their very sustenance, and he begins to feel a sense of discomfort at taking advantage of them and playing with their faith.

So he prepares to bring his series of meetings to an abrupt end but is caught when a real miracle of healing takes place in his meeting. As the sick respond to his "charade" up front to "come to Jesus for healing," the young brother of the waitress comes forward and, in a remarkable moment, is able to throw off his crutches and walk again. The crowd roars in delight and celebration of what God has done.

Nobody is in a greater state of shock than Jonas Nightingale. After all the euphoria has died down, he retires into his quiet room. He has planned to leave the area the next day, but, unable to sleep, he is lying awake as he tries to figure out what has happened. He gets up, dresses, and goes to the tent, where all is in darkness. He walks to the front to a large crucifix, where the miracle of the young lad's healing had taken place. He looks up at the figure on the cross and begins to speak: "Lord, this is ... Jack." For the first time in the movie he calls himself by his real name. He has come to terms with who God is and sees his own name as a true reflection of the person he really is.

Pretense is the cornerstone of our own ultimate failure. To pray as though we have the right to demand what we want without the candor of facing up to who we really are is to make prayer the ultimate charade, even if we think no one is watching.

Alone after making peace with God, Jack returns to his room. In the still-dark hours, he picks up his pack and hitches a ride from a truck driver passing through town. Suddenly he sees a raindrop on the windshield and then two, then three, as the thunderclouds celebrate with teardrops for the healing of a fake healer who has come to faith.

Most interesting to me in such a movie are the insights that even skeptics have into what faith is meant to be, sometimes bearing very little resemblance to what commercialized Christianity makes Jesus out to be. There is probably something deeper here. I wondered why the script writers even gave him the name of Jack. Was it short for Jacob? Do you remember the story of how Jacob pretended to be his older brother Esau and stole the blessing from his blind father? Do you remember that when the day of reckoning came and he was to meet up with his brother who was bigger and burlier than him, Jacob wrestled all night with God and said, "I will not let you go unless you bless me"? God asked him the most unusual question; he asked him for his name. All of a sudden Jacob realized that he was face to face with himself as God knew him to be and as he himself knew he was. He had run from God with the stolen blessing of a fake name. Now, as he was returning home, he knew he was not Esau — he was Jacob, a name that means duplicitous. That day, Jacob admitted to his true name before God and was reborn as a spiritual man; that day a nation was reborn spiritually and its children became the inheritors of the blessing.

"Hallowed be your name" is the opening line of the prayer recognizing both the sovereignty of God and the character of God — a character that is holy and will not lie or deceive, in contrast to our own deceitful hearts. "Father" brings him near, while "hallowed be your name" creates the legitimate distance between a holy God and his creation. His love for us is balanced by his protection of us from that which will make us less than what God intends us to be. That is the pivotal first half of "the equation" of prayer: God is love and God is holy.

"Your Kingdom Come": God Keeps Watch over All of Time

The kingdom of God is neither political nor material. It is spiritual. We tend to define our successes in political or material terms, but God's kingdom is a spiritual rule. It is not a theocracy but rather the imperative of eternity. Life is not subsumed by our "threescore years and ten" (Psalm 90:10 KJV). This is sustained by the implied limitation of the prayer, "Give us *each day* our daily bread" (Luke 11:3, emphasis added). One would think it would be simpler to pray for enough sustenance for the week or even for a lifetime. If enough provision for one day is good, provision for two days is better. Then we wouldn't have to come back, asking for more. But this is precisely the nature of God's provision. We live in bite-sized portions of time and must seek God for strength for the day, one day at a time. We must depend on God *each day* we live. When we live life this way, we are able to face history with the guarantee of his keeping watch over all of time. Unless we live with the eternal in mind while addressing the specifics of each day, we will live as temporarily suspended, with faith always seeking sight.

At the close of Luke's gospel, we see Jesus' disciples disillusioned, confused, and fearful following the crucifixion. In the last chapter, Luke tells us that on the Sunday of Jesus' resurrection, two of Jesus' followers are walking to a village called Emmaus, about seven miles from Jerusalem. They were talking about all that had happened the previous week when Jesus himself came up and walked along with them — but they were kept from recognizing him. He asked them what they were talking about, and they, in amazement asked him if he is the only visitor to Jerusalem who didn't know what had happened there over the weekend. The delightful irony of their question is that he was the only one who *did* know what had happened. His explanation of the significance of these events was detailed, profound, and persuasive, going right back to the writings of the prophets as he unfolded the eternal plan of God.

The seven miles flew by, and before they realized it, they had arrived in Emmaus. True Easterners, they invited Jesus to join them for dinner. He accepted their invitation and as they sat down to eat, Jesus, the universal member of all cultures, became the host as he took bread in his hands and gave thanks to the Father for it. Whether it was the way he broke the bread that may have reminded them of a meal they had shared with him previously, or whether as he did so, they suddenly noticed the wounds in his hands, their eyes were opened to him, and they understood God's eternal presence in *all* things throughout history, even when hope seems lost. As Jesus left them, the fatigue of the miles they had walked that day vanished, and they joyfully retraced their steps to Jerusalem — all seven miles of them — to tell the other disciples the good news Jesus had shared with them.

"Your Will Be Done": From Submission to Crisis

Through Jesus' prayer in Gethsemane we learn the most important thing about prayer — that it is ultimately a conversational relationship in which God does for you what you cannot do for yourself. It is not trying to persuade God to rethink his will but the means through which God reshapes you into a person who desires his will and is content to receive it, regardless of what it entails.

This is not fatalism. It is not defeat. It is not confusion. It is not a cop-out. It is sometimes easier to resist God's will than to have faith and confidence in God and in his specific purpose for each one of us. Only through exercising this kind of faith can the moment be accepted and understood as a small portion of a bigger story. For some of us this may entail a long, arduous journey, but it will be accomplished one moment at a time, one day at a time, each moment and day undergirded by the strength of the indwelling presence of God.

C. S. Lewis resisted writing any book about prayer, for he considered himself to be always a student of prayer. His *Letters to Malcolm* explains why he doesn't think most people are qualified to write on the subject, himself included. His response to the taunting of a skeptic that prayer was nothing more than talking to oneself while thinking there was someone listening at the other end is best expressed in the anonymously written poem he tells us he found in an old notebook:

> They tell me, Lord, that when I seem
>> To be in speech with you,
> Since but one voice is heard, it's all a dream,
>> One talker aping two.
>
> Sometimes it is, yet not as they
>> Conceive it. Rather, I
> Seek in myself the things I hoped to say,
>> But lo! my wells are dry.
>
> Then, seeing me empty, you forsake
>> The listener's role and through
> My dumb lips breathe and into utterance wake
>> The thoughts I never knew.
>
> And thus you neither need reply
>> Nor can; thus, while we seem
> Two talkers, thou art One forever, and I
>> No dreamer, but thy dream.[9]

God's ultimate purpose is to bring us to himself through the relationship made possible by the gift of his Son. The most important point of Gethsemane is that it underscores just how hard that struggle may be at times. Jesus had just finished celebrating the Passover with the disciples, where he had spoken to them about his betrayal at the hands of one of his own. He knew this was the purpose for which he had left heaven for earth, a purpose to which he had fully acceded. Yet in the hours before the inevitable, even he who was fully man and fully God struggled, asking the Father if there was any other way to accomplish the plan.

"My Father," he prayed, overwhelmed with sorrow to the point of death, "if it is possible, may this cup be taken from me. Yet not as I will, but as you will" (Matthew 26:39). And then a little later, "My Father, if it is not possible for this cup to be taken away unless I drink it, may your will be done" (verse 42). I wonder how much time elapsed between the first part of the prayer and the last. Luke tells us the struggle was so great that his sweat was "like drops of blood falling to the ground" (Luke 22:44). It's also revealing to read that at the darkest part of this struggle to align his will with the Father's, God sent an angel to him who strengthened him in his resolve to do the Father's will.

Prayer is hard work. Being aligned with God's will is no light matter. For Jesus, just at his most desolate and agonizing moments, even as he faced the agony of being separated from his Father to make it possible that we would never have to face that total abandonment, he was, in fact, right in the center of his Father's will. How gracious of God to even let us into the struggle of such unimaginable proportions between the Father and the Son!

There are several other instances in the Bible of such urgent struggle to achieve confidence in the wisdom and will of God. Daniel's three friends (Shadrach, Meshach, and Abednego), facing the king's very real threat to toss them into a fiery furnace if they did not bend to his authority, come to the conclusion, "If we are thrown into the blazing furnace, the God we serve is able to save us from it, and he will rescue us from your hand, O king. But even if he does not, we want you to know, O king, that we will not serve your gods or worship the image of gold you have set up" (Daniel 3:17 – 18).

There are numerous reasons given in Scripture for the reality that prayers sometimes go unanswered. But if one understands the purpose of prayer — and, more to the point, the purpose of life — the unanswered prayer becomes more endurable in light of the bigger picture. How many times have we read of someone who was spared from a tragic crash because of some unavoidable circumstance that forced them to miss the plane or train or bus? How often have we marveled at the tales of a lone survivor of a military firefight returning home and being killed within days in a car accident? All of this must point us to the understanding that we all have an unavoidable appointment with God. None of us will be spared that moment. We never know what our last days will be like as we get closer to that final moment.

Before I took the platform to speak recently on the problem of pain, I was introduced by a man who said that in one tragic year he had lost five members of his immediate family, all in different circumstances. As he listed them, one after another — the loss of his wife, his parents, his brother, and one of his children — there was pin-drop silence in the vast audience. Every relationship was tested. Then he added these words. "Our speaker tonight has helped me immensely through those times, and God's presence has been very real through all those heartaches." I sat in silence as he finished his introduction, wondering how I would have fared in the same circumstances. But this is where the grace of God is so uniquely given in the time of each person's need.

UNANSWERED PRAYER

Philip Yancey lists several possible reasons people have given for unanswered prayer and the sense of distance from God that so often is experienced at the same time.[10] We may be focused on ourselves rather than on God and his wisdom; it may be that we are at fault, not the prayer; we may simply be out of fellowship with God; we may be lacking concern for the poor and the needy (the Bible often points to this as a reason for unanswered prayer). Prayer is not magic, nor is it a fixed formula. Sometimes we have placed value in the wrong place — on what we are asking for rather than on what God wants to accomplish in us. Sometimes the delay is not an unanswered prayer but a matter of God's timing and what he needs to have completed in us before he can answer that prayer.

Each of us could make our own list of reasons for unanswered prayer. None of these come from any fresh insight into the mind of God. So we need to focus on what we know to be the purpose of prayer. As I read Scripture, I see five distinct realities that God wants us to know or learn through the process of prayer.

Humility

God repeatedly reminds us that his purpose behind the particular journey in life through which he takes us is that we might see what is in our own hearts. Growing to the place of achieving a humble heart is a double-edged victory. It involves recognizing (1) that none of the blessings he bestows on us are given because we are better than anybody else and (2) that he instead gives them to us as a sovereign act and with the prevailing peace that he is the author and distributor of our blessings, choosing to bestow them according to his own reason.

Years ago as a young preacher, I was asked to call a famous preacher who was in the hospital after having suffered a serious stroke. He was a prolific writer with a double doctorate from Oxford, one of the most eloquent speakers of the day. He was a godly man, yet he had been felled by an unexpected stroke and had lost his ability to speak. Our conversation was difficult. After anything I said, I had to wait for protracted moments before he was able to force out a tentative "Y-y-yes." I could not hold back the tears and struggled to continue the conversation. To hear such debilitation in a voice that once rang with such oratorical skill was a fearsome thing to me, also a preacher. After I hung up the phone, I went straight to my knees and thanked God for the voice I had taken for granted. God's gifts are given at his discretion and may be removed at any time — also at his discretion.

This is not "worm theology," as though we are groveling and treating ourselves as scum. Skeptics love to use this expression to ridicule Christians. Nietzsche called such people weak — the scourge of the earth. That is not what is being espoused here. We are not demeaning our humanity. We are recognizing our fragile nature as we come to God with the recognition that, between our selfish motives and finite glimpses of his perfect will for us, we are prone to think we are more in control of life than we actually are.

When my younger brother was about seven years old, he was stricken with double pneumonia and typhoid fever. As the days went by and his body began to die in front of us, we were grief-stricken. Night after night, though he did not know the Lord at that time, my father would lead us in prayer. That in itself was a powerful lesson to us. He was a tough man who never voluntarily admitted to any sign of weakness. But watching his youngest son at the door of death brought his pursuit for power and success to a halt. Every night we got into bed with fearful hearts about what would happen during the night. My mother sat by my brother's bed for days.

Finally the doctors informed us that his case was hopeless and that he would likely pass away that night. In tears we said our good-byes and went home from the hospital engulfed in a deep sense of loss. My mother stayed by his bedside, refusing to leave him for even a moment. Sometime in the early hours of the morning, she suddenly woke up, still sitting in the chair, and realized she had fallen asleep during the very hours that we had been told he would slip out of this life. In dismay and fear she reached out to touch his face. Something in the way he felt gave her hope that he was better than he had been some hours ago. With the dawning of the day the doctor arrived, expecting to find that my brother had died. He realized there had been a positive change but didn't want to give false hope. "He is defying what we thought would happen," was all he would commit to.

Today my brother, in his fifties, is a doctor in Canada. I often reflect on those days. When all that could be done had been done, when everyone had given all that they could give to him and none of us were even awake, God turned the corner for this little boy and healed his body. I know we don't always see this happen; I've already mentioned the loss of my mother many years later. But we must admit to our own frailty and limitation and realize that sometimes God's greatest work is done when we are least involved in it.

In humility we come to God, and with a humble heart we trust in his character and his wisdom. Any other option flirts with the act of playing God.

Spirituality

Ultimately, a successful life is built by developing the spirit, not the body. Time and matter must always give way to the eternal and to the spiritual. We dislike this inversion. We collectively spend billions of dollars each year trying to look young. I shudder to even think of the possibility of discovering or developing a "fountain of youth" that would eliminate aging and death. What kind of world would that be?

This drive to be as beautiful at sixty as we were at twenty has its last hurrah in the creams and potions we use to disguise death when it comes, liberally lavishing it on the deceased until someone can comment, "He looks just like himself, doesn't he?" I have never seen a corpse that didn't look like a corpse. Death is the absence of life, and no matter how we dress it up, the person is gone from the material shell that housed that great intangible — life. All the things that mattered most and made the person the individual they were — their mind, passions, will, smile, tears, aches, and joys — all are gone. These were the things of the spirit. That is why Jesus said we could not live by bread alone. We are, first and foremost, spiritual beings who must attend to the things of the spirit. Regardless of our pursuits or achievements in life, the hungers of the spirit must always be primary. We must seek first the kingdom of God and his righteousness (Matthew 6:33) — and no one who has done this regrets taking final leave of the body.

Faith

Prayer teaches us faith. It is not a guarantor of getting what we want. It is the assurance that our Lord superintends over our lives in our needs and our dependencies, in our successes and accomplishments. Faith is that sublime hourly dependence on God — our conviction that even though we may not get what we want or think we need, we know and love the One who denies us in this instance for his good reason and for our ultimate good.

The most significant relationships in life are based on this kind of faith, where love and trust triumph over disappointment. In the face of the apparent defeat of unanswered prayer, faith enables us to have victory in the certainty of trusting the One who is in control. Although we tend in our language to interpret *faith* as "containing no basis for belief," this is not the way the Bible uses the word. In fact, in the Hebrew language, faith is more an idea than a word. In the book of Habakkuk, we see the description of "the righteous person" as one who lives "by his faithfulness."

> "Write down the revelation
>   and make it plain on tablets
>   so that the herald may run with it.

For the revelation awaits an appointed time;
> it speaks of the end
> and will not prove false.
Though it linger, wait for it;
> it will certainly come and will not delay.

See, he is puffed up;
> his desires are not upright —
> but the righteous will live by his faith [faithfulness] — "

HABAKKUK 2:2 – 4

Having faith is more than believing; it is living in such a way that the results of faith are evident.

Three of the New Testament books refer to this verse — Paul's letter to the Galatians, Paul's letter to the Romans, and the letter to the Hebrews. These believers all received a reminder of this concept from Habakkuk. The early church was going to be tossed about with fears, dissension, and tensions, and the injunction of the authors of these letters was clearly that they should remain faithful to the teaching they had received, trust in God's timing, and learn from his discipline. By doing so, they would validate their faithfulness before God and men. For the Greeks this was a term of belief; for the Hebrews it was a term with moral ramifications. There are two sides to faith, which is why James declared that faith without deeds is dead (James 2:26).

Fellowship

Walking in the knowledge of service and love with one's heavenly Father results in a unique quality of nearness to him. There is no short-cut to getting there. There is no way to accomplish it by just wishing it or repeating some simple formula. No relationship is built in ten easy steps, especially if it is going to be meaningful and lasting. True friendship comes from being faithful through the thick and thin of the vicissitudes of life. Fellowship with God will always be threatened by unexpected detours.

A powerful story recorded in Matthew 11 shows a side to John the Baptist that should bring comfort to all of us. After all, it was John who introduced Jesus to the world when he declared to all, "Look, the Lamb of God, who takes away the sin of the world!" (John 1:29). Yet even he was nonplussed by Jesus' seeming lack of action when John came under attack by Herod and was imprisoned. John had not expected that Jesus would stand by and do nothing. Perhaps John had been able to face Herod and Herodias so fearlessly because he thought sure that as Jesus' emissary, his safety would be guaranteed.

So when John sent a delegation to Jesus to ask for an explanation and for reassurance that he had not been mistaken about who Jesus was, Jesus first reported to them all the miracles that he had performed, demonstrating who he was and affirming John's ministry. Then he asked them a few questions of his own.

> "What did you go out into the desert to see? A reed swayed by the wind? If not, what did you go out to see? A man dressed in fine clothes? No, those who wear fine clothes are in kings' palaces [and not in a dungeon]. Then what did you go out to see? A prophet? Yes, I tell you, and more than a prophet. This is the one about whom it is written:
>
>> "'I will send my messenger ahead of you,
>>   who will prepare your way before you.'
>
> "I tell you the truth: Among those born of women there has not risen anyone greater than John the Baptist; yet he who is least in the kingdom of heaven is greater than he....
>
> "To what can I compare this generation? They are like children sitting in the marketplaces and calling out to others:
>
>> "'We played the flute for you,
>>   and you did not dance;
>> we sang a dirge
>>   and you did not mourn.'"
>
> MATTHEW 11:7 – 11, 16 – 17

This is a remarkable passage. John is struggling to understand why he is in prison when the Lord of the universe is within earshot. Jesus sends back the message that miracles are on every side for the one who wants to see it. Then he goes on to applaud the greatness of John as an entryway to his main thought that no child of the kingdom is inferior to a prophet, and that the prophet is not above any child of the kingdom. But notice — though Jesus reported to John the miracles he was doing, he did not do a miracle for John and set him free. In this instance, John paid for his love for God with his life.

The inherent danger within all of us is that no matter what God does, someone will wish he had done it differently. The gift of faith is precisely what makes it possible to accept that God works in his own way (which is not always our way), in his own time, and for his purpose. It is our assignment to lay aside our doubts and fall in line with God's purpose, always waiting patiently for the last link to fall into place, finding courage and strength to move forward in the fellowship we have with the Father. It was his fellowship with the Father, sustained by prayer, that made it possible for Jesus to move toward the cross when every fiber of his being was urging him in the opposite direction. God offers us this same fellowship with him.

Understanding

To think God's thoughts after him and to walk through our daily lives *with* him — not ahead of him — is the last of the five distinct realities that God wants us to know or learn through the process of prayer. To understand God is to trust him, even when we don't understand right now what and why something is happening. These are the realities of our walk with him.

Eleven of the twelve disciples died a martyr's death. When they began walking with Jesus, not one of them anticipated how they would die. If they had known where following Jesus would lead them, one wonders whether any of them would have started out on the journey, for as they proved later, they were not particularly brave men. Many, many times I have looked back at my own journey. Had I known the cost it would exact, I am absolutely positive that at the very least I would have had grave reservations and trembled as I stepped onto the road.

I stood one day, as a young man trying to come to terms with God's call in ministry, by a garbage dump in Buôn Ma Thuột, Vietnam, at the grave of six missionaries martyred in the Tet Offensive of 1968. All alone, I pondered the price they had paid for following Jesus. I asked myself whether any of them would have answered God's call on their lives if they had known they would end their lives in a garbage dump. God knows our frailties; how loving of him that he does not allow us to know the future! I prayed there by those graves that God would make me faithful so that I would not focus on the cost but keep my eyes on the mission to serve Jesus with all my heart, soul, and mind and on the sweetness of my walk with him, day by day.

Years ago, I had the great privilege to be in Shanghai in the home of the famed Chinese evangelist Wang Mingdao. He had served twenty-two years in prison for his faith, under the order of Mao Tse Tung. He told us that every day in prison he woke up and sang a hymn:

> *All the way my Savior leads me —*
> *What have I to ask beside?*
> *Can I doubt his tender mercy,*
> *Who through life has been my guide?*
> *Heavenly peace, divinest comfort,*
> *Here by faith in him to dwell!*
> *For I know whate'er befall me,*
> *Jesus doeth all things well;*
> *For I know whate'er befall me,*
> *Jesus doeth all things well.*[11]

At first the guards tried to silence him. When they weren't able to succeed, they reluctantly put up with his singing. Gradually, as the years went by, they would gather near the opening to his cell to listen as he sang of God's faithfulness to him. Eventually, they began to ask him to sing to them and to teach them the words of the song. Such is the impact of one who understands and walks with God.

I was asked to speak at Amsterdam 2000, a conference for evangelists sponsored by the Billy Graham Evangelistic Association. When the renowned soloist George Beverly Shea stood up to sing, he began by recounting the story of how he received the words for the song he was about to sing. One Sunday morning when he was twenty-one, his mother left a poem by Mrs. Rhea Miller on the piano for him to see. George sat down at the piano and in that moment of inspiration put the words to melody. We listened as a ninety-one-year-old man sang again his favorite song, the song he had been singing for seventy-one years.

> *I'd rather have Jesus than men's applause;*
> *I'd rather be faithful to his dear cause;*
> *I'd rather have Jesus than worldwide fame;*
> *I'd rather be true to his holy name.*
> *Than to be the king of a vast domain*
> *Or be held in sin's dread sway —*
> *I'd rather have Jesus than anything*
> *This world affords today.*[12]

When the last note died away, every eye glistened with tears as the ten thousand delegates rose to their feet to honor both God's faithfulness to the man and the man's faithfulness to God. Faithfulness over the long run is the shining example of what faith is meant to be. George Beverly Shea recently celebrated his one hundredth birthday. And the message of the song that has been sung to millions of people over eight decades continues.

The prayer written by the French cleric Michel Quoist is a powerful reminder of our frailty and of God's faithful response to us. To anyone reading this who may be struggling with the guilt of failure, perhaps realizing for the first time that God has not failed you — it is you who have failed to remain true to him when the going got tough — please read this prayer and look up into the face of God, who is faithfully waiting to lift you up.

I have fallen, Lord,
Once more.
I can't go on, I'll never succeed.
I am ashamed, I don't dare look at you.

And yet I struggled, Lord, for I knew you were right near me,
   bending over me, watching.
But temptation blew like a hurricane,
And instead of looking at you I turned my head away,
I stepped aside
While you stood, silent and sorrowful,
Like the spurned fiancé who sees his loved one carried away by the
   enemy.
When the wind died down as suddenly as it had arisen,
When the lightning ceased after proudly streaking the darkness,
All of a sudden I found myself alone, ashamed, disgusted,
   with my sin in my hands.

This sin that I selected the way a customer makes his purchase,
This sin that I have paid for and cannot return,
   for the storekeeper is no longer there,
This tasteless sin,
This odorless sin,
This sin that sickens me,
That I have wanted but want no more,
That I have imagined,
      sought,
      played with,
      fondled,
   for a long time;
That I have finally embraced while turning coldly away from you,
My arms outstretched, my eyes and heart irresistibly drawn;
This sin that I have grasped and consumed with gluttony,
It's mine now, but it possesses me as the spiderweb
   holds captive the gnat.
It is mine,
It sticks to me,
It flows in my veins,
It fills my heart.

It has slipped in everywhere, as darkness slips into the forest at dusk
And fills all the patches of light.

I can't get rid of it.
I run from it the way one tries to lose a stray dog, but it catches up
    with me and bounds joyfully against my legs.
Everyone must notice it.
I'm so ashamed that I feel like crawling to avoid being seen,
I'm ashamed of being seen by my friends,
I'm ashamed of being seen by you, Lord,
For you loved me, and I forgot you.
I forgot you because I was thinking of myself
And one can't think of several persons at once.
One must choose, and I chose.

And your voice,
And your look
And your love hurt me.
They weigh me down
They weigh me down more than my sin.

Lord, don't look at me like that,
For I am naked,
I am dirty,
I am down,
Shattered,
With no strength left.
I dare make no more promises,
I can only lie bowed before you.

[The Father's Response]
Come, son, look up.
Isn't it mainly your vanity that is wounded?
If you loved me, you would grieve, but you would trust.
Do you think that there's a limit to God's love?
Do you think that for a moment I stopped loving you?
But you still rely on yourself, son. You must rely only on me.

Ask my pardon
And get up quickly.
You see, it's not falling that is the worst,
But staying on the ground.[13]

7

WHAT DIFFERENCE DOES CHRISTIANITY MAKE?

I hope that if you have gotten this far in the book, you have recognized perhaps for the first time just who Jesus is and what it means to be a Christian. You have realized that Christianity has not failed you; God has not failed you. It may be that the church has failed you, since it is comprised of human beings just like you, people who often fall short of their own standards and do not always live up to the beauty of their faith and of their Savior. Perhaps your expectations of Jesus and of Christianity were false. But still you are asking yourself, "What difference does it make if I am a Christian or not?"

The difference it makes to you, if this is true, is easy to predict. Without a Savior, there is no one to save you from yourself, no one who knows you completely yet loves you unconditionally. There is no one to guide you through the deep waters and rough seas of life, no one to give you strength and courage to meet each day and face each disappointment, no assurance of an advocate who will plead your cause, no faith to believe that justice for you will ultimately be accomplished. There is no one to welcome you home at the end of life, to open their arms to you and say, "Well done, good and faithful servant." Life is meaningless and purposeless, the monotony of the moments scratched out every day from the poor soil of existence and ending with no hope of a future.

But there are also ramifications for our society if those who have found it difficult to believe in God turn away to live their lives as if he doesn't

179

exist. The words of William Blake and the haunting sentiments of William Wordsworth come to mind in these days when so many seem to have lost their ability to remain faithful to their belief:

> Mock on, Mock on, Voltaire, Rousseau;
> Mock on, Mock on; 'tis all in vain!
> You throw the sand against the wind,
> And the wind blows it back again.[1]

> Milton! thou shouldst be living at this hour:
> England hath need of thee: she is a fen
> Of stagnant waters: altar, sword and pen,
> Fireside, the heroic wealth of hall and bower,
> Have forfeited their ancient English dower
> Of inward happiness. We are selfish men.[2]

There is a payback for mocking the eternal, for jettisoning God's commands and stepping over the boundaries he has placed for us as individuals first and then for the societies and cultures of which we are a part. Something of huge proportions has happened in the West. Thomas Friedman's recent book on world economics, *The World is Flat*, states that the weight of economic strength in the world has leveled the playing field. In my view, Friedman is half right. "Flat" may be an appropriate description in terms of the West's productivity, gross national product, disposable income, and all the other calibrations that economists measure. But there is also a different scale. In the context of moral self-perception, the world has dramatically tilted. Seen for years by the East as a culture in decay and demise, deserving what likely lies ahead for it — a fate echoed in the classic sermon by Robert G. Lee, a famous preacher of years gone by, called "Payday Someday" — the West is increasingly seeing itself that way.

What difference does it make if we walk away from our belief in the gospel message? What difference does it make which society is on top at the moment and which culture is in decline? Is it not just the shedding of worn-out skin? As my professor at Cambridge used to say, "What are these churches now but monuments to what we once believed." I have news for him. The ramifications of such a change in the worldview of the West will not only change the West; it will change the world and will cost more than any gain that could be imagined. Of that I am certain. In the context of our Western nations and of the world, the more pointed question for our times is a question with fearsome ramifications: If not Christianity and the Christian worldview, what other worldview will take its place? It is a question that self-titled "lapsed evangelicals" or "lapsed Christians" must ask of themselves: Is the simplistic notion that the Christian faith is irrational and that naturalism is rational itself rational?

Years ago, Francis Schaeffer gave a simple illustration to demonstrate the conundrum of naturalism, which can offer a materialistic explanation for only some of what it sees. He imagined two glasses of water — glass A and glass B. Suppose that when you leave the room glass A has two ounces of water in it and glass B is empty. When you come back into the room you find that glass A, which had two ounces of water in it, is now empty, and glass B, which was empty before, is now full. The obvious conclusion is that someone came into the room while you were gone and poured the two ounces of water from glass A into glass B. But glass B now has more than two ounces of water in it; in fact, it's filled to the brim. More explanation is needed. It may still be true that someone poured the water from glass A into glass B. But where did the remaining water come from? There was not enough water in glass A to explain the water in glass B.

Now suppose that a wealthy man were to come to you and propose that you build a house for him of the finest quality that money can buy. He is leaving on a trip and may be gone for a few years, but he would like you to build the house in his absence so that it is ready for him upon his return. He tells you that from time to time he will send an agent to check on the progress of the house. Your integrity and reputation are on the line. He will make sure you are well paid. You agree to his conditions, the man sets out on his trip, and the building project begins.

Sometimes you have to admit it would be tempting to pocket some of the advance cash and cheat on the quality. You could build a nice little nest egg for yourself, and the man would be none the wiser. He's been gone a long time now. Will he even know enough about the job you are doing to fully appreciate it, or would he get as much enjoyment out of something that looked good on the outside but was not as substantial as it should be? Could you spend his money on the things that dress up the house and make a good impression, but skimp on the things that make the house a firm, safe structure?

As time goes on and you continue to build, materials are stolen from you by irresponsible subcontractors and tradesmen, and you substitute inferior product. Finally the house is completed. You have successfully camouflaged what is substandard, and the house looks exactly as the man had requested. You alone know that the foundation is a bit precarious because each of your subcontractors were playing the same charade as you, trying to get more than what was due them by putting in less than they had promised.

One day, there is a knock on your door. You open it to see that the man standing before you looks somewhat familiar. You're not sure if you've met him before. He tells you he is the brother of the man for whom you have built the house. He tells you that his brother's return is delayed because of other responsibilities. But he tells you that because you have waited so long for his brother's return and have worked so hard on the house to make sure it is everything he had asked for, his brother is giving the house to you. It is now yours, completely paid for. It is his gift to you and your family, and if there is any money left over from building the house, it is yours too.

These two illustrations sum up the predicament with which we now live in the West, with similar ideas permeating the East. Naturalism seems to have become the reigning worldview, and we think we can explain all of the contents in the glass before us. But the unexplainable extra ounces still haunt us. We can explain matter, but we can't explain why we think in the categories that we do if everything ultimately comes from matter. We have convinced ourselves that we have everything we need and that our minds and our skills will get us through any difficulty we encounter. But we have picked our own pockets. The house we have built with such promise is crumbling because we have cheated on the foundation.

Do you remember Biosphere 2? Biosphere 2 started as a dream. It was built in Arizona during a span from 1987 to 1991. Of immense size, this 3.15 acre spread was an audacious effort to build an ideal biosphere with scientifically engineered precision. "Everything" was planned, calibrated, researched, and thought through to achieve a perfect, hermetically sealed world, a perfect, man-made enclosed ecological system within which to explore the complex web of interactions within life systems. It included an agricultural area as well as human living/working space so that the interactions between humans, farming, technology, and the rest of nature could be studied, allowing scientists to monitor the ever-changing chemistry of the air, water, and soil contained within. It also explored the possible future use of closed biospheres for colonizing space and to glean the scientific ramifications of such an effort without harming the earth's atmosphere. The health of the human crew was monitored by a medical doctor inside and a medical team outside (even with all the combined knowledge and expertise, they couldn't get by without a medical team on the outside). A little ironic, I think, for a "closed system," a system that purports to be able to sustain itself without help from the outside — and telling of the dogmatic insistence of many that our own universe is a "closed system" that does not need God in order to sustain itself.

Costing millions of dollars and at a size comparable to two and a half football fields, it remains the largest closed system ever created. The sealed nature of the structure contained two representative biomes, a 1,900 square meter rainforest, an 850 square meter ocean with a coral reef, a 450 square meter mangrove wetlands, a 1,300 square meter savannah grassland, a 1,400 square meter fog desert, a 2,500 square meter agricultural system, a human habitat, and a below-ground technical infrastructure. Heating and cooling water circulated through independent piping systems and passive solar input came through the glass space frame panels covering most of the facility. Electrical power was supplied from an onsite natural gas energy center through airtight penetrations. At the end of it all, the difference between the hopes and the reality of the biosphere experiment is one word: *embarrassment.*

The first mission group, Mission 1, had a crew of eight people and ran for two years — from 1991 – 93. Following a six-month transition period during which researchers entered the facility through airlock doors and conducted research and made system engineering improvements, Mission 2 — with a crew of seven people — was carried out from March 1994 to September 1994. One month into the second mission, a severe dispute within the management team over the financial aspects of the project led to their ouster from the Biosphere by federal marshals. Four days later, two members of the original team deliberately vandalized the project. After a shuffling of the members of the team and severe rifts among them caused by allegations of bringing in supplies from the outside and tampering with the data, the two-year "experiment in self-sufficiency" looked less like science and more like a $150 million dollar mistake, and the mission itself ended prematurely, a failure by definition.

The rest of the story reads like a plot within a plot, with all kinds of undisclosed and under-the-radar activity. Let me just say that even had the experiment succeeded, it would have proved that it took intelligence to bring this about (which was not their goal).

I visited this site and heard firsthand some of the goings-on that plainly violated the plans and strictures under which the biosphere was to operate. I don't doubt the commendable efforts and perhaps even the goals of such an attempt, but this experiment proved to be a colossal flop. Clearly the experiment was unable to create that perfect sphere and environment, but a key factor in its failure and demise was what lay within the corruption of the human heart, even to the point of vandalizing the controlled environment. In all of our efforts to conquer outer space we have never come to terms with the inner space within each of us.

So as I bring to a close my response to the feeling on the part of some that Christianity has failed them (and the charges against Christianity that are implied), I want you to consider the irrational ends to which the worldview of the skeptic will lead — ends that put at risk the very existence of humanity.

A MESSAGE
TO THE CHURCH

Many of the charges made by some people I have spoken with have a tragic truthfulness to them. They had tried church and found it wanting. They found the church in many ways to be uninformed, unrealistic, and terribly judgmental. If those of us who claim to be Christians do not listen to this criticism, we do so at our own peril. The twin extremes that face us, as I see it — either to be totally complacent about our faith and not deal with sin or to ostracize and condemn anyone who makes a mistake in practicing their Christian faith — risk compromise of fatal proportions. If one person shouts "Fire!" we can excuse him for being mistaken. If two shout "Fire!" it might be wise to take note. If large numbers scream "FIRE!" we would be deaf or irrational to not respond. The church of today must listen before speaking.

That said, by virtue of my work I have visited scores of churches in numerous countries and have found many who have listened and taken note. I have been in a small gathering in China where scholars meet to discuss Christianity. I have spoken in very large churches where the message is clear and the methods are wise. There are many fine pastors and leadership teams who have carefully thought through the questions of our time and are doing a commendable job in their churches. Those demonstrating theological integrity with methodological relevance are the ones I salute during this time of such challenges. So this is not an evaluation of all of Christendom. My challenge is directed to church leaders and members who have either lost the message or resorted to methods that have compromised the message — or both.

Sadly, some churches exist to entertain their audiences with limitless distractions so that they come for the pleasure of enjoying good entertainment in the presence of "good people." I do not intend any sarcasm here. In a world that seems to think entertainment and humor are only to be found by being vulgar or profane or disparaging toward someone, the kind of wholesome and healthy delight that such a church offers is genuinely needed in our times. God is not against entertainment. Unlike the animal world, he has created us to laugh and cry, though there is no premium placed on crying. Laughter and happiness are necessary, especially when most of the daily news we hear is grim.

The problem with trying to worship by such means is that in the end we become no different from the "good" person who has disavowed the gospel; in fact, the private life of this thoroughly entertained Christian may actually be worse than his skeptic counterpart. So what is the point of making this wholesome entertainment the focus of the church when the fragmentation within the church is equal to that outside the church?

Many times I have heard Christian young women say that the Christian young men they meet in church and spend time with are no better than those who claim to have no belief in God — and, in fact, they say some are *worse* than those outside. Sadly, pornography, sensuality, monetary irresponsibility, and dishonesty are equally constant realities in both camps. I even know Christian businessmen and women who tell me they will not hire another Christian because of how they have been exploited by their Christian employees in the workplace — those who expect to be cut some slack for not doing their share of work "because we are brothers in Christ."

This pathetic irresponsibility makes people cautious of those who wear their faith on their sleeves and extremely suspicious of their spiritual talk. Broken marriage vows and business contracts are not exclusively seen beyond the walls of the church; sadly, they are equally prevalent among believers. For this kind of believer, going to church for good entertainment is at best an exercise that puts them in a safe place where they can hear nice things about how nice we are and how nice we should be.

How and why have we failed to produce believers who possess strong characters and exercise self-discipline? There is both a good news and bad news side. The good news is that this "flawed product" is not a new phenomenon in our day. The early church experienced every one of the struggles we face in the church — perhaps even more. Reading the New Testament epistles gives us a catalog of vices that existed within the church that leaves us wondering what was going on in the name of the church and of Jesus. As we meet the disciples and leaders of the early church in the pages of the New Testament, we see bickering, distrust, greed, parochialism, betrayal, even murder — even though they were in the closest contact with the most perfect life ever lived. Any psychologist would declare these men to have been totally unfit for the task. If they had been subjected to leadership testing with all of our present-day methods, I doubt even one of them would have passed. It is absolutely the most amazing thing that Jesus selected them and put up with them.

And if you look at the patriarchs, my word! Even Abraham, the "father of faith," who is claimed by three of the world's great religions, embarrasses us at times. Isaac and Jacob fare no better. David, the greatest and most spiritually minded king, left a trail of blood and infidelity in his wake. Solomon, revered as the wisest man who ever lived, left us the best proverbs by which to live, yet he didn't apply them to himself.

Unfortunately, this affirms to us the bad news — that our inherent personality weaknesses and character flaws stalk us most of our lives. If we do not have a road map to correction, recovery, and change, we will only move from failure to catastrophe and ultimately to the destruction of future generations. The Scriptures give us not a formula for perfection but a way to address our weaknesses and find healing and wholeness. It is the individual choices we make and the selection of our leaders that will put us back on the road of hope and blessing.

So to every charge that those inside the church are no better than those outside the church, the Bible has never taught otherwise. As we have seen, even our heroes in church history may not fare well when put under the critical lens of a skeptic. The Bible reminds believers that we in the church — of all people — must be aware of our own shortcomings. We of all people should be gracious and forgiving of those who fall short of God's standards; we of all people must understand how far we are from what God intends us to be and learn to allow him to conform us to the image of his Son, both in our speech and in our walk; we of all people must learn to be patient with those for whom the journey is still rough.

At the root of the problem with churches that are program driven and lack substance is the appearance of change without teaching people how to think correctly. The church has a responsibility toward believers and unbelievers alike to teach people how to apply the truths of Scripture to their own lives and to ultimately impact society. There is a world of difference between how the gospel works and how every other belief system works. Christianity is not a political theory. It is not even a cultural theory. It is, at its root, all about changing the heart of each man and woman, boy and girl, so that we begin to think God's thoughts and act in accordance with his character.

Think about this. Politics works from the top down, whether we talk about capitalism, Communism, or Fascism. All three begin with an ideology of how a nation should be set up, and the citizens of that nation are governed accordingly. Each system has its own ideologies and rules. This is also true of most religions. Islam is a political and legal theory. In fact, many scholars believe that the history of Islam shows that it began as a political vision and leveraged the "supernatural" to that end. The Pact of Umar in early Islamic conquests of Christian countries clearly made Christians second-class citizens. It is amazing that Muslim scholars actually see their actions as benevolent. From restricting the height of church steeples to the propagation of the message of Christ, Islam put its thumb down hard on Christians. Hinduism also operates from the top down as a way of life for a community in which the individual has little value. So whether we talk of politics or religion, there is a trickle-down effect.

Not so with Christianity. Jesus' resistance to political power was a remarkable caution about top-down belief systems. In the gospel message, the beginning of change occurs in the heart of each individual. This heart change makes a difference in the home, then in the community, and ultimately in the nation — and in turn it shapes the future of a cultural ethos. Eventually, from the overflow of the values of such a society, a ripple effect takes place in cosmic proportions, not because it is imposed from the top but because God has changed the hearts and minds of his people. This is the difference with Christianity. The gospel was never intended to be a political theory that would dictate how societies should be structured.

We must appreciate the wisdom of such belief. The leadership appointed by a people is intended to lead from the moral values and framework by which a people have been identified — a dynamic that will either build or threaten the future. First, the people appoint the leader, then the leader is commissioned to guide the nation according to the values that the people hold. If the leadership fails to do so, the society has begun its journey down the road to destruction. In the microcosm of the church, failure has come not from the people but from the leadership that has led the people into disregard for and even disbelief in the very authority that brought them into being.

Shortly after I came to Canada in 1966, I saw a sign outside a small home that read "Theological Books for Sale." I knocked on the door, and the elderly woman who opened it was obviously surprised to find an Indian at her door. (That tells you how long ago it was!) "These are Christian books, you know," she said. "That's why I am interested in seeing them," I responded. And so she let me in. It was a small library of a couple thousand volumes. "My husband was a pastor," she told me, "and he has passed away. My church is not interested in his books, and so I'm trying to sell them to somebody who would respect this material and treasure its teachings." When she found out I was a follower of Jesus Christ, she was thrilled that I was interested in buying the books. She noticed the books I was choosing, books by men such as G. Campbell Morgan, F. B. Meyer, and so on. "They were among my husband's favorites," she said. Then she added these sobering words. "To watch the death of belief in my church and denomination is the worst kind of death to witness. I never ever dreamed of the day that our leaders would be leading us away from the very teaching that established our churches in the first place. We are truly like sheep betrayed by the shepherds."

The departure of so many church leaders from the teachings of Jesus has led to a kind of death. The handwriting is on the walls of our homes, our communities, and our nations. Solomon, Jeroboam, Rehoboam — one after the other — led their people into seductive and false beliefs. Gradually, they believed things *about* God without believing God himself, until child sacrifice became the preferred act of worship. Once the Book of the Law was lost, generations passed before it was found again, lost in the debris of the house of God. Mourning a similar degradation, Jesus wept over his beloved city: "O Jerusalem, Jerusalem, ... how often I have longed to gather your children together, as a hen gathers her chicks under her wings, but you were not willing. Look, your house is left to you desolate" (Matthew 23:37 – 38).

Do you see the parallels in our day? We have mistaken attendance at church for success and are blind to the desolation within. It is the role of church leadership to sense the heart of God and lead the people toward God — not to build big churches that become monuments to their skill at tickling the ears of those who gather and to their ability to give people what they think they want so they leave feeling satisfied that they have "gone to church."

Capitalism has no more potential for good than any other system of government if the leaders are heading in the wrong direction and have stolen from the people their most fundamental God-given value, their essential human worth. The reason for all the bloodshed in the world is that somebody somewhere has deemed ideology more valuable than human life. This is the endgame of rationalism, where ideas are more important than people. In this kind of environment, the most violent idea wins the day. And the church that has forgotten its purpose and lost its message will have no influence for good in society.

The truths by which we were intended to live are proved within the microcosm of the church. This is where the church must take note and ask hard questions of itself, for without the combination of theological integrity and methodological relevance, our churches will also be a vestige from "once upon a time."

AND FORGIVE US
AS WE FORGIVE

Meeting people where they are hurting is a vital aspect of our call to reflect God to the society in which we live, and the single word that best describes the gospel message is *forgiveness*. Understanding what it means to both offer forgiveness and receive forgiveness is the difficult part of learning mercy. At the beginning of this book, I mentioned a woman who had left her church because she had been effectively cast out. She told us that, to her shame, she had begun an adulterous affair. But even more painful than her horror of what she had done and the pain she had caused her family and friends was that the church never forgot it and never let her move beyond it.

I understand that we in the church have a difficult path to walk in the presence of sin. At what point do we accept something without compromising the message? How do we teach the narrow path of righteousness without becoming legalistic? But surely there is a way to differentiate between someone who trivializes evil and thumbs her nose at God and someone else who stumbles, falls, and seeks to be restored, not just into fellowship with God, but into fellowship with God's people.

I recall a mother calling me one day, greatly upset, and sharing a choice her daughter had made that caused the parents to wonder if they could still have anything to do with her. The story was heartbreaking. They had raised her in a completely different way from the lifestyle she was practicing and was about to seal in a union. I could hear the desolation in the mother's voice and felt it was almost impossible to give her advice that would be incontrovertible. So I advised her that no matter how she chose to respond, she consider doing so in such a way that the daughter she loved so much would not be cut off from her love, her voice, and her reach.

The balance was a delicate one, for if this mother pushed her daughter away, she risked exposing her to other voices and other loves that would appear to be more caring but actually lead her farther away from the One who cared for her most — God himself. If she condemned her daughter, she would probably lose her to a place beyond the reach of her parents. I cautioned her that whatever she did, she should make certain that her daughter understood that her mother loved her and would always be there for her.

There are times when the Father *waits* for the son to return. But there are also times when the husband *goes* and stands in line in a brothel to buy his wife back and love her, as Hosea did with his wife, Gomer. The gospel is an invitation to a relationship, not a legal summons to a hearing.

I know of a tenderhearted, gifted, and capable Christian young man.

During his college years, most of his friends were a year or two ahead of him. By the time he reached his senior year, they had all graduated and he had been left behind. Even though he was part of a Bible study group, that final year was difficult for him spiritually. Beyond anything his family could have anticipated, he developed a friendship that soon became serious with a young woman who had a very different worldview — one of gurus, mysticism, and pantheistic meditative techniques. Under her influence his personality began to change, and he gradually became almost noncommunicative with his family, not responding to them with his normal affection.

His father flew to the town where his university was located and checked into a motel nearby. He told his son he was there for him and would be around for several days. The father suggested they meet for dinner every evening. Every evening, the young man had dinner with his father, but it was obvious to the father that he was there only because it would have been rude for him to not show up. After a few days the father returned home, having no more hope than when he had gone.

The boy came home for spring break, which happened to coincide with his father's birthday. At dinner in a restaurant, the other children presented gifts and cards, but the young man said he had left his gift for his father at home and would give it to him later that evening. The father wondered if the son was telling the truth, or if he just didn't care anymore. And sure enough, back at home there was no gift or card, and his son said nothing. But as the father headed for bed that night, he found a card on his pillow. Opening it, he read, "Dearest Mom and Dad, I am so sorry to have hurt you so much. You were right and I was wrong." From there his son began to unfold how he had lost his way, saying in his own words that he had somehow felt that as a Christian, he was missing out on so much and wanted to experience the world. "But I tried life apart from God," he wrote, "and it doesn't work." With that he proceeded to share the news that he was ending his relationship with this girl, that as much as he loved her, he realized he loved the Lord more. The angels in heaven experienced no greater joy that night than the parents of that young man.

It would have been easy for this father to cut his son off. It would have been easy to heap guilt on his head and say things that would have made life miserable for him. A parent in this situation can't think of anything that can bring the result they are aching to see, and they entertain all kinds of emotions they never could have predicted. But the young man would never have responded to that approach. Instead, it would have pushed him farther away, probably farther than he himself wanted to go, until the way back would have seemed almost impossible. It was because he knew how much his parents and his family loved him and how deeply they were devoted to him — and because of the great mercy and faithfulness of God — that victory in the life of this young man was won.

Isn't the church an extension of the family? Can we not find ways to love that will keep within reach the one who is faltering? Are there not ways to minister to someone who needs healing, rather than having a spirit like Jonah's, which declares in effect, "You are beyond God's reach. He is going to destroy you, and I, for one, am glad of it!"?

As I write this, two major stories made it onto the front pages of the newspapers. The first is the death of Michael Jackson at fifty years of age. His is the truly tragic story of a gifted but immature entertainer whose life was one tangled web of searching for himself. It is telling to see the opinions of people about what they thought of him, ranging from unvarnished hostility to an unapologetic admiration bordering on worship. One does not even have to be buried before the world pours out its judgments of castigation or exoneration. We have become a culture in which we take the prerogative to act as judge and jury before there has even been a trial.

Even more telling is the story of the governor of South Carolina. By his own admission, he has broken the hearts of his family and his friends by becoming involved in a foolishly illicit relationship. As I read his admission and thought of the heartbreak, my heart went out to the ones hurting the most — his wife and his children. This cruel world that celebrates relativism will still burn someone of a different political stripe at the stake for their violation of a moral absolute, and those who despise conservatives, accusing them of judging others, display the venom of duplicity when they, too, stand in judgment on those same conservatives. Someone has said that the charge of hypocrisy is the compliment that vice pays to virtue.

But it is not enough that this governor has admitted to what he has done. The public has become so unfeeling and so heartless that a South Carolina newspaper decided to print emails between the governor and the other party. The glee with which this has been done as they celebrate the fall of someone they have perceived to be a moralizer is incredibly sad. What has become of our society when someone else's tragedy has become entertainment to everyone else?

I think of the talk show host David Letterman. He was ruthless in his comments about the moral stumbles of a young teenager, the daughter of a political candidate from "the other party." Ah! Her story was like throwing him a juicy bone to chew on and spit out. Yet, when his moral duplicity is uncovered, his "confession" is nothing more than a comedic routine because "the show must go on."

This is the point: The world accuses the Christian church of judging others harshly, but when *they* sit as judge, they are equally harsh, cruel, and merciless — unless you buy into their ethos, in which case you are free to live as you please. Both the religious and the not-so-religious extract their pound of flesh when they are in a position to do so. But only the body of Christ, the church, has a Savior whose body was broken and whose blood was shed to bring pardon and healing to the bruised and broken, the fallen and defeated. Only the church that understands the message of forgiveness will reach out to those around it rather than condemning them. And if the church does not reach out, it is a church on which many will turn their backs and never return. Thornton Wilder said, "In love's service only the wounded soldiers can serve."[3]

People make mistakes and stumble. People struggle with failure and defeat. People long to do what is right but often fail. More often than not, people know the truth and still violate it, hoping they will reap more friendly dividends than they do. And when they are in the throes of some defeat, they are most tender, and those moments of hurt and disenchantment and struggle can become critical for reshaping and redirecting their lives.

Professor Wilfred McClay of Tulane University wrote the following after attending the funeral of a friend:

> Where the rest of us had been stunned into reflective silence, awed, chastened by the reminder of the slender thread by which our lives hang, the minister had other things in mind.... He did not try to comfort the family and friends. Nor did he challenge us to remember the hard words of the Lord's Prayer, "Thy will be done." Instead he smoothly launched into a well-oiled tirade against the misplaced priorities of our society in which billions of dollars were being poured into "Star Wars" research while young women were left to die on the operating table. That was all this minister had to say. His eulogy was, in effect, a pitch for less federal spending on defense and more spending on the development of medical technology....
>
> I am willing to concede for the sake of argument that the minister may have been right in everything that he said. All of these considerations are beside the point.
>
> Nothing can alter the fact that he failed us, failed her, and failed his calling by squandering a precious moment for a second-rate stump speech and by forcing us to hold our sorrow back in the privacy of our hearts at the very moment it needed common expression. That moment can never be recovered.
>
> Nothing that religion does is more important than equipping us to endure life's passages by helping us find meaning in pain and loss. With meaning, many things are bearable. But our eulogist did not know how to give it to us. All he had to offer were his desiderata. For my own part, I left that funeral more shaken and unsteady than before. Part of my distress arose from frustration that my deepest thoughts (and those of others around me, as I later discovered) were so completely unechoed in this ceremony and in these words. But another part of my distress must have stemmed from a dark foreboding that I was witnessing another kind of malpractice, and another kind of death.[4]

The church is prone to one extreme or the other in her responses to the world — either legalism that destroys the wounded, or relevance that has no substance and is relevant to nothing. And when the deepest struggles of a person's heart are left "unechoed" or unaddressed, the minister and the members of the church have fallen short of their calling.

MEETING NEEDS
WITHOUT TRUTH

I have mentioned that the church must know its purpose before it can be effective and that it must believe its message and reflect its Savior. Now I want to talk about what the church must affirm if we are going to have an impact on our communities and on our societies. What do we need to believe about what we claim to believe in order to be believed?

Most of us have heard the proverbial story of four blind people touching different parts of an elephant — an ear, the trunk, the tail, a leg — and coming up with different conclusions about what they were touching. This story is supposed to teach us that truth looks different from different vantage points. I am reminded of a research student who wrote a thesis paper about the fly. He extracted one leg from the fly and asked the fly to jump from one hand to the other. The fly jumped. (Insect lovers, please bear with me for a moment.) He removed the second leg and repeated the command. The fly jumped again. He pulled out the third leg and told the fly to jump. Once more, the fly jumped. He yanked out the final leg and commanded the fly to jump one more time. This time the fly did not jump. The student promptly wrote down his conclusion: When you pull out all four of a fly's legs, it loses its hearing.

A deduction based on false assumptions leads to an invalid conclusion, and we simply cannot base conclusions on impeded judgments or limited assumptions. In the earlier illustration, the reason we know they were touching an elephant is that someone who was there *could* see and knew what an elephant looked like.

The Western church in the recent past — and especially in the last decade — has fled from the authority of what Jesus said and taught. In its place we have built a whole new world of Christian spirituality based on individual needs and on definitions that have no source and are based on feeling rather than actuality. The church is supposed to be a community of "called-out ones." We are supposed to be able to transcend the immediate and the material present to lift our sights to the way God has defined our destiny and being. That is what the entire message of the gospel is based on. We are not a community of self-referencing entities. We define ourselves on the basis of a semitranscendent relationship with God.

In my computer bag, I carry a tiny thumb drive. It is the size of my little finger. On that thumb drive are all my books and all the illustrations, anecdotes, and arguments I have collected over almost forty years of ministry. It slips into one of my pockets, and when needed, within minutes I can pull out almost anything you ask for from my writings. But there is something different about this thumb drive and me. Even though it contains everything I have written, it is not me. My will, my longings, my hungers, my passions, my spiritual commitments can never be imparted to that little piece of technology.

Just as that little instrument is a reflection of me, Christians are meant to be accurate reflections of the God we worship, who has made us in his image. But we are not God.

Faced with the incredible challenge of technology and especially the enchantment of the visual, in the last few decades the church has entered into a time of high risk for the imagination. Every advance in technology puts a greater challenge on the value of humanity and the personal touch. This is especially true because we are prone to the error of focusing on alleviating the symptoms of our malady — the outward signs of a society that has turned its back on God — and missing the cause or the disease itself. It is easier to treat the symptoms than to identify and rectify the cause. It is also easier to respond to our feelings toward God or the worship of God than to learn how to think right thoughts in the right way. Because of this, programming has become the buzzword for attracting crowds. The techniques have become more sophisticated, the message has become more simplistic, and the means have gradually eclipsed the ends.

I have often wondered this: if the visual through which we gain most of our enchantment today is truly as persuasive a means as we claim it to be, why did Jesus not wait to come to earth until the camera had been invented? Wouldn't it have made more sense to *show* the miracles, especially with high-definition television available, and let the feeding of the five thousand play itself out on the news rather than just writing about it? Even the news has become a show, and we live in great danger as we find ourselves at the mercy of our fleeting enthrallment span and our collective short memory for news — a dramatic event a day. Instead of "give us each day our daily bread," it is now "give us each day our daily thrill," because the shelf life of thrills is directly proportional to the latest invention or latest story.

In a day's span we move from horror in the streets of Iran to the infidelities of an absent governor to the death of a pop icon to thousands of pages of legislation that legislators don't have time to read before voting — all in a few minutes. The show is all-important, and the news producers choose the stories they will feature based on what will elicit the greatest response from the audience. Perhaps, on second thought, if Jesus had come during our time, his message would have made no greater impact on society than it did then, even though his message would have been available to so many more people. Feeding four thousand people wouldn't have been enough to warrant continued coverage in the news; he would have had to feed five thousand the next day and then ten thousand the next. Even that would eventually become boring. The means have definitely eclipsed the ends.

As I travel, I find myself in places that make me ponder deeply what it means to really live. With each passing year, I begin to wonder whether those of us who live in the wealthy part of the world actually understand life less than those who must by necessity live in dependence for their daily bread. And how has the church reacted to all this? By and large, abysmally. Our buildings and holdings become bigger, grander, more sophisticated, yet we feed people only snippets of truth. We visit needy spots and establish budgets for the hurting and suffering as a momentary response before our lives and attentions return to the high-speed pursuit of the next thrill.

Years ago when I studied at Cambridge, the renowned thinker, Arthur Peacocke, who was then the director of the Ian Ramsey Center for the Interdisciplinary Study of Religion in Relation to Science and a member of the faculty of theology at Oxford, made an astounding statement:

> To be truly "evangelical" and "catholic," the church of the next millennium will need a theology that will necessarily have to be genuinely liberal and even radical — particularly in its relation to a worldview everywhere shaped by science. For Christian theology to have any viability, it may well have to be stripped down to newly conceived essentials, minimalist in its affirmations; only then will it attain that degree of verisimilitude with respect to *ultimate* realities which science has to *natural* ones — and command respect as a vehicle of public truth.[5]

I wonder if Mr. Peacocke wanted us to interpret his statement minimally, or did he want us to take to heart what he said with such forceful intention?

"Minimalist in its affirmations" — isn't that the world we now have? Minimalist in our affirmations, our marriage vows, our contracts, our commitments, the paying back of our debts, our plea bargains; minimalist in our trust of each other, our tolerance of other people's weaknesses, our understanding of each other's values, our ethics, our hope for the future.

Isn't this the church we now have? This is the lie we have believed, a lie that has led us to a religion with minimalist affirmations. It is no longer the calling of the church to inform the world but the calling of the world to inform the church. Thus, from some pulpits now we hear profanity — because people are more comfortable with such language than they used to be and have come to expect it in conversation. We consistently overwhelm the audience with a barrage of the visual, which is supposed to serve as their spiritual food. Eventually, the distinction between the believer and the unbeliever is a minimal one, reduced to a single affirmation: I believe in God and you don't.

Social theorist Ernest Becker wrote many years ago:

> Today religionists wonder why youth has abandoned the churches, not wanting to realize that it is precisely because organized religion

openly subscribes to a commercial-industrial hero system that is almost openly defunct; it so obviously denies reality, builds war machines against death, and banishes sacredness with bureaucratic dedication. Men are treated as things and the world is pulled down to their size. The churches subscribe to these empty heroics of possession, display, manipulation. I think that today Christianity is in trouble not because its myths are dead but because it does not offer its ideal of heroic sainthood as an immediate personal one to be lived by believers. In a perverse way, the churches have turned their backs both on the miraculousness of creation and on the need to do something heroic in this world.[6]

Becker is right. By losing our appreciation for the miracle of life itself, we have turned to the heroics of display and abandoned the true heroism of lives lived for the glory of God. This, to me, is the loss that has made the gospel unbelievable to people. Many efforts by the emergent church are nothing more than a surrender to a postmodern epistemology garbed in the terminology and methodology of "spiritual relevance." What Biosphere 2 was to the scientific world, much of our church entrepreneurship is to the spiritual world. Breaking free from any strictures, we have built a worldview that is a hybrid of naturalism and spirituality. Torn between these various factions, we have vandalized the truth, denying some aspects of it and distorting others in order to accomplish our own goals.

For some, the appeal has been prosperity. They believe not only that they can ask for anything — but that they have a right to receive it. Others are tempted to use Christianity as an opportunity to display or exercise their talents, even if they don't really fit the message. Still others are moved to speak what is popular and what people want to hear rather than the truth because it makes them feel good about themselves and assures an audience. The result? Our youth are left in the middle ground between a materialistic worldview that borrows spiritual talk to soothe their needs and a spiritual worldview that is actually quite materialistic.

So what is the solution? If the problem isn't with God but with the church, what do we do with the church? In a long conversation with Malcolm Muggeridge before he died, I asked him why he didn't go to church. He seemed a bit embarrassed and then said, "I am not quite able to take that which is so much of the soul and institutionalize it." My heart beat a little faster as I tried to respond to this man I so respected and who, by his own admission, was so fatally fluent. I could so sympathize with what he was saying: I have often wondered even in ministry at what point the structure overrides the substance. At what point does your calling become your job?

Such dangers will always lurk beneath the surface. But the answer cannot be to jettison the institution that Jesus established for the propagation of the ultimate truth about life. It was his idea that we gather as a community — the bedrock of where the truth of the gospel transforms lives and from where it is propelled into the wider community. The solution to the failure of the church is not found by abandoning it.

Where, then, do we go from here? What is the way back?

A BLUEPRINT
FOR THE WAY BACK

There is a time to pull away from the cacophony of voices and the clutter of ideas and search one's soul. As the old Irishman said to a man who asked him for directions, "If that's where you want to go, this is not where I would begin." In plain English, "You are so far off the track that you will have to go back even farther before you can start moving forward." In that spirit I ask you now to come away for a while and to think through carefully what all this means for you and for all who come after you. This is absolutely essential.

I was talking to the principal of a seminary in Bethlehem in Israel about the singular loneliness of Palestinian Christians, people whose faith is homeless. Their fellow Palestinians reject them because they are Christians and not Muslims. Western Christians are often not quite sure where to place these Christians in the grand scheme of things. They are a bit uncomfortable with them and reject them in a subtle way because of the covenant promises to the Jews. And the Jews reject them because they are Palestinians, a people with whom they are on constant alert. They belong nowhere, to no community. "We really are orphaned from the world," he said. I attended a service among them. I let the tears flow as I realized that for them, the person of Christ is all they have, and they cling to him with the utter certainty that he will not let them down. I asked the leader what form of ministry he found most effective with such a congregation. He told me it was their "desert ministry."

Every few weeks, he takes a handful of his people who are struggling with particular issues, and they drive into the desert. They mount camels and go deeper into the desert to a secluded spot. There they pitch their tents and spend about three days. "When you're alone in God's creation with nothing to interrupt your thoughts, it is amazing how easy it is to listen to the voice of God," he said. During those three days they study the Scriptures, pray, talk together, and try to resolve their deepest concerns. The world looks different from the desert. He has found that in those alone times, great victories have been won.

The most profound commitments are made when a person is alone. I propose three glories, three supremacies, and three excellencies you need to come to terms with. If you have struggled with your faith, if you feel that Christianity has failed you, take a deep, personal look at what you are called to as a Christian, according to the Scriptures, and then evaluate once again who has failed.

Three Glories

God has spoken in the *glory of his creation*. Do not get bogged down in *how* he did it. Accept that it is a universe of incredible order and beauty. One cannot escape the detail and the fine-tuning of the Creator's hand. To take the issue of "how" to the point of so much contention is to make it something it was never intended to be. "The heavens," states David, "declare the glory of God" (Psalm 19:1). Simply put, the presence of God is manifested even in the created order. Its vastness and intelligibility speak of the grandeur and of the specific complexity that God has put into this world. Just one flame off the sun's surface is forty times the dimension of the earth. Yet, in a single life he has placed the power of intelligence and of the will. God created the world; humanity has created its cities. Look at the contrast, and see where our problem really lies.

God has spoken in the *glory of his law*. None of us like the concept of law because none of us like the restraints it puts on us. But when we understand that God has given us his law to aid us in guarding our souls, we see that the law is for our fulfillment, not for our limitation. The law reminds us that some things, some experiences, some relationships are sacred. When everything has been profaned, it is not just *my* freedom that has been lost — the loss is everyone's. God gave us the law to remind us of the sacredness of life, and our created legal systems only serve to remind us of the profane judgments we make.

God has also spoken in the *glory of the incarnation*, when "the Word became flesh and made his dwelling among us" — "the One and Only, who came from the Father, full of grace and truth" (John 1:14). God entered human history in Bethlehem in the form of a child. Today, instead of being a bustling, vibrant community, the streets of Bethlehem are barren, devoid of commerce. Shop after shop is boarded up, and lawlessness prevails. The streets and walls of Bethlehem reflect the fate of all of us in our personal lives when we reject him. And our personal spiritual state will ultimately be reflected in the state of our communities and our world.

These are the three glories I ask you to dwell on, to reflect on, and to learn from as you seek to know what God has revealed and consider what he principally speaks through, and whether indeed he has failed you. God is the Creator — he has created our universe and has created us to be the complex, marvelous creations we are; God is the Revealer — he has revealed his character to us; and God is the Embodier — our physical world, the moral world, and the human world are all a reflection of who he is. These are the realms in which he has spoken, though in thinking we understand how the physical world came to be — and making that the measure for life — we have impugned the authority of the moral world and the human world, and the world we see bears no resemblance to the world God declared good.

In his recent book *Hot, Flat, and Crowded*, Thomas Friedman takes a look at what we have done to the world. In an instructive section, he talks about our insatiable appetite to destroy and plunder and never to replenish:

> The waters around the 17,000 islands of the Indonesian archipelago hold 14 percent of the earth's coral reefs and more than 2,000 coral reef fish species.... We often forget that "corals are both plants and animals," [Mark Erdmann, a marine biologist] added, "and the main thing they provide is shelter and structure and substrate, like trees in the forest — no more trees: no more leopards or orangutans; no more corals: no more fish." But runaway development and both dynamite and cyanide fishing have imperiled many of Indonesia's coral reefs, which provide the critical habitat for fish and other reef animals. A Western diplomat in Jakarta who follows biodiversity issues told me that one Indonesian fishing fleet company had informed him that in the year 2000, 8 percent of its catch from the waters around Indonesia were small baby fish, and by 2004 that number was 34 percent. As this diplomat put it, "When you are into one-third babies, the end is near."[7]

What neither the diplomat nor Friedman added is that this may well be a metaphor of what we are doing to ourselves by desacralizing life. Creation, the law, and humanity (the incarnation) bear God's imprint. How we navigate through this is given to us in three other glorious truths.

Three Supremacies

When Paul is in prison, he writes to Timothy, telling him, "Do your best to come to me quickly.... Get Mark and bring him with you, because he is helpful to me in my ministry.... When you come, bring the cloak that I left with Carpus at Troas, and my scrolls, especially the parchments" (2 Timothy 4:9 – 13).

Several years earlier, Paul had had a serious disagreement with John Mark and had sent him home. Now as he spends his final days in prison, he asks young Timothy to bring Mark with him to Paul. There is a touch of tenderness here as we hear the need of the older Paul, and it is obvious that reconciliation has taken place — a reconciliation not in name only but in a restored and valued relationship between Paul and Mark. Following this request, he asks Timothy to bring him his cloak, his books, and most of all his parchments.

Paul points us to the three supreme trusts given to us by God: (1) to guard and care for our *bodies*, these temples of God — a trust symbolized by the cloak; (2) to guard and care for our *minds* — a trust symbolized by the books; we read and study and thereby inform our minds; and (3) to guard and care for our *souls* — a trust symbolized by the parchments, the Scriptures; we read and study and apply the Scriptures and allow them to nurture and guide our souls. If we are to understand the world and the God who made it, the church as an institution and each one of us as individuals within it must guard these three individual trusts. Any one of these held in imbalance will distort our growth.

Three Excellencies

From the three glories through which God has spoken and the three supremacies we must guard in order to live a balanced life, we move to the three excellencies that make a meaningful life possible. In his great chapter 13 in his first letter to the Corinthians, Paul writes, "And now these three remain: faith, hope and love. But the greatest of these is love" (verse 13).

These are the elements of life without which it is impossible to live. *Faith* is that aspect which is built on a relationship between the truth we know and the truth we have yet to learn, as we enlarge our knowledge into the unknown. *Hope* casts a long shadow, even in times when it seems to have disappeared. But then comes the greatest — *love*. Think about this: The only way any of this is true is if God exists. Love is the supreme value and the supreme expression in a world where so often hatred seems to have won the day. In the certainty of God's existence, the imperatives of faith, hope, and love follow.

* * *

These three — the glories, the supremacies, and the excellencies — are all derived from the ultimate reality of God the Father, God the Son, and God the Holy Spirit. This relationship between these three — the ultimate reality of the triune God — is as mysterious as it is profound. From this God comes his call to us who are his children to live in the world and not be of it, to honor him and to respect our fellow human beings, and to respect honest questions without abandoning our faith when the going gets tough.

What difference does the reality of God make in our lives, our relationships, and our society?

Some years ago, the movie *The Emperor's Club*, starring Kevin Kline, came to the theaters. It is the story of a class of young men who receive special instruction in classical literature. Once a year, a tradition in the school is to hold a competition and find out which boy has mastered the material most thoroughly. The three finalists, dressed in togas, are on the stage before the student body, and the teacher conducts the test by asking the questions that invariably require completing a quote or referencing a source.

One of the finalists comes from a privileged background as the son of a United States senator and is rather used to making life suit him. He has found a way to cheat throughout the entire proceedings, and the audience — without knowing what is going on — cheers him on to beat his mild-mannered, well-studied competitors. The teacher knows what is happening and the student knows he is under suspicion, but because of the prestige of the boy's father, the headmaster does not allow the teacher to disqualify the boy.

The years go by, and the young man who had cheated has become a successful businessman. He owns a country club, so he contacts the teacher and asks him if he would like to do a rematch at his country club with the two other contestants, both in different lines of work. The teacher sets to the task, the arrangements are made, and the stage is set. A distinguished audience has gathered, and the challenge begins.

Once again, however, when he begins to smell defeat, the man resorts to a back-up plan to ensure a win. And once again, the teacher senses the setup but can't identify how it is being done. The businessman wins, and the evening is over. The disappointed and disillusioned teacher uses the restroom before leaving the club, and his former student comes in and begins a heavy-handed challenge to the teacher. He knows that the teacher knows he has cheated again, and he aggressively tries to justify not only what he has done but the values he lives by. "What's the difference?" he asks. "What difference does it really make?" The teacher gives him a last look of regret and is about to walk out when the sound of a flushing toilet is heard from one of the cubicles. The door opens, and a little boy walks out — the little son of the businessman. He glances in his father's direction, a look of deep, deep betrayal and pain on his face, and walks out of the restroom into the night. No words are spoken.

What difference does it really make that a man cheats and lies to succeed in life? It makes all the difference in the world between a father and his son, between the present and the future.

What difference does our departure as the church from the truths of Jesus' teaching make in the context of the big picture? What difference does it make if you give up on Christianity? It makes all the difference in the world for you and for how you live your life — but not only for you; it makes all the difference in the world for your relationship with the One who made you and this world, who has given you the standards, the rules, by which life is to be lived, the One who gave himself for you so that you could have fellowship with the Father and a future beyond time. It makes all the difference in the world for future generations and the world they will live in.

Let me say this as gently but as seriously as I can. Secularism will not win the day. Atheism will not win the day. Radical Islam is gradually pushing down the walls of secularism in the West because secularism has no foundation. Its walls are built from inferior materials. They may look good on the outside, but inside they are hollow and have no staying power. Radical Islam knows this. We may think our enlightened culture or our technology will withstand their onslaught, but they will not. One of the leaders in the Middle East recently said in a cavalier manner, "Why are we resorting to terrorist acts? We don't need to. Give us another thirty years or so, and the West will be ours. We will take it without an army." This is not a hollow boast. Do you remember when the Soviet Union made a similar boast — that they would not need to fire a shot to win the West because our decay would weaken us so much from within that our walls would crumble and they would be able to just walk in? It is interesting that both these worldviews have recognized that our greatest weakness is ourselves. Fortunately for us, time ran out for the Soviet Union. Islam has all the time in the world. They are prepared to wait. They have been waiting for almost thirteen hundred years since they were turned away by Charles Martel at the Battle of Tours. What's a few more years?

What difference does it really make? It does make a difference. It does matter. It matters to the very freedom of our expression of who we are, who we worship, what we believe, and what we hope for as we look to the future.

It is Christianity that has kept the Western world intact, that has created the environment and the impetus for the success the West has known. It is generations of men and women — fathers and mothers — who drew their strength from God and believed in his ultimate purpose, who built on the foundations others had laid before them, even when it didn't make sense and they didn't see the answers to their prayers they so deeply desired. It is Christians who have stood in humility before the Lord as representatives of their nations, for whom God has blessed these Western nations.

In any situation when Christianity is evicted, I have absolutely no doubt that a radical form of totalitarian religious belief will take over. I have sat with leaders in other parts of the world who have voiced their perplexity that we in the West don't see this reality staring us in the face. The birthrate alone tells the future. We are being outnumbered in that category by nearly eight to one. The handwriting is on the wall. Only Christianity, only the gospel of Jesus Christ that gives us the enormous privilege of sacred freedom without imposing faith on anyone, is strong enough to preserve our freedom and our dignity. Those who mock this faith will find themselves before long under the oppression of an ideological domination that uses religion to gain political and cultural dominance.

The choice for you, if you are among those who think Christianity has failed you, is either to look at Jesus Christ himself and trust God to carry you through the struggles you experience and to bring you to a place of contentment and victory, or to turn your back on this loving Savior, using the failures of the church to justify your unbelief, and to face a meaningless, purposeless existence without any guide to bring you into a future in the presence of God himself — and, sadly, to be brought under the scourge of a freedomless worldview that imposes its belief on all.

THREE TESTIMONIES
FROM PRISON

I want to pull it all together with the stories of three men, each of whom had his doubts, his struggles, and his triumphs. The first is John Bunyan, who wrote the immortal *The Pilgrim's Progress* in 1670 during one of the two occasions on which he was imprisoned for his faith. This book has been translated into two hundred languages and has been read by millions, having never gone out of print since its first publication. It traces the journey of the man Christian from the beginning of his search all the way to his goal — the Celestial City. He is told to keep his eye on the light and not allow himself to be distracted or waylaid. Along the way he encounters several interesting characters, who either help him in his journey or try to prevent him from reaching the Celestial City: Evangelist, the Interpreter, the Formalist, Hypocrisy, Timorous, Legality, Worldly Wiseman, Mr. Sagacity, Lord Hate-good, Pliable, and a few more. He stops and learns valuable lessons at the Slough of Despond, Vanity Fair, Hill Difficult, House Beautiful, Doubting Castle, the Enchanted Grove — you get the picture, even if you haven't read the book. Bunyan did not write much in the way of hymns, but the one he did write is "He Who Would Valiant Be," and each stanza ends with the words "to be a pilgrim."

Exactly one hundred years after Bunyan wrote *The Pilgrim's Progress*, John Newton was born. He was never imprisoned for his faith, but he imprisoned others because he had no faith. He became part of the slave trade as the captain of a slave ship, even though he had personally experienced the horror of being abused, flogged, and enslaved. Caught in a terrible storm, trying to steer his ship to safety, he cried out to Christ to save him. He then dedicated the rest of his life to two pastorates, and his influence in history is undisputed. He was part of the Evangelical

Awakening, and his impact on William Wilberforce to fight the slave trade is a remarkable story. The best known among the many hymns he wrote is "Amazing Grace." One of the stanzas begins, "'Twas grace that taught my heart to fear / and grace my fears relieved."[8]

It is the grace of God that prompts the right kind of fear and brings the right kind of peace. The story of Newton is that of a man who cast doubt to the wind and held firm to the precious knowledge of the grace of Jesus Christ.

One of Newton's parishioners was William Cowper; in fact, Cowper was his music director. Cowper was not imprisoned, nor did he imprison anyone, but he lived as a prisoner of his own mental torment in repeated bouts of depression. His story reads like a roller-coaster ride to the Celestial City, more often in the Slough of Despond than in the Enchanted Grove. Newton touched Cowper's life, and together they compiled the famed hymnbook *Olney Hymns: In Three Parts*. Cowper's best-known hymn is "God Moves in a Mysterious Way," in which one stanza reads,

> *Blind unbelief is sure to err*
> *And scan His work in vain;*
> *God is His own interpreter,*
> *And He will make it plain.*[9]

If you have struggled with some aspect of Christianity and still struggle, don't think you are alone. Others have traveled the same road and have eventually found their way back to joy in their relationship with God. My daughter says that God has the best GPS system. He will bring you back onto the right road, like Christian in *The Pilgrim's Progress*. God's grace along the way will teach you what to fear and what to embrace as you put your trust in him to one day make it all plain to you.

Yes, fellow pilgrim, there are challenges to our belief. Yes, there are dark nights of the soul. Yes, there are questions that may haunt us until we see Jesus face-to-face. But the light of Jesus Christ will carry you through and put your feet on the solid ground of truth and hope. He has done it for others; he will do it for you. And one day you will hear him say to you, "Well done! Well done!"

NOTES

CHAPTER 1: WHO IS JESUS?

1. C. S. Lewis, "Is Theology Poetry?" in *The Weight of Glory and Other Addresses* (1949; repr., New York: HarperCollins, 2001), 140.

2. Thomas Merton, *The Living Bread* (New York: Farrar, Straus & Cudahy, 1965), xiii.

3. James Stewart, *The Strong Name* (Grand Rapids: Baker, 1972), 72–73.

4. Thomas Sowell, *A Conflict of Visions* (New York: Basic Books, 2002), 12.

5. I heartily recommend William Barclay's book *Jesus as They Saw Him* (Grand Rapids: Eerdmans, 1984).

6. Douglas Coupland, *Life after God* (New York: Simon & Schuster, 1995), 359.

7. B. Ramalinga Raju, "It Was Like Riding a Tiger," Outlook India.com, January 7, 2009, *http://www.outlookindia.com/article.aspx?239402* (November 10, 2009).

CHAPTER 2: WHAT DOES IT MEAN TO BE A CHRISTIAN?

1. Antony Flew, *There Is a God: How the World's Most Not;d Atheist Changed His Mind* (New York: HarperCollins, 2007), 77.

2. Reid S. Monaghan, review of *The Science of the Soul: Scientific Evidence of Human Souls*, by Kevin T. Favero, March 13, 2006, *http://www.powerofchange.org/blog/2006/3/13/book-review-the-science-of-the-soul.html* (November 23, 2009).

3. C. S. Lewis, *The Problem of Pain* (1940; repr., New York: HarperCollins, 2001), 91.

4. Reid S. Monaghan, "Thoughts on Plurality," February 13, 2009, *http://www.powerofchange.org/blog/2009/2/13/thoughts-on-plurality.html* (November 23, 2009).

5. David Berlinski, *The Devil's Delusion: Atheism and Its Scientific Pretensions* (New York: Crown Forum, 2008), 9.

6. Ibid., 178–79.

7. Peter Kreeft, *Making Sense out of Suffering* (Ann Arbor, Mich.: Servant, 1986), 51.

8. Gabriel Marcel, *The Philosophy of Existentialism* (Secaucus, N.J.: Citadel, 1956), 19.

9. Reinhold Niebuhr, *Nature and Destiny of Man* (Louisville: Westminster, 1996), 94.

10. Berlinski, *Devil's Delusion*, 179.

CHAPTER 3: POINTS OF TENSION

1. Aleksandr Solzhenitsyn, *Warning to the West* (New York: Macmillan, 1985), 110.

2. William Blake, "The Tiger," in *Masterpieces of Religious Verse*, ed. James Dalton Morrison (Grand Rapids: Baker, 1977), 25.

3. Tessa Cunningham, "How Do You Cope When Your Husband Tells You He Wants to Die?" *The Daily Mail*, May 11, 2009, *http://www.dailymail.co.uk/femail/article-1180210/How-DO-cope-husband-tells-wants-die.html* (November 23, 2009).

4. C. S. Lewis, *Mere Christianity* (New York: Macmillan, 1952), 86.

5. George MacDonald, *Life Essential: The Hope of the Gospel* (Wheaton, Ill.: Shaw, 1978), 24.

6. "Redemption for the Pope?" *Lancet* 373 (March 28, 2009): 1054.

7. G. K. Chesterton, *The Defendant* (New York: Dodd, Mead & Co., 1902), 19.

8. G.K. Chesterton, *What's Wrong with the World* (San Francisco: Ignatius, 1994), 37.

9. Francis Thompson, "The Hound of Heaven," in *Masterpieces of Religious Verse*, 60–61.

10. Saint Augustine, *The Confessions of Saint Augustine*, trans. John K. Ryan (New York: Doubleday, 1960), 43.

11. Widely attributed to C. S. Lewis but the primary source is unknown.

CHAPTER 4: LOOKING INCOHERENCE IN THE EYE

1. A. N. Wilson, "Religion of hatred: Why we should no longer be cowed by the chattering classes ruling Britain who sneer at Christianity," *The Daily Mail*, April 11, 2009, *http://www.dailymail.co.uk/news/article-1169145/Religion-hatred-Why-longer-cowed-secular-zealots.html* (November 23, 2009).

2. Matthew Parris, "As an atheist, I truly believe Africa needs God," *The Times*, December 27, 2008, *http://www.timesonline.co.uk/tol/comment/columnists/matthew_parris/article5400568.ece* (November 23, 2009).

3. Bertrand Russell, *Why I Am Not a Christian* (New York: Simon & Schuster, 1957), 24.

CHAPTER 5: PURPOSE DRIVEN OR REASON DRIVEN?

1. Winston Churchill, quoted in *The Sayings of Winston Churchill*, ed. J. A. Sutcliffe (London: Duckworth, 1992), 42.

2. Robert M. Price, *The Reason-Driven Life: What Am I Here on Earth For?* (Buffalo, N.Y.: Prometheus, 2006), 18.

3. Ibid., 13.

4. Ibid., 8.

5. Ibid., 29, 45.

6. Ibid., 18.

7. Winston Churchill, in a live broadcast from London, August 24, 1941; quoted in Sir Winston Churchill and Martin Gilbert, *The Churchill War Papers* (New York: Norton, 2001), 3:1102.

8. Alfred North Whitehead, *Science and the Modern World* (New York: Free Press, 1970), 12.

9. Cited in Philip Novak, *The Vision of Nietzsche* (London: Element, 1996), 11.

10. Price, *Reason-Driven Life*, 19–20.

11. Ibid.

12. Iris Murdoch, *The Sovereignty of Good* (London: Routledge, 1990), 78.

13. Price, *Reason-Driven Life*, 40.

14. Ibid., 36–37.

15. C. S. Lewis, *Surprised By Joy: The Shape of My Early Life* (New York: Harcourt Brace Jovanovich, 1984), 228–29.

16. C. S. Lewis, *The Silver Chair* (New York: Collier, 1953), 16–17.

17. G. K. Chesterton, "The Convert," in *The Collected Poems of G. K. Chesterton* (London: Methuen, 1933), 387.

CHAPTER 6: DOES PRAYER MAKE ANY DIFFERENCE?

1. G. K. Chesterton, *Orthodoxy* (San Francisco: Ignatius, 1995), 87.

2. Frances Brown, "The Greatest Loss," in *Masterpieces of Religious Verse*, ed. James Dalton Morrison (Grand Rapids: Baker, 1977), 388.

3. C. S. Lewis, *Surprised By Joy: The Shape of My Early Life* (New York: Harcourt Brace Jovanovich, 1984), 228.

4. Cited in Kathryn Ann Lindskoog, *C. S. Lewis, Mere Christian* (Downers Grove, Ill.: InterVarsity, 1981), 118.

5. Saint Chrysostom, "On Prayer," in *Methodist Magazine for January, 1819* (New York: J. Soule and T. Mason, 1819), 115.

6. Robert Browning, *Christmas Eve* (1850; repr., Whitefish, Mont.: Kessinger, 2004), 37.

7. Calvin Miller, *Spirit, Word, and Story* (Grand Rapids: Baker, 2005), 56–57.

8. Paul Waitman Hoon, *The Integrity of Worship* (Nashville: Abingdon, 1971), 164.

9. C. S. Lewis, *Letters to Malcolm: Chiefly on Prayer* (New York: Harcourt, 1992), 67–68.

10. See Philip Yancey, *Prayer: Does It Make Any Difference?* (Grand Rapids: Zondervan, 2006), 222–26.

11. Fanny J. Crosby, "All the Way My Savior Leads Me," in *Hymns for the Family of God* (Nashville: Paragon Associates, 1976), 598.

12. Rhea Miller (lyrics) and George Beverly Shea (tune), "I'd Rather Have Jesus," 1922.

13. Michel Quoist, *Prayers* (Lanham, Md.: Rowman & Littlefield, 1999), 135–37. Used by permission of Sheed & Ward, an imprint of Rowman & Littlefield Publishers, Inc. Michel Quoist, "Sin," translated from the French *Prières* (Les Éditions de l'Atelier, 2003), 144. Used by permission of Les Éditions de l'Atelier, Paris, France.

CHAPTER 7: WHAT DIFFERENCE DOES CHRISTIANITY MAKE?

1. William Blake, "Mock on, mock on, Voltaire, Rousseau," in *The Selected Poems of William Blake* (Hertfordshire: Wordsworth Editions, 1994), 108.

2. William Wordsworth, "London, 1802," in *William Wordsworth: The Major Works*, ed. Stephen Gill (New York: Oxford University Press, 2000), 286.

3. Thornton Wilder, "The Angel That Troubled the Waters," in *The Collected Short Plays of Thornton Wilder*, ed. A. Tappan Wilder (New York: Theatre Communications Group, 1998), 74.

4. Quoted in Os Guinness and John Seel, *No God But God* (Chicago: Moody, 1992), 60.

5. Arthur Peacocke, "New Wineskins for Old Wine: A Credible Theology for a Scientific World," *Science & Spirit* 10 (1999): 32.

6. Ernest Becker, *Escape from Evil* (New York: Free Press, 1975), 164.

7. Thomas Friedman, *Hot, Flat, and Crowded: Why We Need a Green Revolution — and How It Can Renew America* (New York: Farrar, Straus and Giroux, 2008), 300.

8. John Newton, "Amazing Grace! How Sweet the Sound," in *Psalter Hymnal* (Grand Rapids: Board of Publications of the Christian Reformed Church, 1976), 444.

9. William Cowper, "God Moves in a Mysterious Way," in *Psalter Hymnal* (Grand Rapids: Board of Publications of the Christian Reformed Church, 1976), 536.

QUESTIONS FOR DISCUSSION AND REFLECTION

CHAPTER 1: WHO IS JESUS?

1. What is the difference between seeing and recognizing and how is this distinction illustrated?

2. Ravi writes, "A person is more than the physical; personhood involves essence of thought, will, and feeling — a thinking, willing, and feeling entity in relationship." How does this definition help you to better understand God?

3. What two propositions summarize the struggle we have with our expectations of God?

4. "The politics of Jesus were spiritually foundational not morally dictatorial." Explain.

5. This chapter begins and ends with the distinction between seeing and recognizing, which involves relationship and trust. What title for Jesus did you most connect with — or did you hope to connect with — and why?

CHAPTER 2: WHAT DOES IT MEAN TO BE A CHRISTIAN?

1. Why do objective moral values necessarily point to a personal God?

2. How do some atheists reduce all philosophical thought to faith? Do you agree or disagree? Why?

3. Describe two ways that Christianity is unique.

4. What is a "semitranscendent point of reference" and how does this position help you understand your relationship with God?

5. Look at the six bulleted statements of affirmation on page 68. Which one challenges you the most and why?

CHAPTER 3: POINTS OF TENSION

1. What is a half-truth and how does Satan use it to tempt Jesus? What half-truth allures you?

2. When our physical or mental frameworks are not functioning as they should, we usually feel limitations in our spiritual realm as well. When have you found this to be true and how do you meet this challenge?

3. Why do you think Michael's response to Darren transformed Darren's understanding of himself and ultimately his life? What does this story communicate about the way God has fashioned us?

4. What is the third tension addressed in this chapter and how have you wrestled with it personally? Consider taking time to journal and pray about your growing edges in this area and your relationship with God. Is there something for which you may need to ask forgiveness or seek healing?

CHAPTER 4: LOOKING INCOHERENCE IN THE EYE

1. All questions about evil and suffering are raised either by a person or about a person. How does this reality counter the naturalist's and the pantheist's worldviews?

2. If the experience of someone in suffering and pain is valid as a counterpoint to the gospel, why isn't the experience of someone else who has known God's presence in suffering and pain just as valid? Give thought to both perspectives and the role of experience in the search for truth.

3. Examine the three ways we resist pain and Jesus' response to pain. How does Jesus' response expand your view of suffering?

4. Our cultures value the lives of children over adults; most parents would willingly give their lives for their children. What does the counterperspective of the gospel reveal about God and his love for you?

5. What was God's answer to Job? How does this answer trump every argument? Consider how God's response might satisfy your own questions.

CHAPTER 5: PURPOSE DRIVEN OR REASON DRIVEN?

1. Is the reason-driven life in contradiction to the Christian way of thinking? Explore this idea.

2. Why must the laws of logic have transcendent reality as their logical starting points?

3. How does the law of rational inference both challenge and contradict the skeptic's statement that we live in a morally neutral universe?

4. "You are a completely blank slate. It is up to you to create your own meaning." Do you agree or disagree? Why?

5. C. S. Lewis and G. K. Chesterton write poignantly of their conversions to Christianity. What in their stories resonates with you? Consider reading one of the books mentioned.

CHAPTER 6: DOES PRAYER MAKE ANY DIFFERENCE?

1. If you are not a praying person, you are carrying your faith — and trying to carry the infinite is exhausting. Have you tried to carry the infinite in some area of struggle? How might you begin to release this burden to God?

2. How does Jesus' teaching in Luke 11 encourage you to pray? What are one or two affirmations you might reflect on as you approach God in prayer this week?

3. Retelling the scheme of Jonas Nightingale, Ravi observes, "To pray as though we have the right to demand what we want without the candor of facing up to who we really are is to make prayer the ultimate charade." Explore this observation in relation to your own prayer life.

4. Like shared intimacy with a loved one, prayer is conversational relationship that often requires hard work. Does this idea challenge any of your expectations of your relationship with God? What about with others?

5. Name the five distinct realities that God wants us to learn through the process of prayer. Take time to explore each of these in the weeks to come, both in conversation with God and with others.

CHAPTER 7: WHAT DIFFERENCE DOES CHRISTIANITY MAKE?

1. What is naturalism and how does Francis Schaeffer's illustration counter this worldview?

2. Ravi offers a vivid, real-life example to confront the simplistic notion that the Christian faith is irrational and that naturalism is rational. What lessons learned in the Biosphere 2 project debunk the idea that naturalism is necessarily rational?

3. Why do you think many churches struggle to produce believers who possess strong character and exercise self-discipline? How might you experience such transformation in your own community and family?

4. "The single word that best describes the gospel message is *forgiveness*. Understanding what it means to both offer forgiveness and receive forgiveness is the difficult part of learning mercy." Take time to journal or discuss this idea with someone. Is there someone you may need to forgive or ask for their forgiveness?

5. What three realizations do we need to take hold of as we seek to live in relationship with God? Is there one area where you see an imbalance or lack faith? As you conclude this book, consider the growing edges in your relationship with God and others and the ways in which you might move forward to address them.

Author Interview

Danielle DuRant is director of research and writing
at Ravi Zacharias International Ministries

Danielle DuRant: *You've often said that you have a specific individual in mind — a particular person's unique story and questions — when you write a book. Is this the case with this book?*

Ravi Zacharias: In this particular book, I think some of my own early challenges kept surfacing. My struggle came between fifteen and seventeen. In India, you're forced to be much more mature in your thinking because life hits you in the face, especially as far as religion is concerned. You can't escape it; the conflict between religion and culture underlies everything. You just take it day by day and don't ask questions. Yet I had questions. I wondered how it was that tens of millions could believe certain things that I found utterly irrational or possibly much more ceremonially driven than intellectually driven.

But now, many decades later, after having practiced apologetics for so long and meeting honest unbelievers who are not necessarily trying to be difficult but have genuine questions, I don't think a day goes by when I don't meet a believer who has struggled with very serious issues. So this book is a response to the honest questions about the intellectual credibility of the gospel and the pragmatic struggles that emerge when someone does believe. I think this may well be one of the most important books I have written.

DD: *Writing generally comes fairly easily for you, but you've expressed that this book was a difficult one to write. Was this a more personal book than you expected?*

RZ: Yes, it confronted me on two or three levels. First, with my travel — continually being on the road — it's difficult for me to set aside time for the focused attention that a narrow subject such as this requires. But second, I think the range of the struggle in the subjects covered here is very real. Who among us hasn't struggled with unanswered prayer? Also the problem of pain. We wrestle with this every day — not just the intensity of it, but the volume of it. It's all around us. Finally, I interviewed people who had walked away from their belief in God. I think it is crucial that the reader understand this: I'm not dealing with this subject theologically per se; for instance, the issue of eternal security is not a theme of this book. That requires rigorous theological discussion that looks at both sides of the questions. This book aims at people who have experienced what they feel is God's failure in their lives, people who said they once believed and now don't, or are straddling two worlds, trying to find answers to their questions. The questions asked in this book are real questions, not imaginary. This book is relevant to most people, if they are honest; and because there are faces behind these questions, it was much more difficult to deal objectively with the subject.

If we as Christians don't allow people who are angry with God or feel disappointed in him an honest venue in which to talk and share, I think we may become quick to hide behind words and not come out into the open light.

DD: *Have you ever felt that Christianity has failed you, and have you struggled with some of the points of tension you address in your book?*

RZ: The answer to the sharp edge of the question is No. I don't feel that for a moment, and I do not mean to sound very spiritual — I recognize my own failings and shortcomings before the Lord. The two things I need in my itinerant ministry are a very strong back and a very strong voice — and

I have neither of those. I could ask God why he has allowed me to struggle in these two areas that are so necessary for me to fulfill my calling, but you know, in the real drama of existence, they are minor issues. There are many more challenging questions than that. Personally, I don't think I've had a moment of doubt about God since the day I came to know the Lord.

The encounter I had with Christ was so revolutionizing that no matter what arguments fail me, I always go back to what happened on that suicide bed as a young teenager with nobody to help me understand what life is all about. There is no other way to explain what happened in my life than divine intervention. As I look back, I can see how God has used me in both the East and the West.

Of course, I have run into situations where I can see why there are questions. Perhaps I see more of that than the average human being. When I was in my twenties, I was in Vietnam and in Cambodia — places in which people witnessed the elimination of thousands and thousands of people. I remember looking at all of that and wondering, *Where is God in all of this?* Then in the early days of my ministry when I was speaking in Poland and going through Auschwitz, I noticed the silence. Not a word was said as we walked through that place; the only sound was the sound of weeping. I've looked at all that and I think the darkness of sin is daunting to me. So yes, I would have to say that I have asked questions — and still do. To not ask questions would actually be to disengage from reality — but I have never doubted God.

DD: *You seem very familiar with suffering. You've been afforded a perspective through growing up in India and in your travels that many Westerners don't have. Looking back at your own conversion, I think it's fairly unique and special that you had such an amazing conversion experience and that it still carries you through to this day.*

RZ: And that I think is the clue to finding some answers, and I'll tell you why. In India and in many other areas — for example, in Bangladesh or Pakistan or parts of the Middle East — you will see some pretty raw sights.

Many who saw the movie *Slumdog Millionaire* have raised the question, "Is this for real?" People whom I've talked to, who work in that environment, will say, "If anything, it is made more palatable in the movie. The reality is even worse."

One of the most powerful movies ever produced in India is a movie called *Mother India*. Song after song in the movie asks: How do you cope with the poison of living when you have to drink it every day — you don't die immediately, but you are dying a slow death? The Indian culture has learned to cope with the unfairness of life, and the odd thing is that, in spite of it, Indians are the most religious people in the world. Now a psychologist may have a field day with this and question it as a way of coping, along with all the other imaginary ways we look for help. On the other hand, it is a display of the human proclivity toward the spiritual in the absence of any material answers.

Having said that, before I came to the West, I was under this illusion that I'll have my own salary, my own home, my own car, my own everything — and I'll have no questions about life. The Hindi songs became irrelevant to me. The truth of the matter is that if you read Western poets and listen to the country music artists, it becomes obvious that they are the real philosophers of society. They hide behind the poems and the music and tell it like it is: songs of betrayal, songs of brokenness, songs of loneliness, songs of giving up on life. All of them are the same. And to me this is a clue that what G. K. Chesterton said was right. Ultimately, meaninglessness does not come from being weary of pain but from being weary of pleasure. Now if this is true, pain and suffering are not the problem. The problem is finding meaning in a world in which so much is available and yet where true meaning is still so difficult to find.

DD: *You write, "God does not disappoint us. We often disappoint him and ourselves." This seems to suggest that our relationship with God is based on our performance rather than his grace. And if God is all-knowing, aren't his expectations of us viewed through his promise that he who began a good work in us will be faithful to complete it? In other words, can we disappoint God?*

RZ: It's interesting how we attribute emotions to God, whether it's an effect or whether it's an affection that he feels. We can only take God at his word. His analogical use of language is for us to understand God, such as, "How often I have longed to gather you together, but you were not willing. What more could I have done for you that I have not already done?" "If you crucify the Son of God all over again and subject him to public disgrace, no sacrifice for sins is left." Jesus looks on the city of Jerusalem with compassion, and the entire appeal he makes is in the fact he has done so much for them and yet they have responded with so little appreciation and love. When you look at Old Testament books such as Hosea, Malachi, and Jonah, you see the disproportionate response of his people to the abundance of grace God bestows.

I think that's why even the story of the prodigal son does not have a happy ending. He has come back, all is well, let's have a celebration. But now you've got the older brother, who messes it up. It's sort of one of those good news/bad news situations. The good news is that my son who was lost has come back. The bad news is that the fellow who stayed with me is still messed up.

So I think we must understand God's feelings by analogy. In terms of disappointing God, I do not mean that we therefore catch him by surprise. Rather, he would have to say to us, "What was it that kept you away from me?" The emotions of adoration and appreciation are legitimate emotions for a returning child of God. That's what I think we need to be thinking of. The analogical use is to evoke within us a sense of, "'Twas grace that taught my heart to fear, and grace my fears relieved." I think that's a marvelous use of language — using the one expression to show that God induces in us both fear and release from guilt.

DD: *You're speaking of religion in terms of an inviting and intimate relationship with God rather than a performance. The relationship is essential in this question, is it not?*

RZ: Very well put. If our Christianity comes through as a performance, it is unfortunate because that is really not what is intended. The older I get, the more I learn by observing children — and they don't even have to be your own children in order to make these observations. I may be sitting in a restaurant watching a parent-child interaction and notice the child taking advantage of the parent. Or I may go to a graduation ceremony. When a student is speaking, you can easily identify the parents. They are wearing the biggest smiles in the room. We see ourselves in children and in observing parent-child relationships.

When I was struggling with my studies as a boy, my mother's delight when I did well was part of my own reward. The thrill of doing well was not just in receiving a good mark but in going home and showing my grade to my mom. Her pleasure in my achievement was the affirmation I needed. So I think my relationship with God is not by any stretch of the imagination a performance for him. It would be like this: the first time you cook a meal for somebody you love, and if you burn it, you get really upset — not because they are going to love you any less for burning the meal but because you wanted to please them and do something to demonstrate that.

DD: *What do you say to the person who cognitively believes God is good and wants to trust him but, based on a past heartache or a present situation, still struggles to experience him as compassionate and trustworthy?*

RZ: These are what I call the rub questions. They are not easy to answer. And these situations are more often the rule than the exception in our experience. I think about this a lot, and I wonder how much we have been wrongly taught in these matters? Have our expectations for life as a Christian been wrong? In our efforts to be relevant, we have forgotten that some things are going to be irrelevant and unexplainable for us, and it is we who need to become relevant to the truth, not the other way around. We are not God. Imagine trying to force a square peg into a round hole — all you accomplish in the end is to damage the edges of the peg. Sometimes we try to force God to fit our mold for him, to fit our idea of how he should act, and then when he doesn't meet these expectations, we blame him for not meeting our expectations.

I have concluded that the greatest of loves comes at the greatest cost. The greatest of loves will never come cheaply. It takes everything you have to honor that love and everything you have to honor that trust. And the greatest love that any of us could have is our relationship with God.

Look at any athletes who have succeeded. Discipline is an indispensable part of their lives — unless, of course, they cheat. And when you've got the discipline, you've got the marks on your body to demonstrate it. But we sit down Sunday after Sunday, in the West particularly, to a delicious buffet of programming. Then when the first temptation comes, we are walloped; we are thrashed, and we wonder where God is. God is exactly where we have left him — way behind, reshaped into our image.

Something I heard from a Muslim doctor I met in Pakistan who had come to know Christ comes to my mind often. He told me about the two sentences he heard from a preacher that changed his life: "In surrendering, you win. In dying, you live."

This is the counterperspective. So when you say, "I don't feel God here. I'm afraid to trust him here," realize that there are many days when you don't feel the love you want to feel from your spouse, your children, your family. But you have to be big enough to surrender your own needs and keep loving and "kicking against the goads," as it were. I believe when it is over, you will discover that perseverance was what it was all about.

DD: *A number of individuals you allude to in your book are angry with God. Listening to you, I'm anticipating your answer, but I wonder if you ever get angry with God? And what do you do with this difficult emotion in relation with him?*

RZ: That's a good question — do I ever get angry with God? I would have to say I am puzzled by him many times. I have to say that several years ago I would fairly quickly have said no, but in the last three to four years, I haven't done well with the virtue of patience. I like to attribute it to this nagging back that gets me down quite often, and I think there's something to that. But outbursts of anger have not been common for me. Silence, retreating into a shell — perhaps that's been my way of dealing with anger. And this may sometimes carry over into my walk with the Lord too. My prayers become much more perfunctory rather than engendering a deep sense of communicating with God. It's almost like I am saying to God, "You feel I should really be dealing with this. What's the point in my even talking to you?"

But I have to say that many times I have been really puzzled by God. When I look at some of the questions actually raised in the Bible (such as Why do the wicked prosper?), I have some questions for God.

DD: *Given the amazing promises of Scripture and the way the church often proclaims the message that God answers prayer and the desires of our heart if we just have enough faith, it's difficult to not feel disappointed when our prayers aren't answered as we had hoped or in our expected time frame. What advice would you give to the person who once held firm, perhaps even rigid, expectations of God, and now struggles with halfhearted prayers and even resignation?*

RZ: If we were to draw out the really hard questions of this book, this area would be where probably more people have faltered or have found what they feel is a legitimate gripe against God. It would be easy to dismiss this in the simplistic answers — you know, "God wants you to be patient," and "Between the promise and the performance is the parenthesis." The thing is, the parenthesis sometimes seems terribly protracted, so much so that you never see the performance of the promise.

I find it amazing how Jesus dealt with prayer and how in the critical moments of his own calling, he stepped aside to pray. I find it absolutely fascinating that the biblical writers tell us how he prayed and what he prayed. If they had been manufacturing a persona of Jesus, they would never have told us the things he prayed for because clearly his prayers were often unanswered. His high priestly prayer, if anything, is one of the huge gaps between prayer and performance. The parenthesis seems to be very long. Nearly two thousand years have gone by since he prayed that we would be one, and you can't even find us being one in one church, let alone in all of Christendom.

So it says to me, as Jesus reminded us in the Lord's Prayer, that I need to pray much more about my relationship with God and my understanding of his kingdom than with a wish list in front of me. The thing we may be missing most in our approach to prayer is a clear understanding of what communion with God really means. Such an understanding is able to cover a multitude of unanswered prayers and will give us the confidence of knowing that God is with us and that we can depend on him to sustain us with peace and fulfillment and meaning, even at the end of a dark day or in the midst of a dark night of the soul.

Through prayer, God is preparing the wineskin to receive the new wine of grace. This is the work of God. If we think his desire is only to give us what we ask for, we misunderstand the process of preparing the wineskin.

DD: *You have spoken of this parenthesis, and you speak of three tensions in the book that leave many feeling that Christianity has failed them. One such tension is the longing for sexual fulfillment. You write, "If marital consummation is an act of worship, and if the ultimate seduction is false worship, I would dare suggest that those who are longing for a relationship of touch and intimacy — that lesser act of worship which is marriage — seek the greater form of worship until the day they can legitimately participate in sexual love." Why is the single person who is longing for marriage seen as not seeking this greater form of worship because they are also seeking the lesser form, when the married person has also longed for and is now even participating in this lesser form of worship?*

RZ: I think this must be viewed from at least three different lenses. The first lens is an understanding of what consummate relationships are and what they're not. I dare say that people who enjoy this intimacy sometimes fall into the trap of enjoying the feeling and ignoring the cost. I have met many women trapped in a wrong relationship who have told me, as crass as this may sound, that the men who seek them out are more often than not someone who has already experienced sex legitimately and then seeks for it in stolen waters.

But I'll tell you, the moment the human body experiences this kind of relationship, the seduction is to have the experience without having to pay the cost. Yet it is the cost — namely, commitment — that actually preserves the emotional side of the relationship. If there is no commitment, the feeling is merely physical, and the emotion that gives the relationship value ultimately dies. Sex is not just a feeling; it is a commitment, which, when properly expressed, preserves the feeling. If it is improperly expressed, the feeling will die, and the person becomes diminished in the process.

The second lens is an understanding of what marriage is and what marriage offers to you. This may sound shocking, but marriage is not what it's cracked up to be. In fact, I know many young people who, having observed their parents' marriages, will say they are reluctant to become married themselves. I think that marriage has suffered an awful lot because of all the false images and expectations of marriage placed before us. This may be unpopular to say, but the exhaustion of a professional life drains marriage. You cannot serve two masters. Adrenaline keeps us moving throughout the day as we work, whether it's selling shirts or automobiles or computers. When the adrenaline rush is over and you go home to your spouse and children (if you have any), there is little left in your tank to be able to give your family, and it becomes harder and harder to fulfill the obligations of marriage. And when both partners in a marriage work outside the home, the toll on the marriage is twice as great.

The third lens is an understanding that this longing of sexual fulfillment is a God-planted desire in us. And with fleeting time it becomes a fleeting hope. The unrequited God-given longing for this kind of relationship is, I believe, and I say this carefully, one of the most difficult crosses to bear. This is not the Calvary you want. You find yourself asking God if there is any way to be spared from the ache of this longing and to receive the companionship you see so many others enjoying. Of course, marriage goes beyond the consummate relationship of the physical side; it means caring, cherishing, and loving. This should be what you are ultimately craving.

To that person I say, as painful and perhaps flippant as it may sound, just as others who face other unmet desires, you have to learn to receive the strength from the Lord to crucify that desire and make Jesus Christ the focus of your desire to be cared for, cherished, and loved — because only he can ultimately meet this desire, even if you are married.

It's a little bit like doing a puzzle. You've got only three pieces missing out of five hundred, but you just can't make it all come together. I just say, as F. W. Boreham does, that this longing for the legitimate expression of sexual love is one of those painful things that is easier borne by a person who has never experienced it than by the one who daily lives with this sense of loss. In other words, the emotions that are part of this longing cannot be fully understood by one who has not experienced it for whatever reason.

DD: *You've expressed that in any intimate relationship there will be times of distance or even a sense of dryness. So perhaps we ought not to be surprised when we feel this in our relationship with God. What do you do during times of spiritual dryness? Are there particular authors, books, sermons, or disciplines that you turn to when you feel the passion that you long for just isn't there?*

RZ: If there is anybody who has not experienced what you have described, I really want to touch them. It's not only a common thing; it can be a frequent thing. It's like C. S. Lewis's Screwtape telling the junior devil, "Encourage their horror of the Same Old Thing." I think that's actually what's happened to the West right now. We've heard the gospel so much that we're experiencing the horror of the same old thing. So we buy into nonsensical notions that are actually bizarre while sounding sophisticated. They don't make any sense, but they come with mystical, new terminology, and we are wowed by them. This is why, by the way, I think people church-hop. There are no more unexpected moments at the church they've been going to, and all of a sudden, it's the same old thing — and so they move on to something new.

The human ability to remain firm in our convictions and commitments is very, very limited. That's why I think good reading, good viewing, and good friendships are good places in which to find renewal.

There are so many considerations to the dryness we may experience at any given time. You may not feel well, or you may be tired — all of this takes its toll on you. Sometimes a lack of discipline or a lack of perseverance may well be because of lack of sleep. It could be your mind, your body, is tired, and you need a vacation.

You may have become stagnant because your reading material is not helping your growth process. Reading a variety of authors is a good way to light a new spark within you. I love reading biographies. I love reading authors whose language is outstanding because they quicken the imagination by just the right turn of phrase. Sometimes all it takes is one phrase to turn your life around.

You have to have variety in your devotional life, in your relational life, in your church life. And it is important to remain balanced — to keep physically healthy, to keep your viewing life enchanted so that you're looking at the right things. That's one advantage I have in my life: I'm in new places so often that I experience an enormous array of God's diversity.

DD: *You seem to enjoy a warm and trusting relationship with God — it is evident when you speak in open forums and as you write. I wonder, then, even though you had a difficult relationship with your father, you don't seem to struggle with relating to God as an angry or a distant father. Is that true?*

RZ: No, I don't because I don't see anybody as totally reflective of God. Nobody. And I think the moment I put that load on them, I do them a disservice — and especially my father. Because I'm sure if my children were to look for a perfect father, I haven't been that either.

Maybe I focus more on my direct relationship with my heavenly Father than on an indirect relationship. What does it really matter what my father was like if my heavenly Father has shown me who he is? I don't want to be overly critical, but I think we have made nearly everything so scientific in the West that we push so much into a paradigm that is beyond reason. Of course, we would all like our earthly fathers to perfectly reflect God, but very few of us are privileged to experience this in that relationship.

I didn't see my father as either reflecting or not reflecting God. I know my heavenly Father. In fact, I would say I miss my dad in these days. I wish he could have met our children and seen how God has blessed our lives and our ministry. Sometimes in our relationships we push expectations beyond reason. If we've had a warm and loving relationship with our fathers, we should be thankful for it. If we haven't, we have to look beyond that relationship, or we will end up broken — and I don't think that's what God wants from us.

DD: *You've raised many significant points today — that we must carefully examine our expectations of God and our disappointments, not denying them but bringing them to God and asking him to show us where we may be thinking improperly, and that we must come to him in prayer rather than turn our backs on our relationship, asking him to show us more of himself and his love for us.*

RZ: There are two important implications, Danielle. Blaming our poor relationship with our heavenly Father on our poor relationships with our earthly fathers is similar to saying that Christianity has failed us because of what we see or experience in the church. This is a false extrapolation. Yes, the church is flawed; yes, it is broken. But if you think of the twelve men whom Jesus chose — my word! Certainly an insightful Divine Being could have picked better disciples than he did. And out of these less-than-perfect disciples, he took perhaps the least promising — Peter — and gave him the key spot. Then he took a terrorist — Paul — and made him the penman for one-third of the New Testament. So I think we take a great risk if we base our decision about ultimate matters only on what we can see.

Second and very important, one of the chapters in this book is a response to Robert Price and his view of the irrationality and untenability of the Christian faith. This is not a face-value response, but I want the reader to understand this: Examine any other worldview, and you'll find an important difference between it and the Christian faith. In the Christian faith, we may ask the questions, in fact, encourage questions, and while we may not always have comprehensive answers, we have very meaningful answers. In any other worldview, not only do they not have meaningful answers; they cannot even justify their questions.

This is not to say that Christianity is the best of some horrible options. No! I think the questions of morality, meaning, love, destiny, values, sexuality, marriage, friendship, and word over feeling are most meaningfully answered in the Judeo-Christian worldview. I am more convinced of this than I was at the moment I first committed my life to Christ. So examine Christianity against all other alternatives, and I believe with my whole heart that you will find that Christianity has not failed you.

Walking from East to West

God in the Shadows

Ravi Zacharias
with R. S. B. Sawyer

For more than three decades, apologist Ravi Zacharias has shared bits and pieces of his personal life and experience.

In *Walking from East to West*, now in softcover, Zacharias invites you to follow him on a journey through his life: to see and smell the neighborhood in India where he grew up, to feel a mother's love and the consternation of a harsh father—and the lure of a rebellious soul.

In a crisis experience, Zacharias exchanged pantheism for monotheism, and meaninglessness for true fulfillment in Christ. He has traveled from the East to the West and then back again to answer skeptics' penetrating questions about the meaning of life and the existence of a God who is there for his children.

Zacharias invites you to follow him on this journey through his life and into the lives of others and to see how he has become more convinced with each year that Jesus Christ is the one who came to give you life to the fullest.

Is Your Church Ready?

Motivating Leaders
to Live an Apologetic Life

Ravi Zacharias and Norman Geisler,
General Editors

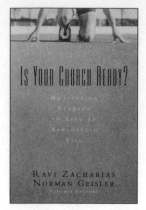

Here is a ministry resource for motivating all Christians to become thoughtful apologists of their faith.

Although apologetics is as crucial today as it has ever been, the classical model for defending the faith often seems irrelevant to the twenty-first century, where people listen with their eyes and think with their emotions. *Is Your Church Ready?* presents a team of highly qualified Christian thinkers — Ravi Zacharias, John Guest, Jay Budziszewski, Judy Salisbury, Dean Halverson, and Peter Grant — who build a case for the place of apologetics in the local church, home, and school. Using personal examples and illustrations, they address:

- How to answer objections to Christianity
- How to equip children in the home and prepare youth to remain committed to Christ after they leave for college
- How to reach international students and the foreign born

Included are discussion questions and a "Church Leaders Resource Guide" to the best books, articles, organizations, and websites on the subject.

Available in stores and online!

ZONDERVAN®
.com

Who Made God?

And Answers to Over 100 Other Tough Questions of Faith

Ravi Zacharias and Norman Geisler, General Editors

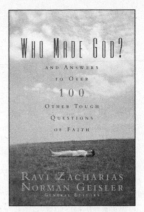

In the quest for the truth, you need to know what you believe and why you believe it. *Who Made God?* offers accessible answers to over 100 commonly asked apologetic questions. Bringing together the best in evangelical apologists, this guide is standard equipment for Christians who want to understand and talk about their faith intelligently.

Part 1 answers tough questions about the Christian faith such as:

> • Who made God? • How can there be three persons in one God? • What is God's ultimate purpose in allowing evil? • Where did the universe come from? • How long are the days of creation in Genesis? • Did Jesus rise from the dead? • Are the records of Jesus' life reliable? • Does the Bible have errors in it?

Part 2 answers tough questions about other faiths, including Islam, Mormonism, Hinduism, Transcendental Meditation, Yoga, Reincarnation, Buddhism, and Black Islam. Relevant stories, questions for reflection and discussion, and a comprehensive list of suggested resources help you dig deeper so you can be prepared to give careful answers that explain the reasons for your faith.

The End of Reason

A Response to the New Atheists

Ravi Zacharias

When you pray, are you talking to a God who exists? Or is God nothing more than your "imaginary friend," like a playmate contrived by a lonely and imaginative child?

When author Sam Harris attacked Christianity in *Letter to a Christian Nation*, reviewers called the book "marvelous" and a generation of readers — hundreds of thousands of them — were drawn to his message. Deeply troubled, Dr. Ravi Zacharias knew he had to respond. In *The End of Reason*, Zacharias underscores the dependability of the Bible, along with his belief in the power and goodness of God. He confidently refutes Harris's claims that God is nothing more than a figment of one's imagination and that Christians regularly practice intolerance and hatred around the globe.

If you found Sam Harris's *Letter to a Christian Nation* compelling, *The End of Reason* is exactly what you need. Dr. Zacharias exposes "the utter bankruptcy of this worldview."

And if you haven't read Harris's book, Ravi's response remains a powerful, passionate, irrefutably sound set of arguments for Christian thought. The clarity and hope in these pages reach out to readers who know and follow God as well as to those who reject God.

Available in stores and online!

The Grand Weaver

How God Shapes Us Through the Events of Our Lives

Ravi Zacharias

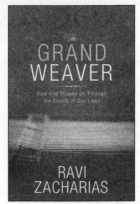

How differently would we live if we believed that every dimension of our lives—from the happy to the tragic to the mundane—were part of a beautiful and purposeful design in which no thread were wrongly woven? That's what bestselling author and internationally known apologist, Ravi Zacharias, explores in *The Grand Weaver*.

As Christians, we believe that great events such as a death or a birth are guided by the hand of God. Yet we drift into feeling that our daily lives are the product of our own efforts. This book brims with penetrating stories and insights that show us otherwise. From a chance encounter in a ticket line to a beloved father's final word before dying, from a random phone call to a line in a Scripture reading, every detail of life is woven into its perfect place. In *The Grand Weaver*, Dr. Zacharias examines our backgrounds, our disappointments, our triumphs, and our beliefs and explains how they are all part of the intentional and perfect work of the Grand Weaver.

Also available: unabridged audio CD.

Available in stores and online!

ZONDERVAN®
.com

Share Your Thoughts

With the Author: Your comments will be forwarded to the author when you send them to *zauthor@zondervan.com*.

With Zondervan: Submit your review of this book by writing to *zreview@zondervan.com*.

Free Online Resources at
www.zondervan.com

Zondervan AuthorTracker: Be notified whenever your favorite authors publish new books, go on tour, or post an update about what's happening in their lives at www.zondervan.com/authortracker.

Daily Bible Verses and Devotions: Enrich your life with daily Bible verses or devotions that help you start every morning focused on God. Visit www.zondervan.com/newsletters.

Free Email Publications: Sign up for newsletters on Christian living, academic resources, church ministry, fiction, children's resources, and more. Visit www.zondervan.com/newsletters.

Zondervan Bible Search: Find and compare Bible passages in a variety of translations at www.zondervanbiblesearch.com.

Other Benefits: Register yourself to receive online benefits like coupons and special offers, or to participate in research.

ZONDERVAN®

ZONDERVAN.com/
AUTHORTRACKER
follow your favorite authors